From Steve

and Steve.

March 25ᵈ 1974.

It's Been a Lot of Fun

It's Been a Lot of Fun

Brian Johnston
an autobiography

W. H. Allen
London and New York
A division of Howard & Wyndham Ltd
1974

Printed and bound in Great Britain by
Richard Clay (The Chaucer Press) Ltd
Bungay, Suffolk
for the publishers W. H. Allen & Co. Ltd,
44 Hill Street, London W1X 8LB

ISBN 0 491 01471 6

With all my love
to
Pauline
who has shared in, and contributed
to, so much of the fun
and to
Joanna
without whom this book would
have been finished three
months earlier!

Contents

8   CONTENTS

Acknowledgements

I would like to thank all my friends who have helped me by jogging my memory and recalling stories or incidents which I had forgotten. Also my very special thanks to Linda Green who has so cheerfully and efficiently deciphered my writing and typed the many pages of manuscript.

1
Early days

MOST PEOPLE SEEM to find it rather odd when I tell them that I was born in an old rectory. But when I mentioned it recently to one of my friends he thought it was highly appropriate . . . 'After all, you *are* a bit of an old wreck and we all know what your politics are!' . . . Fair enough.

Anyway in 1912 I *was* born in the Old Rectory, Little Berkhamsted, a charming village in the midst of the Hertfordshire lanes, yet only twenty-one miles from London. My father was not connected with the Church but was what in those days we called a city merchant. He worked in the family coffee business in the City. This had been founded by my great-grandfather in Santos in 1842 and it was thanks to him and his subsequent partners that as a family we were moderately well-off. I suppose it also helped that my grandfather Reginald Johnston had been Governor of the Bank of England in 1909 and 1910. I was lucky also to have a loving and adorable mother, a sister and two brothers all older than me, and a devoted Nanny who stayed with us until we went off to school.

A year after I was born we moved to a beautiful Queen Anne house called Little Offley. It stood about a mile outside the village of Offley, which straddled the Hitchin to Luton road. A long drive led to the house, which had a farm of about 400 acres and a large garden. It was here that we spent the war years, only seeing Father on his rare home-leaves from the Army in France.

Childhood memories are usually a bore so I will spare you most of mine, especially as I have only vague recollections of anything that happened in my first six years or so. Yet I remember being shown a large hole in the ground where a Zeppelin had dropped a bomb near Hitchin, three miles away. The only casualty from it was said to be one chicken.

Once, I remember, our old sow had a litter of thirteen and to save the youngest or runt from being drowned I took it squealing up to my mother in bed and begged for its life. I believe it was spared but as the way things go in life we probably ate it as bacon later on.

In those days, we travelled everywhere either by dog-cart drawn by our old mare Emma, or in a pony-trap with a temperamental pony called Raffles in the shafts. Sometimes he refused to budge at all; once, when we had been decent enough to get out as we went up a hill, the beast swung round and bolted home with an empty cart. On one occasion he shied at a dog so that one wheel of the cart ran up a bank at the road-side and we were all tipped out on to the ground. Very painful at the time, but except for the strict rationing those were our only troubles during the war.

For four years after the war life settled down, with Father going up to the City every day and my two brothers departing to boarding-school at Eastbourne. My sister stayed at home and shared a governess with me. Thanks to her, there was a quick turn-over rate – about two or three a year. She used to give them a terrible time. I like to think I was better but how I dreaded those wet kisses when we went to say good night.

Looking back, I am amazed at the high standard of living which we enjoyed, despite the after-effects of the war. We had a chauffeur called Wakefield who drove our two cars – a two-seater Ford, one of the original Tin Lizzies, and a coach-built Landerlette Fiat which at that time went at the phenomenal speed of 52 mph. There was a groom to look after my father's hunter and our ponies, a gardener and boy, a butler, parlourmaid, housemaid, 'tweeney' and of course a cook.

We happened to be lucky with our cooks, as normally they tended to be rather fickle and leave at the slightest excuse. This inspired a *Punch* joke about the couple who had a good cook, and as good cooks go – she went. We had one silver-haired butler who one day got at the port and dropped the vegetables into someone's lap. Otherwise they all stayed with us for a long time and seemed perfectly happy. How different things are today. And we little ones were far more strictly brought up than our own children. Little boys were still meant to be seen and not heard, which even in those days was a strain for me! We were also expected as a matter of course to *walk* $1\frac{1}{2}$ miles to church and back every Sunday.

When I was eight I went off to join my two brothers Michael and Christopher at Temple Grove School, Eastbourne. Though homesick at times I managed to enjoy myself for most of the next four years. Temple Grove was the oldest private school in the country and even after three years of peace the food was of very doubtful quality. It was also in rather short supply: we used to gobble up our meals at a tremendous pace in order to be well up in the queue for a second helping. This may be the reason why I have always been a rapid eater. There was also a system of swops. If one did not like kippers one swopped them for someone else's sausages the next day, so that sometimes one had too much to eat, sometimes too little.

The staff were a funny lot! The Headmaster, Mr Waterfield, was for some reason nicknamed Bug. He occasionally wielded quite an effective cane but was otherwise a kindly man. His eye had been knocked out playing squash. The stock joke used to be 'Do you know that Bug has a glass eye?'

'No, how *do* you know?'

'Oh, it came out in the conversation.'

His wife was inevitably Dame Bug, but the only time she interfered in school affairs was on the last night of term when she came up to the dormitories to check that every boy was going home with clean ears.

Mr Waterfield used to give all leaving boys what was called a pi-jaw. It was a brave but incredible attempt at sex-education, to prepare the young boy going out into the world. He always asked the same questions so everyone was prepared. His first question was usually: 'Do things happen at night?' We weren't entirely sure what he meant but knew that the answer he wanted was 'No'. So this is what we all said, all, that is, except a boy called Monck-Mason who panicked and said 'Yes' by mistake. But he didn't get much help from Mr Waterfield who merely put his head in his hands and wailed: 'Oh Mason, Mason' – and went on to the next question which in my case was: 'Do you know where babies come from?'

'No Sir', I said looking innocent. (I was).

'Well', he said, 'you know that hole that women have in front?'

Remembering seeing my sister's navel in the bath at home I replied 'Yes Sir'.

'Well, that's where they come from. Goodbye, thanks for what you have done for us and good luck at Eton.' Thus did I learn about sex. As Douglas Byng was to say later: 'It was sex of one and half-a-dozen of the other.'

The Matron was a large woman called 'Putty' Allen. She had a club foot and a stentorian voice. It was through her I made my first introduction to radio as she had a small 'cat's whisker' crystal set and used to allow us to listen in on the ear-phones.

There was a second matron, Miss King, who looked after the new boys. She was a little old lady in steel spectacles who smelt of seccotine and walked with her toes out as if permanently at attention. Then there were two sisters called Beckwith. One was grey-haired, tall and willowy and always looked as if she was swaying in the breeze. She kept our pocket money and did the shopping. Her sister taught the piano and wore pince-nez at a frightening angle on the end of her nose. She also played the organ in chapel and before I got into the choir I was given the job of pumping the organ during the daily services.

This meant sitting on a stool behind the organ and watching a small lead weight on a string. It had to be kept below a certain line by pumping a wooden handle. When one stopped pumping the lead went slowly up towards a danger line: it was exciting to allow the lead to get within an inch or so before pumping again. If, as sometimes happened, it went above the line then Miss Beckwith could push on the notes as hard as she liked but no sound would come out. She would then leap off the organ bench and glare around the corner of the organ, her eyes popping out against the glass of her pince-nez.

The masters too were fairly odd. Both Mr Fritch and Mr Bellamy believed in physical punishment. Fritch used to bash one over the head with his knuckles – which was not only painful but cannot have done the victim's head much good. This was called a Fiddler Fotch. Bellamy, nicknamed Bowler, was very wheezy and sucked cinnamon tablets. When angry, he used to use a heavy black ebony ruler. However, we survived.

A more gentle kind of a chap was Bill Wigg who had the most beautiful copper-plate writing and tried with great patience to teach it to us. He was an expert on beetles and used to keep his spectacles in a Three Nuns Tobacco tin. Taylor was a bad-tempered man who claimed to have played cricket for Yorkshire. He kept a cane in one of his desk drawers and when annoyed used it to hit boys on the legs. However, this stopped when a boy called Corrie seized the cane as it was aimed at his legs and threatened to use it on Taylor if he ever did it again. Needless to say, Corrie was the hero of the school for quite some time.

There was also Chief Petty Officer Crease who used to teach us rifle shooting and take us in PT and gym. As a school we generally did well in the Ashburton Cup so he must have been quite a good instructor, and I still have a badge which I won as a member of the shooting eight. He was also responsible for our punishments as officially awarded by the Headmaster. These included running round a cobbled yard holding iron dumbbells above the head. This not only made the arms ache but if it was cold the dumbbells were left out overnight to freeze, so you can imagine that this naval discipline was not too popular – but extremely effective.

There was the usual amount of petty bullying but nothing outrageous, except one unpleasant ceremony reserved for new boys in their first term. On the first wet day when there were no games, a 'concert' was hastily arranged in which each new boy was required to sing or recite something in front of the senior boys. A prefect stood behind each performer with a raised book in his hand which he brought down with a thud on the victim's head if he failed to satisfy his audience. What with this and Fritch and Bellamy it is a wonder we didn't wander round with permanent concussion.

It was at Temple Grove that I smoked for the first and last time. We used to slip out and buy packets of BDV – an especially mild cigarette it said on the packet – and smoke them behind the Fives Courts. It was pure bravado as I hated the taste of the smoke. I used to keep the cigarettes in my play-box which was supposed to be sacred to its owner. But one day I spotted Putty Allen ostentatiously smoking a BDV and rushed down to my play-box. My cigarettes had gone. There was nothing I could do, although it was obvious where she had got her smoke. Still she didn't sneak on me to the Headmaster, and I took the hint and stopped smoking.

2
My first ball

In my first summer term at Temple Grove I began to take a real interest in cricket. We had always played in a net in our garden at home, but I remember vividly how at school one day my brother Michael threw me a ball and shouted:

'I'm Jack Hearne, you are Patsy Hendren.'

From that moment on, Patsy was my hero. Each morning I would rush to the daily paper to see how many runs he had made for Middlesex or England. I even wrote to him for his autograph without enclosing a stamped-addressed envelope and he replied by return with three autographs instead of one. He used to sign Hendren – with two short lines under the second 'n' and to this day I do the same thing. I had found his address in a newspaper advertisement for some product like Wincarnis and remembered it clearly – 26 Cairn Avenue, Ealing, London W5. I wonder who lives there now.

I followed Hendren's career closely until his retirement in 1937. When I joined the BBC after the war I had the luck to meet him quite often. And I'm glad to say I was not disappointed. He was a wonderful man, kind, modest and with a great fund of stories. On the field he had been the perfect clown, and off it he had this delightful puckish humour. There are numerous stories told about him. Here are just two of them.

On one occasion he was fielding on the boundary by the famous Hill on the Sydney Cricket Ground. The batsman hit the ball high in the air towards him. As it soared higher and higher into the air a raucous voice from the Hill shouted, 'Patsy, if you miss the catch you can sleep with my sister.'

Later Patsy was asked what he had done. 'Oh', he replied, 'as I hadn't seen his sister, I caught the ball.'

Just before he retired he was batting against Derbyshire on a wet pitch that was slippery with mud. Walter Robins was his partner and was batting against the leg breaks of T. B. Mitchell. Robins who always used his feet to attack slow bowlers, had got into the habit of dancing down the pitch and if he missed the ball, walking straight on to the pavilion without looking round at the wicket-keeper. Mitchell was bowling from the Pavilion end and as usual Robins danced down the pitch, missed the ball and continued walking towards the Pavilion without so much as a backward glance. Patsy immediately shouted 'He's missed it' – so Robins turned quickly round and flung himself on the ground bat stretched out towards the stumps. There was a roar of laughter from the players and the crowd, as Robins slowly got up, shirt, flannels and pads covered in mud. He looked up to see the bails lying on the ground and Harry Elliot the wicket-keeper chatting to the slip, having obviously brought off a neat stumping! When I asked Patsy how Robins had taken it he said that he hadn't been too pleased! Knowing R.W.V.R. I should say that was putting it mildly.

So much for my first hero – I will tell you about my second one later on. Meanwhile I was gradually becoming quite a good wicket-keeper and got into the first XI during my last two years at Temple Grove.

Two years earlier we had had a star batsman called Bader minor who used to score a hundred in nearly every school match. This not only meant that we won most of our matches – but according to an old school custom, whenever a century was scored the whole school was excused prep. Bader became a very popular figure and would I am sure have been a Test cricketer had he not lost both his legs in an air crash before the war. But even so as Group Captain Douglas Bader, D.S.O., D.F.C. he became Temple Grove's most distinguished Old Boy.

We not only played a lot of cricket ourselves but were introduced to first-class cricket at the lovely Saffrons Cricket Ground just over a cricket ball's throw away from our school. We were taken to watch the two Universities each year when they came to play H. D. G. Leveson-Gowers XI. I well remember some of the great names I saw then for the first time. The Gilligans – F. W., A.E.R., A.H.H. – the Ashtons, G., H., C.T. – A. P. F. Chapman, etc. My main memory is of the superb fielding and a wonderful collection of cricket caps, especially the Harlequins. There was also F. B. R. Browne who crossed his legs when he bowled and so was nick-named Tishy after a race-horse made famous by Tom Webster in his cartoons. Tishy the horse crossed his legs on several occasions and so fell and lost the race.

In my second year at Temple Grove, my father died in tragic circumstances. Ever since the war we had gone to Bude in Cornwall for our summer holidays; in 1922 we went as usual to our little boarding-house overlooking the golf-course. The bathing off the North Coast has always been dangerous, especially at low tides.

One day we made a picnic-excursion to Widemouth Bay. It was low tide and we all went bathing. A friend of the family named Marcus Scully, who had been badly wounded in the war, got into difficulties. He was caught in the drag and slowly washed out to sea. In those days there were no beach guards or life-saving equipment so my father, who was a strong swimmer, went to the rescue but himself got caught in the strong current.

Somehow Marcus was rescued by other bathers but by the time they had helped him my father was washed right out to sea. There we all were, waiting on the beach and he never came back. A shattering event for all of us but especially for our mother. His body was washed up further along the coast next day. Even though I was aged ten I couldn't really take in what had happened and will of course never know how my life would have been affected had my father lived. The war had prevented my seeing very much of him and in the four years of peace he was away all day in the City. So I never got to know him as well as the modern boy knows his father.

I do know that he was quiet, honest, strict but kind and highly respected by all who knew him. He never played much with us – certainly not at cricket as he had been a wet bob at Eton and later got a rowing blue two years running at Oxford. But please don't look him up in the record books. He rowed in 1899 and 1900 and in both years Oxford lost after a winning sequence of nine years, at that time a University record. But worse still. In 1900 Oxford were beaten by twenty lengths, still the biggest margin of defeat for either side in the 150 years of the Boat Race!

In 1924 the same Marcus Scully who had been rescued in the bathing tragedy married my mother – who I am sure only wanted someone to help her bring up her four children. Time was slipping by at Temple Grove. Significantly for the future, I had been given the nickname of The Voice, not because of its beauty but because of its constant use.

Even at this early stage I could never resist an attempt to try to be funny and my reports were soon full of phrases such as 'talks too much in school' . . . 'apt to be a buffoon' . . . 'should take things more seriously' . . .

I have always held the theory that making jokes is rather like batting at cricket. If you hit *every* half volley you are bound to score the occasional boundary. And so with jokes. However obvious or corny, have a bash and sooner or later you will get a laugh. And as with batting timing is the vital factor.

3
Floreat Etona

After Father's death, things were not so good financially. Little Offley had to be sold and for the next eight years or so our family became a wandering tribe, spending two years in Dorset, five in Herefordshire and ending up, rather strangely perhaps, at Bude.

Our changed financial position made it necessary for me to try for a scholarship at Eton where I was destined to join my two brothers. Mr Waterfield took me up to Eton where for two days I tried desperately to cope with the examination papers. But I failed hopelessly and had to take the Common Entrance and even then only succeeded in taking Middle Fourth – the third bottom form.

I was sorry to leave Temple Grove. I had finished as a school prefect, a sergeant in the Corps and had played cricket and rugger for the school. It all seemed a very big place then. I went back there recently to have a look and goodness how small everything seems now. The 'big' hall, the dormitories, the chapel, the exercise quad – all had shrunk to Lilliputian size. The school has now moved to Uckfield and the former buildings are now occupied by the Ministry of Health Dental Section. If you ever apply for a pair of false teeth your records will be kept somewhere there, possibly in one of the dorms or the chapel!

Temple Grove is not the only school to have ceased functioning at Eastbourne, which in our day was packed with schools. There was intense rivalry between masters when their schools played each other at cricket or football. Alongside us separated only by a narrow footpath between two walls was St Cyprians whom for some reason we called the Kippers. But strangely, although we played all the other big schools in the town we never in my time played the Kippers. It was said that one of their masters had once stuck their bails on with glue, when they were batting against us, so that even though our bowlers hit the stumps they could not bowl the batsmen out. An unlikely tale and a gross libel on an excellent school, one of whose pupils was Henry Longhurst.

And so I went to Eton and for the next five years enjoyed some of the happiest times of my life. Nowadays it is the fashion for some Old Boys to run Eton down and to reveal all the scandals and terrible goings-on that have taken place there. Perhaps I was just one of the lucky ones. Of course in any school things do happen which would make the editor of a Sunday newspaper lick his chops. But for me Eton was a place where I made many close friends and countless acquaintances among the boys and masters, or 'beaks' as they were known there, and most of these have remained so ever since.

One of the most remarkable things about Eton friendships is that you can meet someone whom you have not seen for years and within a moment you are back on the same wavelength picking up exactly where you left off.

There is no point in denying that Eton is also a wonderful club. Some people call it the best Trade Union in the world. And I would not argue with that. Certainly it is true that wherever I have been in Great Britain or all over the world I usually run into an old Etonian and more often than not he has an important job or is in an influential position. So having been to Eton has been extremely useful and has opened countless doors. But perhaps more than anything about Eton I remember the laughter which was never very far away no matter what I was doing.

I joined my second brother Christopher in the house of R. H. de Montmorency where we shared a room – my eldest brother Michael having left to go to a crammer. 'Monty' was a kind and friendly man who had been an International Golfer and had got blues for both golf and cricket when up at Oxford. He was married and had two attractive daughters. The elder Kathleen used to wake us up as she returned in the wee small hours from parties in London, often with boy friends driving an old Bentley with a strap around the bonnet.

The younger daughter Ann was only in her early teens and too young for that sort of thing but was a decorative part of the scene. I had not seen her since 1927 until I met her again as Jim Swanton's bride in 1958.

The actual building Coleridge House was in Keats Lane and was an absolute rabbit-warren. I am certain it would never have passed the fire and hygiene regulations of today. For just over forty boys there was exactly one bathroom and each boy was allocated ten minutes on *one* night only each week under the eagle eye of a K.C.B. (Night Commander of the Bath). Senior boys took it in turns to do this duty and had to keep a strict check on the time in the bath and the depth of the water. 'Monty' used to call everyone 'little boy' and if he found you in the bath on his nightly round of the house he would say: 'What are you doing, little boy?'

'Having a bath sir.'

'Lucky dog', Monty would always reply and by God he was right! The only other means of washing, after football for instance, was in a tin bath in one's room which one had to fill and then empty – this a particularly tricky job.

Each boy except brothers had a room to himself where he slept, worked and had tea. This was an admirable idea which gave even the smallest or newest boy a feeling of independence and a chance to shut himself off from the noise and bustle of school life. When I was at Eton there were coal fires in the rooms but you were only allowed a fire on three days a week plus Sunday. You can imagine how cold it was on winter evenings when it wasn't your turn to have a fire.

Boys used to 'mess' with each other for tea, sometimes just two but occasionally as many as four together. The room chosen for tea was the one which had the fire on that day. There was a 'night-watch' who used to go round the rooms in the middle of the night, scraping out the grates and taking away the ashes. She was a great character – a little Scots woman with a wonderful flow of language which was given full rein when she tripped over some obstacle or trap which we had deliberately set for her. Nowadays the houses have central heating but at least we had our beds made and rooms cleaned by maids – who are of course in very short supply these days.

The rooms were very comfortable with a wicker armchair, a burry or desk, an ottoman, table and chairs and the bed which was pushed up into a recess in the wall during the day time. As I said Monty used to go round the house each night and visit every boy in his room (or in the bath!). This was a basic part of the Eton education and an admirable idea. It enabled the boy and the housemaster to get to know each other, and to talk over problems of life or work in intimate surroundings. The housemaster could also hand out rockets in a more friendly and effective way than if he had to summon the boy officially to his study.

If you were a lower boy the peace of your room was often shattered by the cry of 'Boy'. All fags had to run to the library which was the sitting-room of the prefects or 'library' as they were called at Eton. The last man to arrive had to do the job so if you had a room right at the top of the house you got more than your fair share of the work. How long you were a fag depended on what form you had taken on entering the school. I took middle fourth so had five half's fagging before I became an upper as opposed to a lower boy.

There are many arguments for and against the fagging system, mostly against. On balance so long as it is not abused and does not interfere with a boy's work I am still in favour. In my time it certainly did affect one's work. I always had one ear cocked for a 'Boy' while trying to solve some tricky mathematical problem. I believe that nowadays there is a 'close season' during the evening when 'Boy' cannot be called, so that lower boys can get on with their prep undisturbed.

Another point in favour of the fagging system is that a new boy often arrives with a slightly swollen head after being a prefect or captain of the XI at his private school. Fagging brings him down to earth and teaches him the idea of service to others. It can help him to understand the point of view of those who provide a similar sort of service in later everyday life, and so treat them with courtesy and sympathy.

At Eton anyway fags also take it in turns to do the teas for their 'masters' and so learn simple cooking, like scrambled eggs. As a result I reckon I am the best scrambler in our family. In his last year or two when it comes to the turn of the fag to be the 'master', he now has a chance to learn how to give orders, to be considerate and not too demanding and above all to be fair. Of course some boys did – and probably still do – abuse these privileges. But they were very rare. If there were a referendum held among schoolboys today I wager a majority would come out in favour of fagging.

For obvious reasons, a similar referendum on corporal punishment would almost certainly show an overwhelming majority against. I would agree with this so far as corporal punishment given by the boys themselves is concerned. At Eton both the Captain of the House and Captain of Games had the power to beat but had to get the permission of the housemaster first. This he usually gave without too much investigation into the case and certainly in most cases not hearing the boy's side of the story. Once again the majority of senior boys played fair but there were undoubtedly grave abuses and I am sure that the beatings did the beater far more harm than they did the beaten good.

There were also grossly unfair things called General Tannings. We had one once in my house when an unknown boy made some rude drawings on the wall of the lavatory. Nobody would own up and so after due warning the whole house was beaten by the 'library', getting about four strokes each. This naturally caused tremendous resentment and would never be tolerated today. A similar thing happened when I was a member of Pop. This was the Eton Society which consisted of about twenty-five of the senior boys in the school. The reason for the name 'Pop' is probably because although certain boys were *ex-officio* members, most of them had to be elected. So, if you were un*pop*ular, you did not get in.

There had been a series of fights between Eton boys and town boys in the area of the Arches which carried the railway line from Windsor to Slough. The headmaster Dr Allington was determined to stop these fights and warned the whole school to keep away from the Arches in future. One Sunday he ordered a swoop by members of Pop and we surrounded the area and took the names of all the boys found there – at least fifty.

The next day before chapel they were all summoned to the Pop room and beaten by senior members of 'Pop', although I am sure most had only been out for an innocent Sunday afternoon walk and had never fought with the town boys. Still, they had been warned. One of the victims, now a distinguished merchant banker, did manage to get his own back. The member of Pop who had beaten him was in the sixth form. This form used to walk in a file up the aisle to their seats in chapel when everyone else was seated. The victim happened to have a seat on the knife board as it was called – the front row of the stalls. As the sixth form walked solemnly by in slow time, he stuck out his foot and tripped up his beater who came an undignified cropper on the stone floor of the aisle!

Another controversial subject is compulsory games. Things have changed a lot now but in my time in the summer everyone on the three half holidays had either to play cricket or row. You were either a dry bob or wet bob. It was as simple as that. Now you don't have to do either. You can play tennis, squash, walk, swim or just play the guitar as my elder son Barry used to do! In some ways this is an improvement on the old system where a boy who hated cricket (there were and are such people, believe it or not!) was made to play in a badly organised game. The pitch was usually appalling and the scorers fiddled the scores and the umpires gave everyone out so that the game could finish quickly. It really was a farce. William Douglas-Home was one of these forced cricketers. At one time the captain of the XI could not make a run for the school and the *Eton College Chronicle* reported that he had struck a bad patch. The following week William wrote a letter to the *Chronicle* saying that if the Captain of the XI would come and play on the sort of pitches William's game had to play on, he would strike a few more!

In the winter in the Christmas half everyone had to play the Eton Field Game, a mixture of soccer and rugger and an excellent game to play. The snag was that the only opponents the school XI – called the Field – could play were Old Etonians. The status of a boy in his House was judged by his skill at this game. Until you were good enough to play for your House you had to wear grey flannel knickerbockers to play in. Shorts were not permitted until you got into the House XI. Just imagine trying to run in such archaic clothing! Anyhow I was lucky because at Eton I suddenly discovered I could run fast, something I had never done at my private school. Speed was a very important factor in this particular game, so I quickly earned my shorts in my second year, and my house colours in my third.

Each day when there was not football against one of the other houses, a boy had to do a 'time' – take some exercise such as a run, fives, squash, racquets, boxing or beagling. In the Easter half there was a choice of athletics, rugger and soccer to add to this list. I opted for rugger and in the end got into the school XV. But we were always very bad and used to get thrashed to astronomical totals by schools like

Rugby, St Pauls, Beaumont and so on. Once again my running stood me in good stead. I was never a great tackler but prided myself on my skill at selling the dummy. Our house became great experts at seven-a-side and won the House Competition in my last year.

I was severely reprimanded after one match when the XV were playing the Welsh Guards from Windsor. They were a tough lot and in great trepidation I once actually fell on the ball in defence. The loose scrum, or ruck as it is called these days, formed round me and I was kicked and trodden on amidst shouts of 'get off the ball'. From deep down I shouted 'get off mine first' which was considered very rude. Not half as rude in a physical sense as a rather fat boy called Burke who used to play in the second row of the scrum and let wind in a series of tremendous detonations. Eventually he had to be dropped from the side as they could get no volunteers to play in the back row of the scrum.

Looking back, the whole system may seem to have placed far too much emphasis on the ability to play games. However, this did ensure that everyone, even those who were no good, did take some sort of regular exercise under supervision. Nowadays boys are left very much to their own devices, which at that age, though more pleasant for them is not necessarily a 'good thing'.

A perfect example of someone who loathed games, and of the bad effect they had on him, was Gilbert Harding. He was at a Roman Catholic school, was short-sighted, fat and hated all forms of exercise. He was so bad and made such a nuisance of himself that his headmaster finally excused him all games so long as he went for a walk instead. This infuriated the young cricket master who was a Blue just down from Oxford. So when the annual match between the Masters and the Boys came along he thought he would get his revenge on Gilbert by ap-pointing him as one of the umpires. The Masters won the toss, the young Blue went in first and hit the boys' bowling all over the field, so that he soon got into the nineties. A bowler bowling from Gilbert's end then got a ball to lift which struck the Master high up on his thigh. The bowler stifled an appeal but not before Gilbert had put his finger up signalling that the batsman was out. The Master was furious and as he passed Gilbert he said: 'Harding you were not paying attention. I was not out.'

'On the contrary', replied Gilbert with great satisfaction, 'I *was* paying attention and you were *not* out!'

Still, I digress. Back to Eton, where my one and only disappointment was my failure to get into the cricket XI. I was still a wicket-keeper and each summer progressed up the scale getting my Lower Sixpenny, Upper Sixpenny, Lower Club and Twenty-two – the various colours awarded to the twelve best players in each age group. But in Upper Sixpenny I blotted my copy book and so only just got my colours.

As usual, I was too frivolous and could not resist the chance of a laugh. I was batting with a boy called Hopetoun at the other end who was rather fat and not too quick over the ground. By some fluke I hit the ball quite a long way and called to him to run. I was pretty fast between the wickets and by the time he was turning to start his second run I had completed two so that we were both then running level towards the bowler's end. I soon passed him again so that I had run four as he was halfway through his third. As you can imagine the whole field collapsed with laughter and when the inevitable happened and the ball was returned to the bowler's end no one could work out which batsman was out. All would have been well had not the Captain of the eleven happened to be watching from a distance and came over to see what all the uproar was about.

To put it mildly he was not too pleased. A similar thing was said to have happened in a house match and they all turned to the square leg umpire for a decision, only to find that it had been his turn to bat and that he was now one of the batsmen concerned!

In my last year a boy called Baerlein who had kept wicket for the school for the last two years decided to stay on for another summer although he was over nineteen years old before the half started. Naturally for a time I felt miserable about the whole thing though everyone was very kind and sympathetic especially our school coach George Hirst, the famous old Yorkshire and England all-rounder. He had a sweet disposition and was loved by all the boys. I used to keep wicket to his bowling and once got a stumping on the leg-side off him much to our mutual satisfaction. Even in those days, aged sixty he bowled a lively medium pace left arm round the wicket, and swung the ball prodigiously.

Anyway he took me under his wing and at the Eton and Harrow match took me around with him, to the dressing-rooms and even up to the scorer's box at the top of the grandstand. I had one slight compensation for not keeping wicket in the match. Eton had two very fast bowlers, one of whom was particularly wild and inaccurate. Poor Baerlein had a terrible time and actually let thirty-five byes. I would not have been human had I not had a quiet laugh. But I expect I would have let many more. Anyway I captained the second eleven or twenty-two as it was called and had far more fun than I would have had in the more austere atmosphere of the first.

The Eton and Harrow match was a great occasion and all the time I was at Eton and for many years afterwards we all used to congregate on Block G – the open stand to the right of the sightscreen at the nursery end. We barracked unmercifully, shouted ruderies and cracked jokes and it became like a club with everyone returning year after year. So far as we Etonians were concerned the stock jokes were usually about the age of the Harrow players or the number of foreigners or foreign-sounding names in their team. In these days of race relations I am sure we would be imprisoned for some of the things we used to shout out. But it was all good fun, and some of my best friends have been those same Harrovians about whom we had been so rude.

In fact until a few years ago we ran an annual match at Hurlingham between Old Etonian *v*. Old Harrovian Block G teams. The only man who ever took the slightest offence was an unsuspecting Harrow father sitting with his son watching the match. While he did so we fastened the end of his immaculate tailcoat to the seat with drawing pins, so that when he rose to leave he found himself attached to the seat. Childish I admit but we had to laugh and so did he in the end.

4

Best of the beaks

The great strength of Eton lay in the quality and character of its masters. I may be falling into the old trap but they certainly seemed greater characters then than the masters are today.

By far the wittiest was Tuppy Headlam who ruled over his house with a light rein. He seemed to inspire wit – or an attempt at it – from others. He was called the Master with a soft 'a' and was the first port of call for many Old Etonians when revisiting the school, for he dispensed drinks or dinner with great generosity. During our time there he was especially friendly with the well-known film actress Anna May Wong. He taught us history and his classroom was in his house, and as he often received telephone calls we all took it in turns to go and answer them for him. One day, just after Anna May had been down to see him, the telephone rang and Martin Gilliat (now the Queen Mother's private secretary) was on telephone duty. As he left the room there was much speculation among us and Tuppy himself as to whether the caller would be Anna May. So there was quite a lot of excitement and then a hush as Gilliat returned.

'Who was it?' asked Tuppy.

'Sorry sir', said Gilliat without a smile on his face, 'Wong number.'

On another occasion I was to learn the importance of timing in making a successful joke. I discovered that however bad the material if it is put over well, with the right emphasis at the right time it can produce laughter.

We were doing history and Tuppy was talking about the wives of an historical figure called Henry – I forget which one.

'His first wife died,' said Tuppy 'and now let's talk about his second one, Henrietta.'

'Did he really?' I said quickly from the back of the class. Bad joke, but big laugh which Tuppy enjoyed as much as anyone. His own wit could be mildly malicious. Of four headmasters under whom he served he said: 'A was a greater man than me, B a better man than me, C a cleverer man than me, and D (long pause) a deafer man than me.'

Another character was Hope-Jones. He had black curly hair, a very loud voice and was a physical fitness fanatic. A tremendous enthusiast in everything he did, he was a very keen Scoutmaster. One rather cold day he told his scout troop that he would be the hare and they the hounds. He would have a five minute start leaving a trail behind him and they were to see how soon they could find him. He went off and headed straight for a fairly deep pond by one of the playing-fields. He jumped into the water and waited for his scouts to appear. When they did so he disappeared under the surface with just his nose above water so that he could breathe. Although the trail ended rather obviously at the edge of the pond the scouts pretended they could not find him, and searched all round the adjoining fields. Poor Hope-Jones had to stay submerged in the cold water.

One summer holiday he had a bit of bad luck. The headline in our morning paper read: 'Eton Master caught bathing in the nude.' Poor chap. He had only gone for an early morning swim on some secluded beach in Cornwall and some nosey parker had sneaked to the police. In those days it was quite something and I believe he was fined for indecent exposure, so you can imagine all the talk when we got back to Eton.

Then there was Sam Slater, a frightening man with a red face and horn-rimmed spectacles. He used to let out the most enormous sneezes during class. This went on for quite a long time until the master in the next door room could stand it no longer. His name was Lt.-Col. J. D. Hills, later to be headmaster of Bradfield. He commanded the corps and thanks to his habit of somewhat immodestly reminiscing about his wartime experiences, was known as 'the man who won the war'. Anyway he was determined to win this one and instructed everyone in his class to wait for the next sneeze from Slater and then at a signal from him, all were to sneeze as loudly as they could. The effect was magical. When Sam let out his next sneeze he was amazed to hear a deafening chorus of ah-ti-shoos from Hills' classroom. He took the hint and in future sneezed in a more gentlemanly manner.

'Jelly' Churchill was a great rowing coach and spoke with a lisp. He brought the house down one day when he told a boy: 'Stop thucking your pen.'

Mr Crace was a gentle person and looked like Mr Pickwick. We were in his class one day when a messenger brought him a note. He read it and for some reason seemed annoyed. It was from the Treasurer of the Eton mission who asked him if he would please collect from his class *in the usual way*. It was these last four words which got under his skin and he promptly announced that for the next week he would be pleased if we would give what we could afford to the Eton mission but NOT in the usual way. We were to do it in any way we liked so long as it was not usual.

We thought up all sorts of ideas. We balanced piles of pennies on top of the slightly open door so that when Mr Crace came in they all fell on his mortar board. We arranged to throw coins on to his desk as the school clock struck a particular hour or quarter, so that without warning, possibly while talking to us, a shower of coins would descend on him. If we knew he was likely to refer to a certain book we inserted coins between the pages, or if he was going to use the blackboard we filled the duster with pennies. He loved it and so did we and at the end of the week the Eton mission received a record collection but definitely NOT collected 'in the usual way'.

There were quite a few parsons on the staff. One of them, the Reverend C. O. Bevan was a very pious man as befitted his station. Once a friend of mine named Charles Villiers had been annoying him all morning until in the end 'Cob' Bevan really lost his temper.

'Villiers', he said in his gruff voice, 'just because I'm a parson you think I can't swear. But I can. Damn you, Villiers, and (*a long pause while he plucked up courage*) . . . damn you again.' I doubt whether he ever forgave himself.

Quite different was 'Satan' Ford, a very fierce man who was a terror to be up to and for some reason had a strong nasal American accent. He prefaced most of his remarks with 'Boy' and one of his favourite expressions was: 'Boy, your breath smells like last week's washing.' Charming! He once wise-cracked to a stupid boy: 'Boy, you have as many brains as a snake has hips.' But he came off second-best when he was reprimanding a friend of mine called Jimmy Ford. After a few explosive comments about Jimmy's work 'Satan' said: 'Well boy, what's your beastly name?' 'Ford sir,' replied Jimmy smartly, with a smile. He knew he had won.

Mr H. K. Marsden, the Master in College, knew Bradshaw's Railway Guide backwards and it was impossible to stump him with any train to anywhere from anywhere. Mr Adie on the other hand enjoyed motoring and used to boast that he always passed other cars on the corners as they were then going so much slower. The Provost was M. R. James, a friendly genial man who wrote all those ghost stories. One of the real treats when one was an older boy was to be asked to supper with him and listen to him reading P. G. Wodehouse out loud until tears of laughter ran down his cheeks.

The headmaster was Dr Cyril Alington, a keen writer of detective stories and later Dean of Durham. He was a distinguished grey-haired figure with an imposing presence, greatly respected by the boys. He was perhaps most famous for his Sunday evening chats from the pulpit of College Chapel. All the lights were turned off and there were just two candles lit on the lectern of the pulpit. His talk lasted about ten minutes, often less, and there was always complete silence throughout the congregation of five hundred boys, except for the occasional cough.

He always finished with a strong punchline, paused, and then slowly blew out the candles – puff puff. Another pause, then up would come the lights and it was all over. Beautifully staged, and very effective. One always felt like applauding. I remember that in one of his talks he was trying to show how the story of Jesus' trial and crucifixion would not have been sensational news in those days. For Pontius Pilate it was just another job, similar to hundreds he had to deal with. Dr Alington illustrated this by telling the story of a writer who some years later wanted to find out more about the trial of Jesus. So he obtained an interview with Pontius Pilate. 'Jesus of Nazareth,' said Pilate. 'No, I don't remember the name. Who was he?' Puff-puff.

Although normally so calm and dignified Dr Alington was slightly taken aback one day when giving communion in College Chapel. He gave the Holy Bread to a boy called Danreuther who for some unknown reason put it into his pocket. The Doctor's hoarse stage whisper echoed round the altar steps: 'Consume it here,' and the crisis was over.

An unusual character was A. C. Beasley-Robinson, a highly religious man who ran the Boy Scouts and was always understood to be extremely rich. He drove an open yellow Vauxhall tourer and during the holidays was a keen rider to hounds. He prepared me for my confirmation and when he took over his house he had one of the rooms converted into a chapel. I doubt if the whole time he was at Eton he ever missed a single service in either upper or lower chapel. When he finally left he treated himself to a full season's hunting in the shires, then gave up everything to become a monk.

Just after I left Eton there was a boy called Trotter in his house who was an expert at all things to do with radio and electricity. In fact when I joined the 2nd Bn Grenadier Guards during the war he was the signal officer. Anyway he put his knowledge to good (?) use by wiring up the house and placing microphones in strategic places, including under Beasley-Robinson's dining-room table in the private part of the house.

I wonder if Beasley realises today how many of his dinner party conversations were monitored. Trotter soon became one of the best-informed boys in the school and knew most of the gossip about the masters, boys and even the dames! But even if Beasley had discovered Trotter's secret I am sure he would have forgiven him. He was that sort of man.

One of the doctors at Eton was called Amsler, a tough character who stood no nonsense. It was his job every summer half to issue any 'excused camp' certificates to members of the OTC. Some people disliked the idea of camp, though in fact it was great fun. One summer half there was a bigger queue than usual in his surgery of boys trying to get off. He listened patiently for some time to their feeble excuses, carrying out brief examinations of the more genuine cases. But after an hour or so he lost his temper and his patience. This was bad luck on a boy called Stirling, later to become the Lord Mayor of Westminster. He genuinely had a bad attack of rheumatism, and was bent double as he struggled up to Amsler's desk. Amsler must have thought he was trying to be funny and putting on an act. He interrupted Stirling's 'Please sir I've got rheumatism' with a curt: 'Next man please' and poor Stirling had to go to camp.

Amsler also used to referee at the school boxing. One year there was only one entrant for the heavyweight division, a large boy called Balmain. This meant that he would have a walk-over and automatically win the cup. But by the regulations if there was no fight there was no prize money which normally went with the cup. So Balmain found another boy in his house called Congreve to whom he offered £1 just to enter for the heavyweight division. Congreve had never boxed before but agreed to the proposal when Balmain promised not to hurt him in any way. There was a packed house in the gymnasium when the final bout of the evening was due to start and a surprised ooooh from the spectators when they saw Congreve step into the ring, hardly knowing which corner to go to.

When the bell went the two boxers danced around, bobbing and weaving, but making sure never to get within striking distance of each other. The crowd roared with laughter. But not Dr Amsler. After about a minute he stopped the 'fight' and warned both boxers that if they did not box properly he would stop the contest and declare it null and void. This would of course have meant no cup nor prize money for either boxer. What came over Congreve I don't know, but at the words 'Box on' he rushed at Balmain, swung his right arm and with a tremendous hook of which Dempsey would have been proud knocked the astonished Balmain flat out on the canvas. Pandemonium erupted and the look on Congreve's face when he realised what he had done was worth going miles to see. But it was nothing to the look on Balmain's when he finally came round to find that he had not only lost the cup and the prize money but also the £1 he had paid Congreve to enter!

After two years my housemaster Monty retired. Our new man was an old Wykehamist who years before had made a hundred against Eton in the annual match. A red-haired man called A. C. Huson, his face was completely purple as he was said to have one skin less than anyone else. He was a bachelor and a really wonderful person and as near the perfect housemaster as could be. He had a great sense of humour, was kind and understanding and I owe him as big a debt as anyone else in my life. He died ten years after I had left as a result of a strangulated hernia brought on I am sure by a strange habit he had.

In those days the Eton housemasters used to live very well and entertained each other at super dinner parties with only the best wines and beautifully cooked food. Furthermore they always changed for dinner. Immediately after the meal the other housemasters used to return to their houses for their nightly rounds of the boys' rooms. When these were completed they would return to the party for brandy and cigars.

In my last year Huson had been bitten by the keep-fit bug and used to do all sorts of exercises. One of his favourites was to lie on his back and raise his legs up 90° into the air, lower them without touching the ground, up in the air again and so on. Try it and see how many times you can do it before your stomach muscles pack up. You will be lucky if you do ten. Well Huson used to come to my room in his dinner-jacket straight from one of these dinners, lie down on the floor and do one hundred of these leg exercises. It was a crazy thing to do following a big meal and it is no wonder that he died in the way that he did.

One of his great friends was another red-haired master called Routh who also had a sense of humour and used to snort through his nose every time that he laughed, which was often. His sense of the ridiculous was a great help to William Douglas-Home, when Mr Routh marked one of the history papers we had to do in 'trials' at the end of the half. One question was:

'Write as briefly as you can on one of the following subjects:
1. *The Future of Coal.*
2. *The decline of the British Empire.*
3. *Whither Socialism?*'

William chose the first question and bearing in mind the instruction to be brief wrote as his answer the one word 'smoke'. To his eternal credit Mr Routh awarded him seven marks out of ten. After all, the answer was both accurate and brief.

It is an unusual thing to be able to say but the food in our house both with Monty and Huson was always excellent. It cost a lot to feed and run a house even in those days. I remember Mr Huson saying that when King George V asked for an extra week's holiday for the boys to celebrate a visit to the school, it was as good as giving £100 to the Huson bank account.

Not all houses were so well fed, especially one on the corner of Keats Lane, which had better be nameless. About six years after I had left one of the boys in this house tried to commit suicide. Luckily he failed, but the housemaster was determined to find out why the boy had tried, and summoned the whole house into the dining-room. He asked if they knew any reason why this should have happened. Was the boy being bullied, was he in financial difficulties, was he worried about his work?

As usual on occasions like this there was a deathly silence. So the housemaster repeated his questions, saying he was determined to get to the bottom of the affair, even if it meant them all staying in and missing their half-holiday.

Thus threatened a boy at the back of the room held up his hand: 'Yes, Ormsby-Gore,' said the relieved housemaster, 'what is your theory?' And Ormsby-Gore – now Lord Harlech – replied with an innocent air: 'Please sir, could it have been the food?' Collapse of housemaster!

There are also splendid stories told about some of the housemasters' wives, one or two of whom were fairly formidable ladies. One was once at a charity concert given by the local Women's Institute. Somewhat rashly, one of the performers struggled through a recitation of a poem in French. When she had finished to enthusiastic applause the house-master's wife turned to her neighbour in the front row and in a loud whisper said: 'Beautifully spoken, and how wise not to attempt the French accent!'

Another wife found that her servants were pinching cigarettes from the various boxes in the private side of the house. So she put notices in each one which read: 'Please don't help yourself'. Unfortunately, when the fourth of June came along and they had a lot of parents to lunch and tea she forgot to remove the notices before the boxes were handed round to the guests.

It was quite the opposite at the local Eton flower show, when there was often intense rivalry between the various Eton houses as to who had the best displays of fruit. There were baskets of apples, raspberries, gooseberries, etc. on display, with the usual cautionary notice stuck in front: 'Please don't touch.' One housemaster's wife feared that a rival's apples were better than hers so she waited for an opportune moment when their owner had left the show tent and placed the following notice in front of her rival's apples: 'Please take one'.

Something peculiar to Eton was the office of Dame. Each house had one – they were called M'Dame – and they were a sort of super matron, substitute-mother, state-registered nurse and catering expert all rolled into one. Usually they were even more than that. They became the confidante, comforter and friend of all the boys in the house. They acted as a kind of buffer between the boys and the house-master and library. They were mobbed, mimicked and laughed at, but at the same time in a funny sort of way were respected and loved. Tea with M'Dame was a regular date each half and there was a saying we used to use about people or things: 'very good but very old – just like M'Dame's cakes'.

Dames were responsible for the health of all the boys and were expected to deal with emergencies like cuts or injuries at games. In the unmarried houses they did the catering and of course ran the house-hold – the maids, cleaning, linen, etc. To be good they had to be saints and very often were. We had two while I was there, Miss Sealey and Miss Hancock. They both took a great interest in the house and often stood on the touch line in icy weather watching some juniors playing in a house-match.

Our Dames also had to deal with the real mothers who varied from the difficult to the impossible with their demands on how 'my boy' should be treated. God bless them both and my grateful thanks and my apologies for the many ways in which I am sure I must have made their lives more difficult.

In this chapter, I have purposely dealt mainly with the lighter side of Eton life. Many others more qualified to do so have written about its ancient traditions and education. All I would humbly like to say is that the system of each boy to his own room, with his own tutor to guide and help him was invaluable, and that the traditions and customs helped to create a solid base on which to found one's life. So speaks – a bit pompously I'm afraid – at least one very satisfied old Etonian.

5
And so to Bude...

For the first two years of my life at Eton we lived at Hellens an old Jacobean house in the quaintly named village of Much Marcle in Herefordshire. It was a lively village and we took part in all the activities. My mother ran the Mother's Union and Women's Institute and my sister and brothers and I used to try to provide entertainment at the 'do's' in the village hall. We formed a rough sort of band and also tried our hand at a spot of drama.

I remember one sketch called 'George's Ghost'. It involved my brother Michael wearing a false moustache. At the most dramatic point of the plot I had to offer him a light for his cigarette. I struck a match as detailed in the script and promptly set fire to his moustache which he was forced to rip smartly off his upper lip, rather spoiling the dramatic climax. It certainly got one of the biggest laughs I have ever heard and after that we decided to stick to comedy.

Our groom in those days was called Dean. He had enormous ears which he could tuck in. He taught me how to do it and I can still tuck in my right ear today. This is a trick very few can achieve – a lot depends on the texture and pliability of the ears. I have only met two people who can do it – Mike du Boulay an old friend from Winchester, and John Woodcock, *The Times'* cricket correspondent.

At Hellens we also had a very sweet parlourmaid called Mrs Jones who had the biggest tummy-rumbles in the business. I don't know if it was because she was always hungry or what. Anyway when we had guests and her tummy started to rumble, my stepfather used to ostentatiously kick his spaniel 'Shot' who lay under the table and tell him to behave himself. Rather like the apocryphal story of the day when the Queen was meeting an important Head of State at Victoria Station. They were driving back to Buckingham Palace in an open state coach drawn by four well fed Windsor Greys. When the coachman flicked one of them with his whip the grey let out an ear-splitting fart. The Queen and the Head of State were busy waving to the crowds and the Queen, still smiling, graciously muttered to the Head of State: 'I'm sorry about that' and went on waving.

'Ah, Madam,' replied he, 'the honesty of you English. Had you not apologised I would have thought that it was one of the horses.'

It was at Hellens that my stepfather bought our first ever radio, a big event in those days. A man came to install it so that he could listen to it and decide whether to buy it. It was a super eight-valve set and the whole family assembled as it was switched on. After a minute or so my stepfather commented with disappointment to the man, 'But that sound is just like a gramophone record.' With a gleam of triumph the man replied: 'That sir, is exactly what it is. We are listening to one of Christopher Stone's gramophone programmes.' So the radio was duly purchased.

From Much Marcle we moved to Bude in North Cornwall to a much smaller house, and there on my holidays from Eton I played cricket and tennis in the summer and continued hunting in the winter. Hunting for some reason I thoroughly enjoyed, possibly because so many funny things happened, although I was pretty scared at times. We hunted with a small hunt called the Tetcott which covered wet and boggy country with banks instead of hedges to jump. This meant that the horse had to jump on to the top of the bank and then off again – which made it difficult if by any chance you suddenly encountered a fence. The horse was so used to banks that it would usually jump right on top of a hedge instead of clearing it, with disastrous results.

The field was made up of farmers with a few retired colonels and majors and even one General and a few like me at home for the holidays. We used to pull the legs of the retired military by pretending we had suddenly seen the fox. We would gallop madly off shouting 'gone away', hoping the field would follow us. Sometimes they did and then our day was made.

Once when it was very wet my stepfather, who always wore full hunting pink complete with top hat, was talking to the General outside a cover which was being drawn by the hounds. He was riding a brand new chestnut hunter which he had just bought in his home-country – Ireland. As he was swopping some wartime experience with the General the chestnut began to sink slowly into the ground as if going down in a lift. They had been standing in a bog. Luckily it was not too deep but it was a marvellous sight with most of the horse under the mud and my stepfather visible only from the waist up. He had to dismount and struggle through the mud in his spotless white breeches and pink coat. The horse was eventually pulled out but I imagine that if he was watching, even the fox laughed.

Another time the MFH, a retired Captain, came to dinner and my stepfather who was very proud of his port sought the MFH's opinion. 'What do you think of this port, Dudgeon?' (Note the use of the surname – a military habit.)

A long pause while Dudgeon sipped his port. 'Do you want my candid opinion, Scully?' 'Yes of course, Dudgeon,' replied my stepfather. 'Well, I'd say it tasted like sea-weed.' As I have said my stepfather was Irish and after a second's incredulity, he exploded. We were all sent out of the room from which heated voices could be heard for some time.

During one summer holiday something happened which I always try to recall whenever I feel in need of a laugh. We were sitting by the swimming pool at Bude which is full of seawater and built out of the rocks beneath the cliffs. As in most pools one end was very shallow and the other deep enough for people wanting to dive. On this day the water was very murky and a man in a rubber helmet came and stood by us. After taking a good long look at the water, he held his nose, took a terrific leap into the air and jumped into the water. Unfortunately we were sitting at the shallow end which was only two feet deep. Instead of sinking slowly down as he had intended his legs crumpled up underneath him as his feet landed on the bottom. As he collapsed spluttering into the water I am ashamed to say that we roared with laughter.

6

Oxford

By the time I was due to leave Eton at the end of the 1931 summer half I still had no idea what I wanted to do with my life. I had a feeling that I ought to go into the family coffee business, as my elder brother Michael had gone off to farm in Canada, and the other, Christopher, was up at Oxford prior to going into the 14/20 Hussars.

Mr Huson persuaded me to go to Oxford while I sorted myself out. So I went up to New College where my father had been thirty-one years before. I doubt whether I really passed the rather cursory entrance examination, but in those days the family connection was all-important and made entry practically certain. Very different to today when in some colleges, including I am afraid New College, it seems to be more of a handicap than a help.

We were very lucky with our dons, who were most delightful characters. The Warden was H. A. L. Fisher, a brilliant historian who for a short time had been Minister of Education in Lloyd George's Government of 1922. He had a habit of bringing into the conversation the phrase 'when I was in the Cabinet' which caused a lot of amusement among his French friends (*cabinet* in French means a W.C.).

The chaplain was called Lightfoot and he used to tell us how he had once been 'crucified' with croquet hoops on the college lawn by some undergraduates who were celebrating. My own tutor was a friendly man with a snorting laugh called Wickham Legge who once got an unintended laugh when talking to us about Henry VIII and the bad fevers from which he suffered.

'Personally', said Wickham Legge, 'if I am in bed with a fever I toss off everything within reach.'

The Dean was a charming man called Henderson who spoke with a broken German accent. He was an expert in dealing with rowdy parties and employed sound psychology. One night some visitors from another college were throwing stones in the quadrangle and had broken one or two windows. The Dean appeared on the scene and quickly summed up the situation. 'Let's all break one more window,' he said to the astonished revellers, 'and then all go off to bed.' So saying he picked up a small stone and threw it through a window. This apparently satisfied the students, who dispersed quietly and returned to their own colleges.

In other ways, the Dean was a bit old fashioned in his outlook. For example, some of us once went out with a friend to test his new car. We topped 75 mph – very fast in those days – and were stopped by the police and reported for speeding. The Dean got to hear of it and requested us to see him. We all agreed to say that we had only been doing 37 mph as we knew that he disapproved of fast cars. So when he asked us how fast we had been going, as one man we all answered innocently, 'Thirty-seven miles per hour, sir'.

The Dean stepped backwards as if startled, and a low whistle escaped his lips. 'Ach', he said, 'if you go at such speeds you must expect to get into trouble.' We were gated for a few days, but goodness knows what would have been his reaction or our punishment, had we been a little more truthful.

Another don who taught me history had the splendid name of Ogg and there was also an earnest Wykehamist in spectacles whom we saw from time to time. But he deserted teaching for politics and did not do too badly. His name was Richard Crossman.

In my first term I made great friends with another freshman called Jim St John Harmsworth. He came from Harrow and had a wonderful sense of humour and a very funny, pompous way of talking. He is now, by the way, a highly respected stipendiary magistrate in central London.

Together, we decided to have a go at the hunting set, who had their headquarters in some digs in the High. They were all famous point-to-point riders, hunted most days of the week and kept their horses and grooms at some stables outside Oxford. Jim and I asked whether we could call on them for some advice and in some trepidation went round to beard them in their rooms.

They received us royally, offering huge glasses of sherry at eleven o'clock in the morning, as they stood warming their bottoms in front of the fire, every now and again slapping their riding boots with their canes. There was Lord Rosebery's son Lord Dalmeny, John Pearson now Lord Cowdray and John Lakin, a famous figure in the hunting and point-to-point world.

Jim and I pretended that we each had several hunters and wanted to know how many we needed to bring up in order to hunt at least two days a week. We also asked whether they would advise us to bring up our grooms as well. Naturally we had neither hunters nor grooms, but they seemed to believe us and offered us good advice and lots more sherry. We also enquired about the point-to-point racing, saying we were very keen to take part in the Grinds or point-to-points next term. This set John Lakin off and he proceeded to tell us some hair-raising incidents in races in which he had taken part. To this day I remember well one of his remarks: 'I had Geoff Fitzhornby racing on one side, Harry Kennard on the other. As we came down the hill I stuck the daggers in and left them standing . . .'

We departed firm friends, leaving them with the impression that we would be regular members of the hunting set. A week later we were asked to attend a party for all the horsey men up at Oxford. Eventually they found out that we had been pulling their legs when no horses or grooms arrived. But they seemed to bear no malice and went on happily slapping their boots whenever we met them.

Jim and I did in fact ride in one race in our last year. So did William Douglas-Home which was extremely brave of him, as he had never really ridden before, whereas Jim and I had at least done some hunting – as boys. William and I took some practice at a riding school at Headington where it was decided that William should have a large black docile horse called Nero, and that I should ride Tiptop. He was more lively and a nice-looking bay who was said to be a half brother of Tom Walls's Derby winner April the Fifth – though which half they never told me. Jim by this time had bought a horse of his own, so was better mounted than either of us.

For some reason we were never allowed to jump either of our horses in practice beforehand, so we had no idea whether we would ever get over the first fence. As the day of the race approached I was terrified at the prospect and wished I had never entered. I had tried to pick up some tips by reading various books on riding, and was impressed by the arguments in favour of the forward seat, and was determined to try it. As it turned out I was very lucky to have been allotted Tiptop, whom I rode in a racing snaffle, and though of course he did not know it, he could have stopped whenever he wished.

When the starter's flag went down we were left at the post, but Tiptop set off in pursuit of the others and flew over the fences as if he imagined he was Golden Miller. My forward seat theory went for a burton and I found myself leaning so far backwards that my head nearly hit his quarters each time we went over a jump. We somehow got round without me 'leaving the plate', though once or twice I nearly 'went through the front door'. We finished fifth, one ahead of Jim Harmsworth on his chestnut gelding.

Poor William was not so lucky. Nero refused at the first fence but scrambled over at the second attempt, encouraged by shouts of 'Nero my God to thee' from some irreverent undergraduates. But he was a long way behind the other horses and did not fancy jumping the second fence on his own. So William reluctantly had to call it a day.

When I returned to the unsaddling enclosure I was given a few cheers by one or two friends, but was surprised to receive a somewhat hostile reception from the other race-goers. It turned out that before the race my friends had gone round the bookies backing Tiptop and with loud stage whispers saying what a good chance he had. As a result Tiptop had started third favourite and had also been tipped by an old tipster friend of mine called Captain Dean. He had some wonderful patter such as: 'There's a horse here today which could jump the first fence, lie down, smoke a cigarette and then get up and win.' Or, 'They've sent a horse all the way from Leicester. It's so thin that it reminds me of Napoleon in exile. They couldn't have St Helena horse,' and 'I've got as many pound notes as Sir Thomas Lipton had tea leaves. I tell you what I'm going to do. I'm going right through the card and at the end of the day when you've backed all my winners I want you to come up to me and say, "Good old Captain Dean. You and I have got a lot in common. Common have a drink!" '
But I think he summed up our performance in the saddle perfectly when he said: 'There are jockeys here today who couldn't ride in a railway carriage unless the door was locked.'

Inspired by our attempts at equestrianism we organised a race meeting in the summer on Port Meadow, a large open space by the river. We hired some old hacks and had enough runners for a card of four races. A local bookie shouted the odds and I took over Captain Dean's role as tipster. Everything went fine until the start of the third race when the favourite, rightly deciding that his jockey was no great expert bolted straight for the river. Unfortunately he failed to stop at the bank and jumped straight in, jockey and all. So the races had to be abandoned, while horse and jockey were salvaged.

At Oxford I read for my degree in history. I averaged around one lecture a day and read books suggested by my tutor for whom I had to write one essay a week. Looking back, I feel ashamed at the small amount of work I did, devoting most of my time to games and getting up to stupid pranks with friends.

Together we formed a club called the All Sorts, playing rugger against neighbouring schools or soccer against various sides in the town including a side of waiters from all the hotels. We had numbers on our backs and before every match lined up to be presented to some 'dignatory' with bowler hat and rolled umbrella who was needless to say one of us disguised with false moustache, etc. The matches used to be reported in the *Oxford Mail*, an excellent evening paper which, however, once made an awful bloomer.

It was during the gold crisis which occurred while I was up at Oxford, resulting in the formation of the National Government. Everyone was asked to economise, so quite a few of the colleges decided to cancel their commemoration balls which normally took place at the end of the summer term. This news was headlined by the *Oxford Mail* as follows: UNPRECEDENTED EVENT. UNDERGRADU-ATES SCRATCH BALLS! I hasten to add it was only in one edition – which was of course a sell-out.

On some summer evenings we would go up to the Trout Inn and after a good supper get into a couple of eights and have a boatrace back. It was usually Eton *v*. Harrow with Eton the winners as befitted a rowing school, though all of us were dry bobs. In those days there was always something going on.

One Sunday night there was a concert in New College Chapel so I disguised myself as a tramp and sat down outside the gate with some old hunting pictures which I had taken down off the wall of my room. I had a cap on the pavement and when the concert was over and people began coming out I started to beg in a whining voice, saying I had a wife and six children to keep, etc. Some friends mingled with the crowd and tossed coins into the cap murmuring 'Poor fellow' 'What a shame' and so on. This encouraged the others to throw in a few

pennies. Eventually the proctor was seen approaching with his two
bulldogs so we quickly gathered up the pictures and fled. But I had
collected about five shillings, the first money which I had ever 'earned'.

New College was a fairly tough place to live in at the time. The rooms
were comfortable enough but if one wanted a bath one had to go across
the quadrangle in a dressing-gown in all weathers. Why we did not die
of pneumonia I have no idea. Each staircase had a scout who used to
clean the rooms, serve breakfast or lunch if required and generally
act as a sort of super Jeeves. I had a marvellous man called Honey who
needless to say we nicknamed Bunch.

Honey had been my brother's scout and always called me 'our kid'.
He was a part-time fireman and had to work overtime on 5 November
when the whole city was ablaze with fireworks. This was the only
occasion in the year when there was ever any real trouble between the
police and undergraduates.

New College was very cosmopolitan. It had a large number of
Rhodes scholars from the Commonwealth as well as a sprinkling of
Americans. One of these, Bill Crandall, was in his late twenties and
had a Yul Brynner haircut (not intentionally). He was full of charm and
always tried to say the nicest things to everybody. Unfortunately, he
was not always successful. For example, one Sunday some of us went
to lunch at the home of one of the undergraduates, and Bill, always
ready to help, volunteered to carve the chickens. When it was time for
second helpings he went to the sideboard and called out to our hostess,
'Would you like some more breast Mrs Tollemache?' She happened
to be the owner of a very large pair of bosoms so you can imagine
our reaction when Bill noticed she had not yet finished and went on to
say, 'Oh sorry, I see that you've still got plenty in front of you.'

On another occasion he was trying to congratulate Elizabeth Alington (daughter of the Eton headmaster and who later married Sir
Alec Douglas-Home) on being a personality in her own right.

'Miss Alington,' he drawled, 'I'd like to congratulate you on being
yourself without the help of your father.'

So far as games went, I played rugger and cricket for the college,
being captain of cricket for two years. I had two unusual experiences
at rugger. In one cupper – or inter-college cup-tie – I found to my
horror that I had to mark H. G. Owen Smith at centre three quarters.
He was a Rhodes scholar who had made a hundred for South Africa
against England at cricket, and had also played full-back for England at

rugger. During the match as I had feared he frequently penetrated my defence. But once when in front of the posts he shaped up to try to drop a goal.

Instead of tackling him, as I should have done, I sneaked up behind him and whipped the ball out of his hands. He was obviously amazed – that sort of thing just did not happen in the high-class rugger in which he usually played. My triumph was short-lived. Before I could do anything with the ball he swung round and flung me into the mud. In another match, my shorts were torn off when I was tackled. I went and stood on the touchline while someone rushed off to the pavilion to get me another pair. A friend who was watching lent me his macintosh to put on to cover my confusion! As I stood there the ball came down the three-quarter line so I joined in on the wing, took the final pass and amidst uproar from spectators and players alike scored a try between the posts in my macintosh. The referee was laughing too much to blow his whistle so he allowed the try to stand, though as I hadn't signalled my return to the field of play, I doubt if it was legal.

I used to play cricket at least four times a week not only for the college but for teams like the Oxford University Authentics, Eton Ramblers and I Zingari. This was delightful cricket though naturally my work suffered. In fact I played just as much in my third and final summer when I had my exams to do for my degree. I was able to do this thanks to a crammer called Mr Young. Several of us went to him, and his method was very simple. He taught us the outstanding facts and events in each period of history and told us that we must weave these into our answers, no matter what the questions were. The idea was to impress the examiners with our knowledge, and it evidently worked as we all got degrees of sorts.

However, I nearly gave the game away in one of the questions about Anglo-Saxon times. They had a piece of land called a fyrd, but when Mr Young talked about this I thought he had said third. In the exam I was in a bit of a hurry so to save time wrote 'the Anglo-Saxon $\frac{1}{3}$rd'. One of the dons pointed this out to me during my oral and I am glad to say that I had the grace to blush! I must also add that I now feel very guilty about resorting to such tactics to gain a degree, which I did – a third in history.

In spite of playing so much cricket I was never quite good enough to get a blue, though in my second year Brian Hone the University Captain did play especially in a match for New College in order to assess my form. He did this as it seemed possible that the old blue P. C. Oldfield would not be available through pressure of work for his degree. Oldfield was one of the best wicket-keepers I have seen, amateur or professional. He was very quiet and unostentatious and played for the Gentlemen at Lord's in 1934. The annoying thing about it to me was that he loathed cricket and gave it up as soon as he went down from Oxford. He much preferred point-to-point racing. Had he really enjoyed cricket and had the time to play it I feel sure that he would have been near to the England side.

The great Wally Hammond once made Oldfield look rather foolish when Gloucestershire played Oxford in the Parks. The giant Christopher Ford – six feet eight and a half inches and twin brother to Edward Ford who later was one of the Queen's secretaries – was bowling very fast and bringing the ball down from a great height. To counter this Hammond stood a yard outside his crease. Ford and Oldfield noticed this and at a prearranged signal, Oldfield who had been standing a long way back, began to creep up to the stumps as Ford started his run. The obvious intention was for Ford to bowl a slower ball and for Oldfield to bring off a surprise stumping. But the great man must have sensed something was up or possibly heard Oldfield approaching from behind. Anyway just as Ford was about to deliver the ball, coinciding with Oldfield's arrival at the stumps, Hammond simply stepped aside signifying he was not going to play the ball. Ford stopped in his tracks and a very sheepish Oldfield turned round and went back to his old position, looking just like a boy who has been spotted moving in a game of grandmother's footsteps.

7

Fun AND games with the Ramblers

I am not really entitled to criticise the University education, since I was so busy enjoying myself that I failed to take real advantage of it. But I have always been surprised that each term only lasts for eight weeks. It seems to be an absurdly short percentage of the year – less than half.

By the time one had settled down in the first week of term and attended all the farewell parties in the last, there was not much time left in between. An undergraduate was of course meant to work at his books during the vacation, but even in those days and much more nowadays many students took jobs especially in the summer.

If there is any value in having a tutor to direct and explain one's studies, it does seem ridiculous that for twenty-eight weeks of the year he is not available to do so. But it obviously suits the dons and so it did me, as it enabled me to play cricket non-stop throughout the summer holidays!

Based at Bude I travelled miles to play anywhere usually for the 'Eton Ramblers' and went on tours staying in private houses for something which has now nearly disappeared – country house cricket. The host would put up an eleven of his friends and there would be a long weekend or even a week of cricket played on his own private ground against visiting teams. It was the perfect mixture of good – though not too serious – cricket in beautiful surroundings mixed with great hospitality and conviviality in the evenings. I'm bound to admit that we got up to some terrible tricks.

Once we were staying in Yorkshire with some great friends called Lane Fox. One of the guests was to be Colonel Cartwright, then secretary of the Eton Ramblers and now their revered President. He has always been known throughout the sporting world and London clubland as Buns and is a remarkable character. For over sixty years he has been seen at almost every main sporting function, Ascot, Lord's, Twickenham, Wimbledon and so on. In 1946 when the Moscow Dynamos were touring England he and I after a generous lunch at White's stood wedged in the crowd at Stamford Bridge to watch them play Chelsea. The crowd was 81,000 – still I believe a record for the ground and I have seldom been so frightened in my life. We were against a crush barrier and even the massive figure of Buns was nearly crushed and winded every time the crowd pressed forward.

Buns has always been a bachelor but has never let that state interfere with his pleasures. On one occasion a friend of mine said he had met a Colonel Cartwright on holiday in Yugoslavia. He thought he was good value and added . . . 'and what a charming lady Mrs Cartwright is!'

Anyway back to our cricket tour in Yorkshire. We persuaded our hostess to tell Buns when he arrived that owing to the late departure of the last guests the maids had not had time to do his room out properly. So would he please excuse anything that had not been tidied up or cleared away. We asked her to do this because we had got hold of a chamber pot and filled it with lime-juice, sausages and loo paper and placed it under his bed. We made sure that it was just sticking out so that he would be bound to see it. Sure enough he did, though we were not able to see his reaction when he first spotted it. Anyhow when he discovered its true contents he chased us all round the house and threw it all over us.

In another house at a dinner party we placed a 'whoopee' bag under the cushion of his dining-room chair. We arranged for everyone to be quiet when our hostess asked us to be seated. The explosion as Buns sat down was shattering. But our hostess (duly rehearsed) remained calm. She summoned the butler and said: 'Meadows, would you please open the window. Colonel Cartwright has . . . ' Then there was uproar.

But our practical jokes did not always come off. Every summer we used to stay with Edgar Baerlein and his family during the Eton Rambler tour of Lancashire and Cheshire. He was the old Tennis and Racquets champion and even then at the age of fifty-six was still a wonderful games player. I remember when we were staying he decided to take up lawn tennis, so engaged a professional from Manchester to come over and teach him the basic techniques. We left them to go and play cricket which as it happened finished a little early. When we returned they were still playing but there was no doubt who was winning. With his marvellous eye, the cut he got on to the ball and his instinctive placing Baerlein had the professional chasing all over the court. In his championship matches he had always been famous for never giving up or admitting defeat, which is why we met our match.

Before dinner one night we filled some of his favourite chocolates with toothpaste, and after the port had gone round we waited in expectation, hardly able to suppress our laughter. He offered the chocolates around but we all refused one. Suspecting nothing he took one himself and popped it into his mouth. He was engaged at the time in a long argument with someone about games – he had a theory that golf was a competition not a game, as nothing could be done to interfere with one's opponent's play (other than by cheating). We waited breathlessly for him to spit the chocolate out as soon as he bit on the soft centre. But we waited in vain. He carried on with his conversation as if nothing had happened, chewing away at the chocolate apparently quite unconcerned, though froth was oozing out of the corners of his mouth. In the end he swallowed it without turning a hair. He had called our bluff and our joke fell flat.

One trick which I would not recommend was played on a member of our team called Gerald Best. He was so tall that he used to sway in the breeze and was nicknamed Percy Pinetree. We bought some kippers and tied them on to the cylinder block of his car engine when he was not looking. At the end of play he got into his car, started up and then had to wait a few minutes in a queue to get out of the ground. Almost immediately smoke and a horrible smell came from under his bonnet much to his amazement. I am sorry to say that a passing dog sniffed the odour of the kippers and leaped at his car and tried to scratch his way through the bonnet. We were NOT popular.

At the end of one of these tours some of us went to Blackpool to savour the delights of the Golden Mile. We 'did' the funfair, including paying sixpence to see the Rector of Stiffkey sitting in a large barrel. Poor chap. What a way to earn money, sitting there all day with hundreds of people peering through the bung-hole at you. We also tried one of those talking weighing machines. When I got on the voice said 'Eleven stone four pounds' – I was a slim young chap in those days. Then it was the turn of Buns. On he got and the voice said 'One at a time please'!

Playing cricket for the Eton Ramblers was tremendous fun and we travelled miles to get a game. The Ramblers is a club like the Free Forresters or I Zingari – it has no home ground of its own but plays up to eighty matches every season. A friend of mine named John Hogg was due to play with me in one match against Sandhurst at Camberley. At the last moment he could not play for some reason, so obtained a replacement, another Old Etonian called Scaramanga, who was a very good bat but could only bowl friendly leg breaks. John on the other hand was a very good all-rounder and a top-class medium-pace bowler. The manager of the match was a rather irate Colonel called Darrell who had been relying on Hogg's bowling to get the opposition out. So he was obviously very annoyed when I explained to him what had happened. He turned to Scaramanga and testily asked him his name. 'Scaramanga sir,' he replied, to which Darrell snapped: 'Stop joking boy. What's your proper name?'

Another family with whom we used to stay a great deal were the Turners. The father Geoff was extremely rich and had huge business interests in India. They lived in a fabulous white modern house with a large estate near Hungerford, with wonderful shooting and fishing for those who enjoyed that sort of thing. They were exceedingly hospitable and the comfortable, centrally-heated house was always full of guests. The whole family used to enjoy a drink or two and it was funny to see the different ways in which it used to affect them.

Geoff used to start reminiscing about the time he had spent in Japan, prefacing his remarks with the phrase, 'You boys all know why I went to Japan.' None of us including his family had the slightest idea, though his stories were full of vague hints about secret service. When he died after the war I remember writing to one of his sons Nigel who was my particular friend. After the usual condolences, I added a PS. 'Now we shall never know why he went to Japan.' And we never did.

Mrs Turner after a few drinks used simply to drop off to sleep even at a dinner party – just like the doormouse at the Mad Hatter's Tea Party.

One of the daughters used to get a bit annoyed and once picked up a Christmas pudding off the dining-room table and hurled it through the serving hatch into the kitchen where it luckily missed the cook.

The effect of alcohol on Nigel's brother John was once nearly disastrous. After rather a good dinner he went to throw a log on to the large open fire. Unfortunately he forgot to let go and went on to the fire with the log but luckily was quickly pulled off.

All these antics were capped by Pinnock, the butler, who one evening at dinner had obviously been at the port. As he swayed round the table serving the vegetables Mr Turner shouted to him: 'Pinnock, you're drunk.' 'Well sir,' replied Pinnock dropping a few peas into the lap of one of the guests, 'it's about my turn'!

When I was at Bude during the long vacation I used to run the cricket side, which played on the tennis courts on the edge of the cliffs. It was always very windy which made the judging of high catches very difficult. The old tennis court lines also led to a certain amount of confusion. My stepfather was once going for a short run against the New College Nomads who were on tour in Cornwall. He flung himself at full length with bat stretched out and was furious when given out. 'But look,' he said to the umpire, 'my bat is over the line.' It was gently pointed out to him that it was the base-line of one of the tennis courts.

I also used to play a lot for a team which was run by Lord Carrington, father of the present peer. The team was called Millaton after his house in the little Devonshire village of Bridestowe. It was a beautiful ground, very small, with a thatched pavilion and very short boundaries.

There were always two or three parsons playing, especially an old boy called Arundell. He was mad about cricket and was said to say 'over' instead of amen at the end of a prayer. He kept wicket as he was not mobile enough to field anywhere else. A local rule had to be made that boundary byes counted two not four otherwise extras would always have been top scorer. Arundell was inevitably nicknamed the Ancient Mariner as 'he stoppeth one of three'. I first heard the following story as referring to him, though in later years it was always told about that grand old actor A. E. Matthews. It was said that each morning Mrs Arundell used to take her husband up a cup of tea and a copy of *The Times*. He would drink the tea, read *The Times* right through, then finally check on the Obituary Column. If he wasn't in it, he got up!

Bude was a happy place in those days with lots of young people of my own age. One of them was called Mickey Thomas. He had a very attractive sister called Marjorie with whom I was 'friendly'. Nothing serious of course but she used to come and see me at Eton during my last year and afterwards at Oxford. One holiday-time she said she had an actor friend coming down to stay. He was in the Liverpool Repertory but was 'resting' at the moment. He was a bit hard up for cash, so would we be nice and kind to him. So of course we were, and saw a lot of this amusing actor who was very short-sighted and wore a monocle when he wanted to see anything at all clearly. He had a high squeaky voice with a slightly querulous tone, and was not much good at table tennis. Shortly after this holiday in Bude he married Marjorie who promptly changed her name to Colette, and became the first of his five wives. He then got a part in Terence Rattigan's *French Without Tears* and after that, as they say, Rex Harrison never looked back.

8
A taste of coffee

In June 1934 it was time for me to go down from Oxford. I had enjoyed three very happy years, not too productive maybe in the development of my knowledge, but of great value in helping me to understand and live with my fellow beings. But I was no nearer to deciding how I wanted to earn my living. After a series of family conferences, it was decided that I should go into the old Johnston coffee business.

It was now a public company – the Brazilian Warrant Co. Ltd – and its Chairman a kindly if occasionally irascible man called Arthur Whitworth. He was a big 'noise' in the City and among other things was a director of the Bank of England. He had also rowed with my father at New College and his brother had been a famous housemaster at Eton. So he knew something about me, and took great trouble to plan my future for me. I shall always be sorry that in a way I let him down. But more of that later.

The present plan was for me to learn the business in the London office for a year and then go to our agents in Hamburg for a few months. After that I was to go out to Brazil for two years to see how the coffee was grown, graded and shipped. Looking back it all sounds terribly dull. Anyway after a final cricket fling for the rest of the summer, I reported in October to No. 20 King William Street.

I had a new pin-stripe suit, which was too tight under the armpits, white stiff collar and shirt and the inevitable bowler-hat and rolled umbrella. I went to live with a very rich cousin, Alex Johnston, who was also my godfather. He was a pillar of the City being chairman of a large insurance company and deputy chairman of one of the 'Big 5' banks. He and his wife lived in a large house in Queen's Gate. They had no children but made up for it in staff! There was a butler, footman, housemaid, under-housemaid, cook, 'tweeney' and chauffeur.

My relatives were kindness itself and I was thoroughly spoilt with

Edward the footman appointed to look after my every want. I had my own latch-key and I am afraid that I treated the house as an hotel or base for my social life. But I paid my rent regularly once a week by staying in to play bridge. Cousin Alex was a fantastically good-looking man with impeccable manners, a wicked twinkle in his eye and a liking for the opposite sex to whom he paid outrageous compliments.

One elderly lady nearly fainted with joy when he told her, 'Many seasons have passed you by since I last saw you but Spring is the only one that has touched you.'

He also told a good story and was quite a wit himself. One evening we had been playing bridge and his male partner had made a series of terrible calls, so that they were going down a large number of points. At the end of a particularly disastrous rubber the friend asked to be excused to go to the lavatory. When he had left the room cousin Alex commented 'Well, for the first time this evening I shall know what he has got in his hand!'

His wife Audrey treated me like a son and thoroughly spoiled me, but bullied cousin Alex unmercifully. The main character in the house was the old butler with the splendid name of Targett. I used to go 'below stairs' to watch him play endless games of cribbage with a friend of his, who was a one-legged tailor. By that I mean that he had a wooden leg which he used to unscrew and park under the table, not that he made one-legged trousers. Targett was a great betting man and used to give me tips in a hoarse whisper as he handed round the fish or the veg. So I enjoyed two years or so of luxury living at no cost to myself, and learnt how the rich live and why they become rich. Cousin Alex used sometimes to take me to the theatre for which we would normally put on a dinner-jacket. But if it was the chauffeur's night off we always went there and back by tube – never by taxi.

To start with the office was like going back to school, and I felt just like a new boy. But the office staff were all very friendly and helpful and gave me a warm welcome. I was put into the cable office and learnt to type with one finger or two if I was in a desperate hurry. It was our job to decode all the telegrams which came in on the telex from our agents in Europe. These usually contained orders for so many bags of coffee and we had to forward these on to Brazil in freshly coded cables. The code was not for secrecy but for economy. 'We accept five-thousand bags of coffee at forty shillings – FOB' being represented by two or three letters.

I soon got used to the routine and was even allowed to taste the samples of coffee. This meant sucking it up into one's mouth out of a spoon, swilling it round and then spitting it out into a big spittoon. It was not too good for the digestion and I must admit that in later years I have often tasted coffee in restaurants to which I would have liked to have given the same treatment.

The man put in charge of me had been with the firm for many years. His name was Frank Copping and he was a true blue conservative and an amateur actor of some repute in Croydon. We had a lot of fun and I used to get on to the telephone in another room and with a phoney foreign accent pretend to be an agent complaining about the quality of our coffee. In between cables we used to play a betting game with coins. One of us would put a pocketful down on the desk and the other had to call heads or tails. We were doing this one day when we heard footsteps coming down the corridor. We hurriedly covered up the coins with a letter just as Mr Whitworth came into the room. He wanted to see a letter from one of our agents and as luck would have it it was the one covering our coins. We had to hand it to him and there on the desk were revealed about a dozen pennies and sixpences. He never said anything but he must have wondered what was going on.

On another occasion I made myself slightly unpopular by cheeking one of the senior staff who gave me a mild rocket for being late.

'Mr Johnston,' he said, 'you should have been here at 9.30.'

'Why,' I could not resist replying, 'what happened?'

But I was not cut out for the City life and never understood its jargon – draft at ninety days sight, cash against documents less $2\frac{1}{2}\%$, etc. My friends used to meet me for lunch at clubs or restaurants in the City and occasionally we used to sneak off to the Savoy to have steak and kidney pudding on a Thursday. One of the people with whom I used to lunch was Tuppy Headlam, who had retired as a housemaster from Eton. A rich friend of his had given him a 'job' in his stockbroking office in gratitude for the many occasions on which he had been entertained by Tuppy at Eton. All the job seemed to consist of was sitting at an empty desk doing *The Times'* crossword.

On one occasion Tuppy wanted to write to a friend about some shares, but did not know his address. So he decided to cable at great expense a mutual friend who was then big game hunting out in Kenya. The reply paid telegram read: 'Do you know John Smith's (or whatever the name was) address?' The next day back came the reply: 'Yes.'

My evenings were spent occasionally at deb dances but more often at the theatre or one of the many music halls like the Palladium, Holborn Empire, Victoria or Chelsea Palace. I had a passion for variety and saw most of the great artists of that time. Billy Bennett – almost a gentleman – was one of the funniest stand-up comics ever with his red nose and hair smarmed down over his forehead. He was Queen Mary's favourite and used to crack gags like: 'My brother has a hair on the end of his nose. It's so long that everytime he sneezes he nearly flogs himself to death.'

The immaculate Randolph Sutton in top-hat, white tie and tails used to sing *On Mother Kelly's doorstep* with tremendous pathos. Nellie Wallace, Layton and Johnstone, the Western Brothers, the big bands like Jack Hylton, and of course the Crazy Gang and Max Miller were all my favourites.

In those days you could usually catch one or other of the big names at one of the many London music halls. I saw Flanagan and Allen before they became famous with the Crazy Gang. They appeared at the Holborn Empire and finished their act with an unknown song called *Underneath The Arches*. They were a wonderful double act with Bud getting all the place-names wrong. King's Cross became Her Majesty's Annoyed and so on. They used to finish each gag with the word 'Oi'.

Bud
I've been up to Scotland, where all the Scotsmen were wearing kilts.
Ches
Did you see the Trussocks?
Bud
No, it wasn't windy.
Both
Oi!

Max Miller, the Cheeky Chappie, was of course the most daring comic of the time, with his white hat, outrageous outfit of gaudy plus-fours and his wicked eyes flashing and winking at the ladies. But if anyone accused him of being blue, he blamed it on the dirty minds of his audience. He made sure that his *double entendres* really could be taken either way, such as: 'A young girl of twenty-one married an old man of eighty-five and on her first night she prayed "Oh Lord, make me as old as my husband." And even as she was praying she felt old age creeping upon her.'

In the theatre I went to musicals and farces, especially those by Ben Travers at the Aldwych. I saw all of them and no matter how funny the modern farces may be there can surely never be two better actors of farce than Ralph Lynn and Tom Walls.

After a year in the City I went to Hamburg where I worked in our agent's office. He was an ex-U-boat captain from the Great War, and his assistant was an enthusiastic member of the Nazi Party. Whenever he mentioned the Führer his eyes would fill with tears. It was he who took me to a large Nazi Party gathering in one of the halls of Hamburg to hear Dr Goebbels speak. I felt very conspicuous in my London suit among all the brown shirts.

Goebbels ranted on and on and of course I did not understand a word. But suddenly he raised his voice to a high-pitched scream and everyone in the hall sprang to their feet, gave the Nazi salute and shouted out one word. My friend quickly translated as I too scrambled to my feet. It was the famous moment when Goebbels offered the German people the choice of guns or butter. Even I could tell that the one word they were shouting was NOT butter, and I felt very much alone and apprehensive of the future.

After Germany it was back to the City with occasional business trips round the ports of Europe before setting off for Brazil in June 1936. I went by liner from Southampton and was very unhappy at having to leave all my friends, my cricket and London life for at least two years. But nevertheless I enjoyed my first-ever trip on a liner and was re-signed to fate by the time we reached the hot, steamy port of Santos, through which every year millions of bags of coffee and thousands of bales of cotton were exported. As our liner passed through the estuary to the harbour we passed Johnston island, where in the mid-nineteenth century sailors were billeted to escape from the yellow fever which raged on the mainland.

When I arrived there was a terrific tropical thunderstorm booming and I remember being taken to a house on the beach where I sat on the verandah feeling miserable and homesick. Some trouble had come up about my work permit so I was rushed up-country to one of the company's fazendas or coffee plantations to spend a dreary month looking at miles and miles of coffee trees and piles and piles of coffee beans, and little else. Incidentally, I had started off literally on the wrong foot on my journey up-country. Before getting into the train which wound its way round the mountain up to São Paulo I had unknowingly stepped into a dog's mess. I did not discover this until we had started on our journey and it was then too late to do anything.

You can imagine what it was like especially in that heat. But at least it ensured that my companion and I had a carriage to ourselves. When my permit was in order I went down to Santos where I spent the next eighteen months trying to learn all about the coffee business. I was not much use as I could never tell one bean from another (which was important for grading) nor taste any difference between various types (which was essential for assessing the value of the coffee). So it was not surprising that I was never given any job with any authority or responsibility.

I even failed on a PR job which I was allotted. An important client from New York was due to stop at Santos for a day in a cruise liner. He was a big buyer of our coffee and it was very important that we should keep on the right side of him. So I was instructed to lay on a day's entertainment for him, his wife and two daughters. Accordingly I ordered a big open car to take them up the mountain road to São Paulo for the day. I was at the docks to greet them early in the morning and they were delighted at the prospect of a drive up to the interior.

The buyer was in a white palm beach suit, a panama and smoking a large cigar. The ladies were wearing gay summer dresses with parasols. What they did not know – nor unfortunately did I – that once the tarmac road had reached the top of the mountain it became a dirt track and in the dry weather the dust was so thick that it was like driving through a sandstorm in the desert. Everytime they got behind another car or one passed them they were showered with dust. Needless to say theirs was the only open car on the road. The Brazilians knew better.

I was ignorant of all this as I waited by the liner to welcome them back and could hardly believe my eyes when I saw them approaching. It was Black and White Minstrel time. Their faces were black with just the whites of their eyes and their teeth showing. All their tropical clothes were ruined. They brushed me aside as I tried to apologise. As they disappeared up the gang-plank I feared we had lost our most important client. We had. He never bought another bag from us.

There was quite a big colony of English and Americans in Santos and the social life was centred round the Anglo-American club. Besides playing quite a bit of cricket on matting, including a triangular tournament with Rio de Janeiro and São Paulo, we also tried our hand at baseball. Every Sunday morning our American friends used to play us on the beach. Then came the great day when an American cruiser visited Santos and we challenged them to a baseball game on the cricket ground. What a different game it is to cricket.

When it was my turn to be striker the catcher kept up a running commentary: 'Come on boys, this limey is no good. He's nervous, he'll never hit a thing . . .' and so on. I missed the first two balls the pitcher sent down but was lucky enough to connect with the third (my last chance). It soared over where mid-off would be at cricket, but for some reason the Americans had no man out there. So I raced round and had the thrill of scoring a home-run before anyone could retrieve the ball. How I envied the catcher being allowed to talk like that. If wicket-keepers had been allowed to do the same at cricket I reckon I would have played for England.

There was also a large German colony and with Hitler behaving as he was in Europe we were very suspicious of them all. One man whom we definitely suspected of being a spy, used to travel on the same train as us to and from work. We discovered his name was Herr Kürl and with a name like that imagine our joy when one day he took his hat off and we saw he was as bald as a coot!

It was at the club in Santos that I first tried my hand at acting and revue work. I compèred the various shows we put on, and did the occasional cross-talk act based on all the gags I had heard in the old Holborn Empire days. I also played my one and only star role – the silly ass in the Ghost Train. I did the silly part more or less OK, with a monocle and a highly pitched voice.

However, the last scene called for the silly ass to reveal himself as a policeman in disguise, and to become deadly serious as he explained to the assembled cast exactly how the gunrunners had worked the Ghost Train. I remember my big speech started something like . . . 'It was really quite simple. What they did was . . .' and there and then on the first night I dried up completely. It may have been simple but my mind went blank and I could not remember a single line. I think the audience thought it was part of the play. At any rate it got about the biggest laugh of the evening. The play was produced by the British Consul in Santos at the time. His name was James Joint and he later became our commercial attaché at Buenos Aires, where appropriately enough he had the job of negotiating with the Argentinians over meat prices. It was lucky he never had any children, as otherwise I am sure they would have been known as the 'two veg'.

People used to stay in Santos for years, some of them without ever going home on leave to England. One of these was a coffee man called Jack Edge who had come out from Lancashire as a boy and had been in Santos for twenty-five years. At last he decided to go home to see his old mother to whom he had always written regularly. So he sailed home and took the train to Liverpool. He had not warned her he was coming as he wished to give her a surprise.

He rang the bell of his old home and after the noise of bolts being shot back the door opened to reveal a sweet old lady. 'Hello mother, I'm your son Jack from Brazil,' said Jack. His mother peered at him carefully through spectacles for a second or two and then said: 'You're not my Jack!' and slammed the door in his face. I believe he later managed to persuade her that he was the genuine article. But what a welcome home!

One of the high spots of life in Brazil is the annual carnival in February, when everyone goes mad for three days on end. All businesses and shops are closed down and the streets are crowded with singing and dancing people. They never seem to stop in spite of the terrific heat which at that time of year is in the nineties plus maximum humidity. The revelry goes on all night with bands playing and long lines of people dancing through the streets like a giant Palais Glide. Most of the dancers carry a scent spray which they squirt over each other – a wise precaution in that heat!

It was after one of these carnivals when I had been in Santos just over eighteen months that I was suddenly struck down by a strange sort of paralysis. It was a frightening experience as I gradually began to lose the use of my arms and my legs, and after two days could hardly drag myself along. It was diagnosed as Acute Peripheral Neuritis and I was rushed down to Santos to the house of a member of our firm, whose wife happened to be a doctor. They were Jerry and Dorothy Deighton and for six weeks between them they nursed me like a child.

To start with, I could not do anything for myself, and I even had to be fed. It was all very frightening and I began to wonder whether I should ever use my arms and legs again. But once again I was in luck, as there was a wonderful Brazilian doctor called D'Utra Vaz who had had experience of this sort of disease before (it was a sort of beri-beri). He prescribed for me a diet of raw vegetables, lots of tomatoes which I hate, daily injections in the bottom (I had over ninety) and lots of massage and sunbathing.

Gradually, I began to get better and one day to my delight I was able to wiggle one of my toes. What a relief that was! From then on I slowly began to learn to walk again, though I was very weak and had lost a tremendous amount of weight.

I shall never forget the debt I owe to the Deightons. They gave up everything to nurse me and were always cheerful and comforting. I remember asking Jerry why he was called that when his real christian name was something quite different. 'Oh,' he said, 'it's because all the women sit on me and the men hold me at arms length!'

As soon as I was strong enough I was put on a liner back to England accompanied by my Mother who had been rushed out to Brazil to be with me. The cause of the disease was all a bit of a mystery. Some people said it was due to a deficiency of vitamin B and it *is* true that I had not eaten many fresh vegetables while I was in Brazil. Dr D'Utra Vaz also added that it was often brought on by excessive drinking or childbirth. Whether he was joking or not I don't know, but I was a bit worried, as my average intake of *drink* was only about one gin and tonic a day!

I was sorry to leave all my new friends in Santos but I had to admit that I had hated my work in the coffee business and was already trying to work out how to escape from it all into something I could enjoy more. Meanwhile, ahead of me lay the happy prospect of seeing all my old friends, recuperating from my illness and enjoying an English ummer once again, especially as the Australians were to be the visiting cricket team.

9

Back home with Home

England in May 1938 was not the happiest place to come back to. Hitler was ranting and raving and the headlines in the press were daily more sensational and depressing. But come to think of it, they were nothing compared to what we have to put up with now every day.

Still, it was a nerve-racking summer and there was a general feeling of resignation and despair.

However, for me personally there were many compensations, though I had to keep to a rigid programme of rest, exercises, no drink, injections and early to bed. Nor was I allowed to play games. But I was able to catch up with all my friends, and spent most of the summer either visiting them, going to the theatre or watching cricket. I was lucky enough to see the second Test against Australia at Lord's where Wally Hammond played one of the great Test innings of all time – a majestic two hundred and forty in which he hammered poor Fleetwood-Smith unmercifully with some of the fiercest driving I have ever seen.

There had been one or two family changes while I was away in Brazil. My eldest brother had married and both my mother and sister had been divorced. Our home in Bude was sold, my stepfather re-married and my mother went to live in a picture-postcard thatched cottage in the village of Chearsley in Buckinghamshire. I visited her as often as I could and she lived there very happily, busying herself with good works and her garden. While on the boat out to Brazil she had made great friends with a Major Black, who by chance lived in the next door village of Haddenham. He had an equally delightful cottage and was also an enthusiastic gardener. But though they saw a lot of each other, they remained just friends.

Yet I think we all missed Bude a bit, despite its sad associations. My mother told me a splendid story of something which had happened to her there just before she left. She had gone into the local ironmonger to buy a garden hoe, went up to the assistant behind the counter and said, 'I want a hoe please'. 'Yes,' replied he without a smile, 'china or enamel?'

The circumstances of my sister's divorce were rather unusual. She and her husband had four children, the youngest one, a boy, being only a baby. When her husband told Anne that he had met someone called Margaret whom he wanted to marry, she said something to this effect: 'Right. Ask her to come and stay with us for a week. If I like her and think that she would be a good stepmother to the children, I will divorce you and go off with the baby, leaving the other three children for you and Margaret to look after.' And this is exactly what happened!

Margaret came to stay, Anne approved and left more or less immediately for South Africa where she has been ever since! I still think it an amazing decision for a mother to make, especially as Anne was very fond of her three eldest and they of her. Anyway, she remarried an ex-police officer and game reserve warden and has lived happily ever after in a fishing village called St Lucia Estuary, about 150 miles north of Durban. It's an idyllic spot with hippos at the bottom of the garden, crocodiles in the river, and monkeys swinging from tree to tree across the lawn. The climate is perfect and there is a small colony of white people. I have been lucky enough to see Anne on my various trips to South Africa but doubt if, after forty years, she will ever come back to England.

On my return to London in 1938, I went once again to stay with my godfather at Queen's Gate, where I was fussed over by all the servants and treated as a semi-invalid – which I suppose I was in a way. But it was not long before I moved to No. 35 South Eaton Place to join William Douglas-Home in rooms kept by a remarkable couple called Mr and Mrs Crisp.

The husband was a retired butler and she a cook and they had met when serving together in a large house owned by some peer of the realm. Mr Crisp – or Crippen as I used to call him – was a mixture of Jeeves and Robertson Hare and really was the perfect gentleman's gentleman. He had a wonderful sense of humour and sometimes when we had dinner parties would wait at table complete in powdered wig and knee-breeches. If there were any strangers present we used to ask them if they knew of any good butlers who were free, as we were thinking of making certain changes on our staff. Crippen would then pretend to be overcome with shock and would drop a plate or dish on the floor – or even over the unfortunate guest on one occasion.

He had some good stories about his early days. He told me how once when he was a pantry boy in a big London house, he was looking out of the basement window, which had bars in front of it, presumably to keep out burglars. But two passers-by must have thought differently, as they looked down and saw him peering through the bars. Crippen heard one say to the other, 'Poor boy – and so young too.' He was also a football fan and he and I used to go off to watch the Arsenal and saw such great forwards as Hulme, Jack, Drake, James, Bastin, and defenders like Hapgood, Barnes, Male and Copping. On one occasion we even saw wee Alex James, baggy pants below the knees, score three goals, which was a soccer sensation as he normally 'made' the goals for others with his brilliant footwork and dribbling.

Mrs Crisp – or Gert – was an absolute saint, and a super cook. She treated us just like children, spoiling us if we were good, or scolding us if we did not meet her own high standard of manners and behaviour. They had two rooms vacant at this time, one of which had been occupied by Jo Grimond who left to get married. So I took his room and another friend John Hogg – now a highly respected banker – had the other, and in spite of the recurring crisis we managed to have a thoroughly enjoyable summer.

In August I went up to Yorkshire to stay with James Lane Fox and his family. When I was at Oxford I had had a sealyham dog with one black eye called Blob, and I had given him to the Foxes on my departure to Brazil. Blob had always gone everywhere with me, especially to all the cricket matches in which I played. He used to sit and watch from the boundary edge and then when we came off the field, would rush out to meet me and proudly carry in my wicket-keeping gloves. One Saturday, the Lane Foxes lost him and searched everywhere for him. Finally they ran him to earth on the village green, where he was quietly sitting on the boundary edge watching the local village cricket match. Rather touching.

Blob was a dog of great character and though very pleased to see me again it was obviously better for him to stay up there in the country rather than live in London. I pinched one of the current music-hall jokes of the time and nicknamed him Larwood – because he had four short legs and his balls swung both ways!

During my stay I remember we went on a picnic and listened in on the radio to Howard Marshall commentating on the 5th Test against Australia at the Oval. His deep burbling voice suited the atmosphere of cricket perfectly and we were able to hear him describing Len Hutton's then record Test score of 364, interspersed with such typical comments as . . . 'Bradman standing there, arms akimbo' . . . or 'the Oval sparrows are pecking away in front of the Pavilion gate' . . . He was a marvellous commentator and unlike some past commentators in other sports, would be totally acceptable today, so far advanced was his technique.

In September, the crisis finally caught up with us, and with Neville Chamberlain flying off to see Hitler at Bad Godesburg I began to deliver gas-masks to some of the embassies.

Then came Mr Chamberlain's dramatic announcement in the House of Commons that Hitler had agreed to meet him yet again . . . 'He is coming halfway to meet me at Munich in order to save an old man another such long journey' . . . At that time William Douglas-Home's eldest brother Alec, then Lord Dunglass, was Mr Chamberlain's Parliamentary Private Secretary, and was going to Munich with him. But he was caught by the sudden announcement and came rushing round to us to borrow a clean shirt, which I was very proud to lend him. William, Gert and I went to see them off at Heston airdrome and also met them on their return. We saw Mr Chamberlain wave his little piece of paper and say: 'Out of this nettle, danger, we pluck this flower, safety.' He looked a frail, tired old man with his black homburg, stick-up collar and umbrella. And what a tiny plane it was in which they flew. None of the posh VIP VC 10s of today.

Whatever people may now pretend, there is no doubt that at the time the Munich agreement was a tremendous relief to the country as a whole. The crowd in Downing Street reflected the feeling of most of us as they cheered Mr Chamberlain when he looked out from a window of Number 10 and shouted, 'It's peace in our time.' It was at least peace for another twelve months and a breathing space in which to build up our forces.

Shortly after this, Mr Chamberlain and I became joint godfathers to one of Alec's daughters, Meriel. It made my day when I read a report of the christening in The Times which stated that the two godfathers Mr Neville Chamberlain and Mr Brian Johnston were unable to be present.

By October I was passed fit again and returned to the office. Since I was now supposed to know something about coffee after my stay in Brazil, I was promoted to be Assistant Manager with a salary of £500 a year and a room of my own with an enormous desk which had belonged to my grandfather. I paid a few visits to our agents in Europe including one to Hamburg. I found this rather frightening.

The Germans, though still outwardly friendly, seemed far more arrogant, and intolerant of all those who did not support Hitler. He had given them complete confidence in their ability to take on and crush the rest of the world if necessary. I was very relieved to get home. But I found myself less and less interested in coffee and the City. All I really wanted to do was to be an actor. But I had not got the guts to get out of the rut, in spite of two things which should have encouraged me.

First, William was now not only writing plays but also acting in the

(*Top*) The Temple Grove 1st XI 1925. Wicket-keeper Johnston in the front row. (What big ears we all had!)
(*Bottom*) The Temple Grove 1st XV 1925. Fly-half Johnston sitting on the ground.

Member of Pop–Eton 1931.

In the last few weeks of bachelor-hood.

(*Top*) The start of an unsuccessful business career. My first day in the office of the Brazilian Warrant Company.
(*Bottom*) Eton 1931 – with four cricketing friends: Nigel Baker, Tony Allen, Mike Gosling and coach Wilf Payton (Notts).

A warm handshake with rival Captain Jim Harmsworth before an Eton *v*. Harrow Rowing race at Oxford in 1933.

Wicket-keeper extraordinary!

The Mad Parson (see page 67).

'Somewhere in Europe' – 1944 with two of my technical staff M.Q.M.S. Cross and Sgt. Reid.

West End. In addition he even got himself temporarily engaged to Ronald Squire's daughter. So there was plenty of theatrical talk and atmosphere at No. 35.

Secondly, I decided to go to a well-known lady fortune-teller to help me to make up my mind. Everything she told me indicated that I was destined for some sort of career in the entertainment world. She even asked me to sign her two visitors books, one which she kept for all her clients and the other which she said was for people who would eventually become well-known or famous. I was highly flattered to be asked but even this spur could not persuade me to take the plunge.

I went to stay once or twice with William's family at the Hirsel, their home near Coldstream in Berwickshire. They were a large and united family, and the Earl of Home was as near to being a saint as any man I have ever met. To him, everyone was good and I never heard him say an unkind word about anyone. Although a huge land-owner he was kept on a very tight pursestring by his agent. There was a good reason for this, because he was so kind that otherwise he would probably have given it all away. Anyway he was driven around in a battered old Wolseley and when he went to London he was given £25 in cash by the agent. Once this pocket-money ran out he used to return to Scotland. It was always said that he spent £5 of it in tips by the time he arrived at Brown's Hotel, where he and the family always stayed.

Lady Home too was a marvellous character – on the surface the most unemotional and placid of women. She would sit quietly knitting, listening to all the noisy conversation which was always going on around her. Then promptly at 10 pm the 'wee Lordie' as Lord Home was known would call out, 'Lil, bed,' and she would gather up her knitting and go off without a murmur. She was a wonderful mother to her large family, though they used to pull her leg unmercifully. In true female style, she had no sense of logic. On one occasion at Brown's Hotel she was in bed with a slight cold so I went up to say goodbye as they were leaving the next day. I knocked on her door and she immediately called out 'Come in.' So in I went, only to be greeted with: 'What are you doing? You shouldn't come into my room like this.' 'But,' I replied, 'you told me to come in.' 'I know,' she rejoindered, 'but I thought you were only one of the waiters!'

Everyone now of course knows Alec Douglas-Home but at that time, except for his connection with Mr Chamberlain, he was an ordinary MP who had never held any office. I attended one of his political meetings on Lanark race-course, just after Hitler's invasion of Czechoslovakia. Sir John Simon, then I think Foreign Secretary, was his chief speaker and referring to the invasion uttered the not very helpful remark: 'Who knows where it will end?' If he didn't know, it was not much use asking us!

What people may not know about Alec is that he is one of the best after-dinner speakers in the country, with a good fund of stories, many of them collected by his wife Elizabeth. On a recent occasion I heard him speak about a man who asked a friend where the Virgin Islands were. 'I don't know for certain,' was the reply, 'but I imagine they must be some considerable distance from the Isle of Man.'

The second brother Henry was a retired Major and a famous ornithologist known throughout Scotland as the Birdman. He also painted birds with great skill and accuracy, and I am in fact still waiting for one of a pheasant which he promised me as a wedding present over twenty-five years ago.

Henry was a very good broadcaster and on one occasion was broadcasting Birdsong for the BBC from a Surrey wood. This was a very popular programme which for many years used to go out 'live' at about 11 pm in the early summer. The main object was to get the song of the nightingale but there was also the joy of hearing and trying to pick out all the other birds as well. Before the war, the BBC used to place a well-known cellist called Beatrice Harrison in a punt by the side of the wood and hope that the sound of her cello would entice the nightingale to sing, though whether in complaint or competition was never made quite clear.

After the war we went one better and got Percy Edwards to do his famous bird imitations as a challenge to the real birds. More often than not they would sing back in protest at this invasion of their territory by another 'bird'. A control van used to park outside the wood and from this long microphone leads were run out to four or five chosen spots in the wood where the bird expert thought there would be some birds singing. The vital microphone was of course the one placed to catch the nightingale, and this would involve several nights of research. But once discovered, the nightingales seldom left their selected territory.

On this occasion there were four microphones placed in strategic positions. One by a bluebell glade, another by a small bridge over a stream, one near some fir trees and the nightingale one over a group of rhododendron bushes. The programme was due to start at 11 o'clock – 'live' remember, not recorded – so with five minutes to go Henry thought he would have a final check to make sure all the microphones were working. The engineer brought up No. 1 mike and they heard a willow warbler, No. 2 produced a wood pigeon and No. 3 a frightened black-bird. No. 4 was hanging over the rhododendrons and as the engineer switched it on, to Henry's horror there was no nightingale but the unmistakable sound of a couple making love.

There were now only three minutes to go before the broadcast, so Henry rushed round to the bush from where the sounds were coming. He shouted to those inside to come out, and a shamefaced but thoroughly annoyed couple emerged, the man hurriedly doing up his flies. They protested about this intrusion into their privacy but were somewhat mollified when Henry explained that in a few minutes' time he would have said to the waiting listeners all over Great Britain something like . . . 'Now let's listen to the dulcet tones of the nightingale . . .' and goodness knows how far the couple would have got by then!

While staying with the Douglas-Homes, William persuaded me to play a practical joke on his uncle and aunt who lived near by. He also persuaded Lady Home to ask them over to tea to help entertain a strange clergyman who was staying at the Hirsel. He was deaf and behaving in a very eccentric way. Needless to say I was the clergyman, with a thick pair of horn-rimmed spectacles, hair parted down the middle (I had some then) and dressed in the appropriate black clerical gear out of the dressing-up chest.

At the time they were expected I began to walk up and down the middle of the drive reading a Bible. When their car approached I pretended not to hear so that they had to stop and hoot. I then stepped gingerly aside, raising my hat as they drove past. This set the scene ideally as they too were now convinced that I was a 'case'.

Later, I joined them at tea where I was seated next to the aunt to whom I immediately began to make amorous advances, putting my hands on her knee and so on. As I was meant to be deaf I pretended not to hear any of the conversation and they were soon saying rude things about me. The family, who were in the know, were in hysterics, especially when William purposely dropped a hot cup of tea all over me and I let out a very un-clergyman-like expletive.

When we went into the drawing-room after tea the aunt sat down on the sofa, and pretending that I could not see very well, I sat down on her lap. She let out a scream especially when I asked her to come for a walk with me in the shrubbery. Her husband was becoming more and more annoyed and began to say things like . . . 'What the hell does the lunatic think he's up to . . .', etc. I then asked to be 'excused' for a minute and left the room.

I quickly changed into my sports jacket and flannels, removed my spectacles, parted my hair at the side instead of in the middle, and then strolled unconcernedly back into the room. William introduced me as myself explaining I had been into Edinburgh. It took quite a few minutes before the aunt and uncle realised what had happened, and I am glad to say that they took it very well.

20

My military début

After the invasion of Czechoslovakia it became more and more obvious that war was not only inevitable but imminent, and some of my Eton friends and I thought we must do something to prepare ourselves for it. We had all been in the Corps at school and at one of our lunches in the City decided we should try to get on to the reserve of some regiment. We were unanimous in thinking that if we had to fight we might as well be in the best and most efficient regiment. So we went right to the top and applied to the Grenadier Guards, the senior regiment of the Foot Guards.

My first cousin 'Boy' Browning was then commanding the 2nd Battalion. They had just returned from two years in Egypt and were stationed at Wellington Barracks. 'Boy' was later to become the founder and first Commander of the Airborne Division, and it must have been due to him that I and five or six others were accepted for training by the Grenadiers, and placed on the Officer Cadet Reserve. This involved reporting on one or two evenings a week throughout the summer of 1939 to Wellington Barracks, where we were taught weapon training, basic tactics and regimental history and traditions.

We reported for the first time one evening in May, coming straight from the City in our bowlers, white stiff collars and dark city suits. We were welcomed in the officers' mess by 'Boy' Browning, who offered us drinks and gave us a short informal talk. This was fine, we thought, as we sipped our drinks and sat in deep comfortable armchairs. A great institution the Army!

When we had had a second round of drinks 'Boy' smilingly suggested that we might like to meet the Regimental Sergeant Major who he said was waiting for us out on the parade-ground. Innocently we left the comfort of the mess and walked out on to the steps. As soon as we emerged a roar rent the air as the RSM bellowed out to us to get into a double and fall in in front of him. Before we knew what was happening we found ourselves marching up and down the vast parade-ground in double quick time, being told we were a lazy lot of so and sos. About turn, quick march, right turn, mark time, halt. The orders came out like machine-gun fire and we were soon sweating and panting for breath, wondering why on earth we had ever volunteered.

After twenty minutes of utter hell we were dismissed with a 'Goodnight gentlemen. See you later in the week,' from RSM Tom Garnett – a wonderful man and soldier with whom I was to serve for most of the war. We had experienced Guards' discipline at its best – or worst, depending on how you looked at it. We limped back to the mess and sank into our chairs as 'Boy' Browning dispensed some badly-needed drinks. We were definitely in a state of shock.

He then gave us an enthralling talk about the Brigade of Guards and the reasons for their fanatical emphasis on discipline in all their training of officers and guardsmen alike. Keith Bryant in his book *Fighting with the Guards* has put it all very succinctly when he details the six basic qualities instilled into every guardsman – cleanliness, smartness, fitness, efficiency, pride and invincibility.

The acceptance of these six qualities demands a tremendous amount from any man, but if achieved, result in the perfect fighting machine – a man who can obey any order without question, no matter how bloody it may seem. Hence the endless, and to the outsider, seemingly pointless, hours of drill. Naturally this automatic acceptance of an order demands an even higher standard for those in command. It becomes absolutely essential that every order is the right one and practicable, something of which I was very conscious when I became an officer later on.

But meanwhile we were slowly being put through the mill as the summer advanced, and after our first experience always made sure we were suitably dressed. Bowler-hats and suits were replaced by grey flannels and cricket shirts, and after each parade we used to retire exhausted for supper to the houses of those who were married.

The political clouds were gathering, so I got in as many games of cricket as possible, mostly for the Eton Ramblers. Also, whenever I was in London for the weekend I used to go round the corner to St Michael's, Chester Square, to hear Canon Elliott preach. What an actor he would have made! He had a deep voice, a fine appearance and used to lean over the front of the pulpit and just talk – no notes, no reference books. He had the rare gift of making each member of the congregation think that he was talking to them personally.

One Sunday he made a plea on behalf of poor families, who due to high unemployment were desperately short of food and clothing. He suggested that members of his congregation should adopt a family and look after them. He had a list of deserving cases and I decided to carry out his suggestion, and was given a family in Durham. They were a married couple with four children. The husband was unemployed and not in the best of health and as a consequence his family were pretty badly off. I got in touch with them, wrote to them regularly and sent them a little money or groceries from time to time. At least they could feel that someone was interested in their plight.

I also asked Elizabeth Dunglass to visit them when she was staying with her father Dr Alington, who had become the Dean of Durham. This she kindly did but for various reasons I have never managed to visit them myself, a fact of which I am rather ashamed. But two of the sons once came to see me in my BBC office when they were down in London, and to this day I still write to Mrs Corbett and send her a small present every Christmas.

At this time I was rather keen on a very attractive girl called Cynthia, though I don't flatter myself that she was at all keen on me. However, we used to have a lot of fun and after weeks of trying I at last persuaded her to go out with me to a theatre and supper. In order to impress her I persuaded Nigel Turner to dress up as my chauffeur disguised with fake moustache and spectacles. But I spoilt it all by getting carried away when he nearly had an accident, and sacked him on the spot. Cynthia thought this was unnecessarily harsh and told me in no uncertain terms what she thought of me. So I did myself more harm than good. She did not even think it at all funny when Nigel whipped off his disguise and revealed who he was.

I was due for some holidays in August, and after a cricket tour in Yorkshire, James Lane Fox, William and I were crazy enough to go off to Cap Martin in the South of France. We realised the possible danger of being stranded by the outbreak of war but thought we would have one final fling. The Kennedy family were also there. We knew them in London and used to go round to see them in the Ambassador's house in Prince's Gate. We were particularly fond of Jack, who seemed to appreciate even our worst jokes. But we had only been in France for a few days when there was a general panic and everyone was advised to return home at once. The weather was terribly hot and the trains and steamers were packed. So we had a very uncomfortable journey back home, arriving on the last day of August.

We had only just made it, and promptly got down to filling sandbags. We were doing this outside Westminster Hospital on Sunday, 3 September when the frail voice of Mr Chamberlain announced over the radio that we were at war with Germany.

Shattering though the news was, it came in a way as a relief after all the months of tension, and we continued shovelling sand into the sandbags. But we were soon rudely interrupted by the air-raid siren, and were all rushed down into the mortuary for shelter. We reluctantly had to hand it to Hitler for being so much on the ball that within a few minutes of war being declared, his bombers were approaching London. As it turned out of course it was only a false alarm but it had given everyone quite a fright and we returned somewhat chastened to No. 35 to tuck into Mrs Crisp's roast beef and Yorkshire pudding.

The next few days were full of activity. William, who was an admitted pacifist and conscientious objector immediately joined the fire service and I tried to do the same. But when they learnt that I was in the Officer Cadet Reserve I was told to wait for instructions from the Army. So I looked into the office from time to time but there was little business and an air of unreality about everything. I realised, too, that once I had joined up I would never return to the City, no matter what happened to me in the war. It was the break I needed to escape from a business life. Hitler had done for me what I had not had the guts to do for myself, though I had a strong feeling of guilt at letting the family business down. But I was probably flattering myself, as I imagine that they must have been as relieved as I was.

After a week or so and much badgering of the Grenadier Headquarters I was ordered to report for a medical inspection. With a lot of other naked men I had to go through some fairly undignified routines and as a result have always appreciated the old joke about the recruit who started to run as he thought the doctor had said 'off' instead of 'cough'. Very painful!

I passed all right but there was one awkward moment when I could not read all the letters on the card with my rather short-sighted right eye. But the doctor must have realised how disappointed I would be if I failed or perhaps they were short of budding officers. Anyway he made it easy for me by opening the fingers of his hand which was covering my left eye, so that I could read all the letters with that eye.

My other friends also passed and in October we reported to the Royal Military College at Sandhurst for a four months course. It was being turned into an OCTU and we were its very first victims. There were lots of people like myself, most of them in the middle twenties who had come from jobs in the City or one of the professions. It was just like going back to school, but the great thing was that we did not have to think. Everything was organised for us and we were told exactly what to do and soon automatically did it.

After the first shocks of reveille at 6 am and long doses of PT and drill, we soon settled down and began to enjoy ourselves. The course was a strange mixture of war and peace. We still each had a room to ourselves with a batman to look after us, and our Company Sergeant Major – a great character called 'Dusty' Smith – would call us 'Sir' with one corner of his mouth and hand out the most terrible rockets with the other: 'Mr Johnston, SIR, stop being so dozy and get a . . . move on.' That sort of thing.

It was even funnier with the Regimental Sergeant Major. We had to call him SIR as well. He used to say, 'I call you sir, and you call me sir. The only difference is that you mean it!'

We soon became physically fit and moderately efficient, and unless we were on guard duties were free from midday Saturday to midnight Sunday, which meant a mass exodus to London as soon as the last parade was finished. This led to complete chaos on the first Saturday. We kept our cars in a garage in Camberley and had asked for them to be brought up to the parade-ground by midday Saturday.

We were out on our first route march, and were marching back to be dismissed for our first week-end off. We rounded the bend to go on to the parade-ground, and it looked like a car park at a football match. All the cars were parked in the middle and we had to be called to a sudden halt and dismissed where we were. Our Company Commander was naturally very annoyed and from then on we had to go down to Camberley to collect our cars.

On the occasional week-ends when we were not given leave we had to attend church parade and go to chapel. One Sunday the padre accused us of not putting enough in the collection and urged us to be more generous in future. This rather annoyed us. So the next time we went to chapel we all filled our pockets with pennies and halfpennies. A friend called Tom Blackwell who was richer than most of us even had several pounds worth of coppers in those paper bags issued by banks.

When the NCOs came round with the gold plates we poured out our coins and the plates were soon full to overflowing. Pennies were spilling out all over the aisle and more plates had to be fetched from the altar. The look on the NCOs' faces was a mixture of anger and disbelief that such a thing could happen in their chapel. But they could do nothing about it. There was even more chaos up at the altar when they tried to transfer the contents of each plate on to a master plate for the padre to bless the offering. The master plate had to be taken several times into the vestry to be emptied and each time it was filled the padre had to try to bless it. But the weight of the coins made it very difficult for him to raise it above his head to make the sign of the cross, and from behind he looked just like a weight lifter straining to beat a world's record. I think we got our own back. At least there were no more slurs on our generosity.

Once again my inability to resist playing jokes got me into slight trouble. We were all out on a TEWT – or tactical exercise without troops – where the instructors posed various military problems which they asked the cadets to solve.

We had stopped at the top of a hill and looking down at the valley below the instructor turned to me and said, 'Johnston. You and your platoon are defending this ridge. Suddenly at the bottom of the hill you see a troop of German tanks advancing. What steps would you take?' 'Bloody long ones, sir,' I replied and was deservedly 'put in the book' and had to report to the Company Commander next day for a reprimand.

While the 'phoney' war continued in Europe we were gradually being turned into officers. The various Regimental Colonels came down to vet us and check up on our progress, and by February we had all been accepted. Then came the final passing-out parade and finally that last day when we put on our officers' uniforms for the first time. The NCOs who had been ordering us around and handing out rockets for the last few months now had to salute us, and I shall always remember the twinkle in Dusty Smith's eye when he 'tore me off' a beauty as I drove away.

It was quite a moment – a Commissioned Officer in the Brigade of Guards. A bit prefabricated perhaps, but at least there was the one pip on my shoulder to prove it. I must confess that it was highly embarassing walking about the West End and having to acknowledge salutes, as well as give them.

We had been granted a few days leave before joining our Regiments and I spent mine seeing all the theatre shows I could, and I especially enjoyed the wartime jokes of Tommy Trinder. Take this one: A man walking down Whitehall stopped a passer-by and asked him if he knew which side the War Office was on. 'On ours, I hope,' was the somewhat unhelpful reply.

But my leave was soon up and I was ordered to report to the Training Battalion of the Grenadier Guards at Windsor . . .

11

New boy Johnston

Although we were now officers, life at Windsor was not much different from that at Sandhurst. We were drilled in a special Officers' squad by RSM 'Snapper' Robinson, and the Adjutant kept an eagle eye on us as we continued training in weapons, tactics and motor transport.

Some of these duties took place on the tiny grass square in the middle of the barracks which in peacetime had been used for cricket and had the shortest boundaries of any ground I have ever seen. They were so short that they only counted two runs and the batsman had to hit the ball *over* the boundary to score four runs. To get a six he had to hit it clean out of the barracks.

We did have certain duties such as kit inspections and we also learnt what it was like to be put in charge of a platoon of guardsmen. These inspections were pernickety affairs with the kit laid out on the bed in a set pattern. The greatcoat and blankets had to be folded in a certain way, knives and forks put in a special order and so on. Everything too had to be scrupulously cleaned and scrubbed. The slightest deviation and the guardsman was 'put in the book'.

We also began to attend the adjutant's 'orders' where discipline was meted out. We had our first insight into the rough justice which was administered for minor offences such as long hair, idleness on parade, untidy kit, etc. There was a fearful clatter as the accused was marched into the room in double quick time by a Drill Sergeant shouting at the top of his voice. The charge was read out and if the accused wanted to say anything in his defence he had to wait to be asked to do so by the Adjutant. He would then say: 'Thank you sir for leave to speak' and would be told to go ahead. If he spoke before he had done this the Drill Sergeant would shout to him to 'stop talking'.

This also happened if the accused's excuse appeared to be a lame one, or even if it went on for too long. If the Adjutant thought he was guilty he would ask one of us if we had anything to say. This was the chance for the Platoon Commander to put in a good word for his guardsman if he wanted. ('A good man sir. Tries hard. This is his first offence.') Alternatively he could report adversely on the accused if for instance he was a regular troublemaker.

For more serious offences there were all sorts of safeguards and procedures and for these the accused definitely got a fair deal. He could be sent before the Commanding Officer or ask for a private interview with his Company Commander when no one else would be present. Finally as a last resort he could ask for or be sent to a court martial.

Five years later when I became a Company Commander I had to take company orders and never enjoyed them. I felt I was called on to give judgement far too quickly in an impossibly noisy atmosphere. I also felt sympathy for the accused who by the way he was treated was made to appear guilty before his case was heard. I often used to postpone my decision to the next day in order to give myself adequate time to sort it out. I am afraid my NCOs sometimes thought I was a bit of a soft case.

After a few weeks at Windsor we were considered sufficiently trained to take our turn as one of the junior officers on the guard at Windsor Castle. This involved twenty-four hours in the guard-room up at the Castle and a nightly patrol of all the sentry posts to see that all was well. Since the Royal Family stayed in the Castle a great deal – it was the wartime home of the two Princesses – we at last felt we were doing something practical to help the war effort.

However, I am not sure how effective our methods of guarding really were. In these days of small automatic weapons, hand-grenades or bombs it seems a bit archaic for a sentry, if he heard footsteps approaching, to call out into the darkness: 'Who goes there?' If there was more than one person the answer would then come back: 'Mr Johnston and others.' The sentry in that case would reply: 'Advance one and be recognised.'

But it does seem to be inviting trouble to order a possible enemy to approach any nearer, even if the sentry has his finger ready on the trigger. There was an hilarious occasion at Sandhurst when an officer cadet was on guard late at night and heard footsteps approaching. Of course he did not know it but they belonged to a new officer instructor with a very long name who had only just arrived.

'Who goes there?' challenged the sentry.

'Blundell-Hollingshead-Blundell', replied the officer from the darkness.

'Advance *one* and be recognised,' said the sentry.

We had various training schemes in Windsor Park and also used to guard the polo grounds there against possible parachute landings. I shared one night's vigil with the Duke of Beaufort who was commanding a troop of the Household Cavalry. I often wonder what would have happened had the parachutists landed. By the end of April things were hotting up in France and Belgium and one by one officers from Windsor were being sent out to join fighting battalions out there.

In the first week of May Hitler started his offensive and I was among those told to get the necessary injections at once, collect my full fighting kit and report to Wellington Barracks to await orders to join the 2nd Battalion. It turned out to be quite a long wait which was occupied by guard duties and strengthening various defences in Whitehall. Then I got my orders to leave, and said all my goodbyes. I even proposed to a girl with whom I was friendly. Goodness knows what would have happened if she had said 'Yes'. I was in no position to marry anyone, nor was it a very good time to do so. Luckily for both our sakes she had the sense to say no.

Then came a terrible anti-climax. The BEF were in retreat and our 2nd Battalion with everyone else fell back on Dunkirk, from which they miraculously escaped without too much loss, except for all their kit. All my orders were cancelled and after a few days I was sent to Shaftesbury where the Battalion now was. I found everyone exhausted after days of tough fighting and no sleep, and sensed a slight state of shock that the Army had been so hopelessly overrun and beaten in its first encounter with the Germans.

The Battalion had to be re-equipped and my first job was to help in the distribution of all the stores as they arrived. We were in Monty's 3rd division, and it was being given priority to be brought up to fighting strength in order to defend the south coast against possible invasion.

It was here for the first time that I came upon a ridiculous custom of the Brigade of Guards, namely that in the officers' mess no one spoke to a newly-joined officer except in the course of duty. I gather in peace-time this could go on for quite a time but in wartime, at least in our Battalion it lasted for a fortnight. Even friends whom one had known before would avoid or cut one dead. Then suddenly at the end of the period everyone began to smile and talk and from then on could not have been friendlier. I suppose it was intended to put the new boy in his place and prevent any possibility of him getting a swollen head. But frankly it made all those who took part look not only ridiculous but boorish and bad-mannered and I cannot believe that it did anyone any good.

I wish I had known then the following story which I should have enjoyed telling them. A newly-joined officer was ordered to report to his Commanding Officer, who was determined to make him feel welcome and at ease.

'You'll soon settle down with us, I hope,' he said. 'We are a friendly lot and pride ourselves on making everyone feel at home in the mess. For instance, on Mondays we always have a get-together with plenty to drink. We really let our hair down and if anyone gets a bit drunk we turn a blind eye.' 'Excuse me, sir,' said the officer, 'but I'm afraid I don't drink.' 'Don't worry about that,' said the Colonel, 'there's always Wednesday nights when we invite some of the girls from the WRAC and nurses from the local hospital to a bit of slap and tickle in the mess. Great fun. A bit of sex does no one any harm. You'll enjoy it.'

'Excuse me, sir,' said the new officer again, 'but I don't really approve of that sort of thing.' The Colonel was taken aback, and after a pause said: 'Good gracious. Are you by any chance a queer?' 'Certainly not, sir,' replied the new officer indignantly. 'Pity,' said the Colonel, 'then you won't enjoy Saturday nights either'!

As soon as we had been re-equipped we left Shaftesbury to take up positions on the beaches near Middleton-on-Sea in Sussex, where I was thrilled to see Charlie Kunz, the pianist with the soft touch, sunbathing in front of his house. But as the danger of invasion receded we moved first to Castle Cary in Somerset and then to Parkstone in Dorset.

To start with I was put in charge of the mortar platoon though I had never seen one fired nor in fact ever did fire one in practice as we were conserving our ammunition. For equally good reasons I was given command of the motor-cycle platoon – I had never ridden one in my life! Still I soon learnt and even used to ride up a ramp and 'jump' the machine over some barrels. But I could never manage to start the wretched thing with the kick-starter, and was sometimes left stranded as I desperately tried to do so.

The platoon consisted of about twenty clapped-out secondhand machines which the Army had bought off the general public. On manoeuvres or in action I was meant to lead my platoon riding in side-car – the sort of machine in which you can see father taking his wife and two kids to the sea-side on a bank holiday.

It was our job, if the invasion came, to proceed down a main road towards the coast until we met the advancing Germans. What was to happen then was not too clear, though I had a pretty shrewd guess! We had no protective armour of any sort and the guardsmen were only armed with rifles slung uncomfortably across their backs. I was even worse off as all I had was a revolver. We had no radio link of any sort, so if we had not been shot-up first, all we could have done was to belt back up the road and warn our Battalion. But on our machines we should have been pushed to get there before the Germans.

It's funny now looking back, but rather frightening when you remember that my platoon was to be the advance guard of the crack 3rd division on which the defence of southern England relied. In spite of *Dad's Army* I still cannot understand why Hitler never invaded. We thought he had on one night in September.

We were playing bridge in the officers' mess when the telephone rang. The duty officer, who happened to be dummy went to answer it and came back after a few minutes looking white and shaken. He told us it had been Brigade Headquarters who had said: 'Codeword Cromwell' and then rung off. The duty officer had gone to the orderly room, looked up the files and found that Cromwell meant that we were to mobilise the Battalion at once and get ready to move off, as invasion was either imminent or had already taken place.

I wish I could say that we did a Sir Francis Drake and finished our rubber. But in fact we all rushed into action. The Battalion was scattered over a large area and as there was no radio contact, the companies had either to be telephoned or warned by despatch riders, who also had to winkle the guardsmen out from pubs, cinemas and so on. In spite of apparent chaos it all worked quite well and the Battalion was standing by ready to move off in about two hours. I'm still not clear what really happened that night and whether it was a genuine false alarm or a test of our mobility.

Anyhow, as the advance guard, I had been sitting all night in my side-car at the head of the Battalion waiting for the 'off' and as you can imagine I was immensely relieved when we were eventually told to stand down.

In the autumn we moved to Parkstone and it was obvious that my superiors felt I would never make a good fighting soldier. From the motor-cycle platoon I was sent on an MT course at Minehead, with a view to becoming the Transport Officer, although I was not the least technically minded. But I had a bit of luck.

At the end of the course there was to be an exam which I was dreading. On the night before, a friend who had been on the course with me was duty officer, and to his surprise found next day's questions in the IN tray in the Adjutant's room. When he came off duty he rushed round to me with a copy and we hurriedly looked up the answers. As a result I passed with flying colours, though ironically my friend only just passed!

On returning to the Battalion I was congratulated on my report and became the Transport Officer. It was a good job to have. We were left very much to ourselves, as everyone else knew even less about it than I did. I had a small élite staff of fitters and storemen and was never short of volunteers since we escaped most of the 'bull' and drill parades.

It was about this time that I indulged in my habit of giving people nicknames. In a most unguardsmanlike way I gave people on my staff such names as Honest Joe, Burglar Bill, Gandhi, the Admiral, and even extended it to the officers' mess where the Mess Sergeant became Uncle Tom.

Uncle Tom was a lovely person and looked after us superbly. He had been a cook and made the best chocolate pudding I have ever tasted. I even indoctrinated the regular officers so that in no time one could hear the Commanding Officer saying: 'Another pink gin please, Uncle Tom.' Scarcely credible really when you consider the traditional discipline of the Brigade of Guards. I was especially pleased with my nickname for one of my fellow officers called Neville Berry. He was known as The Hatchet. Got it?

Our Headquarter Company was stationed in an evacuated girls school and some of the guardsmen slept in one of the old dormitories. They were delighted to find a notice on the wall which read: 'Please ring this bell if a mistress is required during the night'! We had three visits which I especially remember. The first was from Harry Hopkins, President Roosevelt's special envoy who was flying back to America from Hurn Airport after a visit to Mr Churchill. He stayed the night in our mess and breakfasted with us on powdered eggs. He was a quiet, friendly man, who looked pale and sick. He quizzed us about living conditions in Britain, and showed special interest in our families and their reaction to the bombing and blackout, obviously for the benefit of his master.

The next visit was from the Press who descended on us in a public relations exercise organised by the Army. The idea was for them to see how a Battalion worked, so when they came to me I decided to give them good value. I gave a lot of pennies to one of my clerks and sent him out to ring my office every few minutes from a call-box. While I was being interviewed by the Press my telephone hardly stopped ringing and as a result I got a jolly good 'press' the next day saying how hard an MT officer had to work.

Our most important visit at Parkstone was from Monty – he came to inspect the Battalion. We had good warning and we prepared what we thought would be an interesting display when he visited our work-shops. We had an engine in the process of being taken out of a truck, we took a wheel off one vehicle and jacked up another, with a mechanic lying underneath it.

When Monty arrived I saluted and offered to show him round. But he would have none of it and hardly looked at our display. Instead he walked straight up to one of the trucks parked near by and asked the driver to switch on his side-lights. The driver went to his cab and turned the switch. But no lights came on. Monty went to the next truck and asked the driver to do the same thing. Again no lights.

To my horror, this happened twice more and Monty in triumph asked one of the drivers why none of the lights came on. I was as eager to hear the answer as he was. The driver explained that a lot of bulbs had been pinched out of parked vehicles so that now whenever they left their vehicles they used to put the bulbs in their pockets. Monty had obviously been tipped off about this habit and wanted to put a stop to it. He told me what a bad habit it was as if there was an emergency and the driver was in a cinema or somewhere, his vehicle would have no lights if someone else was ordered to drive it.

I thought I had better not make things worse by telling him that the vehicles probably would not start anyway. The reason for this was that the drivers used to immobilise them by removing the rotor arms from the distributors and putting them in their pockets too.

I remember too that at lunch Monty pointedly quizzed our Commanding Officer, Lt.-Col. Mike Venables-Llewelyn, on how the weekly five-mile run was going. This was Monty's keep-fit campaign in which everyone in the division from the highest-ranking officers to the lowest other ranks were required to go for a five-mile run once every week. Monty must have asked the question with his tongue in his cheek as Mike had what you might politely call an ample figure and could not have run one mile let alone five. He got away with it but I must admit that not many of us ever did carry out the order.

We used to set out from the mess at a trot looking very businesslike in shorts and gym shoes. But once round the corner out of sight we used to go for a walk round the block and sneak back to the mess through the back door. There was not much danger of being found out. The only risk was that one might run into Mike doing the same thing!

Whilst at Parkstone I had my first experience of a court-martial when one of my staff was due to be tried for being absent without leave.

An accused man was always allowed to pick any officer in the Battalion he wanted to defend him. My chap chose me although he was going to plead guilty on the main charge. But there was a charge of losing some kit which he denied and he also thought I might put in a good word for him and make an impassioned plea for mercy. I accepted the case as I was bound to do, and told the court consisting of a major, captain and second lieutenant that my 'client' was pleading guilty on the first charge but not guilty on the second.

This brought the prosecuting officer – our own Adjutant Neville Wigram – to his feet to read out a list of the kit that was said to be lost. They included small items like a mess tin, knife and fork. When he had finished I thought I would try to show how trivial this charge was against the overall cost of the war and ask for it to be dismissed. So I rose from my seat and advanced towards Neville like Perry Mason used to before he took to a wheel chair. I walked up to him, tapped him on the chest and looking straight into his eyes said: 'Captain Wigram I put it to you . . .' But I got no further and no one ever knew what it was that I was going to put. I am ashamed to say that Neville winked at me as I was talking and I burst out laughing and couldn't say another word. I tried to turn it into a coughing fit, went very red in the face and retreated hurriedly back to my seat, muttering something about no further questions.

When I had recovered I did get up to plead for my client, saying what a good chap he was and that there had been extenuating circumstances, taking care not to reveal what they were, as I had not the slightest idea myself. But I am afraid he had to pay for his kit. On reflection it does seem rather rough justice that he had to be defended by an officer who knew nothing of military law, court procedure nor how to conduct a case.

12

Technical Adjutant Johnston

In May 1941 I received two bits of news, one bad, one good. The bad news was that No. 35 South Eaton Place had been wrecked by a landmine which had fallen on the corner of Ebury Street. The Crisps, luckily, were only badly shocked but otherwise unhurt. Most of my things were salvaged including a bottle of champagne which, however, I never saw again. Nigel Baker who was on leave at the time, went round to see how the Crisps were and spotting the bottle quite rightly opened it and drank to their lucky escape. The house was impossible to live in again, and for the rest of the war the Crisps looked after a retired colonel in the village of Long Crendon just near to my mother.

From then on, whenever I was on leave in London I used to stay at the Savoy, a suitable base for my twice daily visits to the theatre. But for the first twenty-four hours I always used to stay in my room overlooking the river and have all my meals in bed. Not only was this a much-needed rest but it was such a treat to be alone and in complete quiet. One of the worst things in war were the people and the noise, and one was seldom alone, not even in the bathrooms or the loos. So you can imagine what a luxury it was to be cut off from the world for twenty-four hours, even if there was the occasional interruption from the bombers overhead.

The good news was that a Guards Armoured Division was to be formed and that several Battalions were to be mechanised and turned into tank battalions. This meant that all that summer we went on a course to Bovington and I found myself being groomed for the job of Technical Adjutant. This involved learning some highly technical matters – which I never really came to understand.

The other battalions all sent similar people to myself and of about the same age. I think the reason for this was that the job of Technical Adjutant was a vital one in a tank battalion. He did not *have* to be highly technical but needed to be a good organiser and administrator, and able to stand up to the four company commanders or squadron leaders as they were to become.

So far as the tanks, scout cars and vehicles were concerned the Technical Adjutant's word was law, and if he said a vehicle was not fit for action then the squadron leader could do nothing about it.

Two of my companions on the course were a distinguished barrister called Gerald Upjohn who after the war rose to the heights of a Lord of Appeal and the other an old Cambridge golf blue called William Whitelaw of whom you will all have heard. I met him again in 1971 when Mr Heath entertained the victorious MCC team at No. 10 Downing Street.

Willie reminded me of what had happened during the test we all had to do at the end of the course. We had to carry out various practical repair and maintenance jobs on vehicles and tanks. Upjohn, Whitelaw and I had been detailed to strip down an engine and then put it all together again. The stripping was easy enough but putting it together again was a different matter. We had tried it before and knew that we would have a few nuts and bolts left over for which we could not find a place on the engine. The inspecting officer knew that this was liable to happen and that when it did, people slipped the spare bits into the pockets of their overalls, and pretended that the engine was complete.

Before he reached us we saw the officer asking the other teams to turn out their pockets. So Willie Whitelaw and I took out the few nuts which we had in our pockets and slipped them into Gerald Upjohn's without him knowing. When he came to us the officer looked carefully at the newly assembled engine, and said: 'Very good gentlemen. That looks fine. But just as a matter of routine will you please turn out your pockets?' Willie and I did so promptly and of course there was nothing there. But as it happened Gerald Upjohn had not had any nuts over. He was older and more distinguished looking than us with fine silvery hair and could be a bit tetchy. He resented being treated like a schoolboy and protesting strongly that he had nothing to hide, turned out his pockets. To his horror out on to the ground fell our nuts and bolts.

The officer could not help laughing – I suspect he knew what had happened – but 'Daddy' Upjohn as we used to call him was not too pleased with us. Had we been in the dock, and he on the bench at that moment I reckon he would willingly have ordered us the cat! But luckily we all passed out and in August I reported back to our Battalion at Warminster.

I was given an old civilian garage as a workshop and had a staff of about forty fitters and was responsible for the care and maintenance and repair of about seventy-five tanks and over a hundred trucks and scout cars. It was a splendid job as once again no one interfered with us and we were left to our own devices so long as we kept all the vehicles 'on the road'.

I was to remain Technical Adjutant for the next four years until the Guards Armoured Division was disbanded in July 1945. This must be something of a record in wartime when people are usually moved all over the place. But I was happy and I suppose the Battalion must have been too. So it suited us both.

When we became armoured we all had to wear berets and I had to adopt some psychological tactics. I knew what a clot I would look in one. So on the day the berets were issued, I paraded all my staff and said something like this: 'I have called you together so that you can see me in my beret. If any of you want to laugh – and I don't blame you if you do – you may laugh now for two minutes. But after that if ever I catch anyone laughing at me he will be put into close arrest for insolence.' It was a bit unorthodox, but they had their laugh, and I never actually caught anyone laughing at me afterwards. So I suppose it can be said to have worked.

We took part in a lot of tank exercises over Salisbury Plain and in the course of these I suffered two physical mishaps. First my scout car pitched into an old shell-hole and I smashed my face against the armour plating and severely damaged my nose. It was too big and too tough to break, but it was an awful mess and had to have a great many stitches put in it. I still bear the marks today.

The other injury was more serious. We used to have to change the tank tracks or replace them if they came off, and this meant lifting heavy weights. Somehow or other I ruptured myself and had to have a hernia operation in the military hospital at Salisbury. (This recalled the old joke about the man who went on a holiday to Hernia Bay, stayed at a Truss House Hotel and had a rupturous time.) I was in hospital for three weeks and spent another three recuperating at my mother's cottage, where she had been housing two evacuees from London.

Soon after I had returned to the Battalion I was sent up to the English Electric factory at Stafford to see how our Covenanter and Crusader tanks were made. I was looked after by their new PRO, a Mr Attock. They told me an intriguing story about him.

Earlier that year he had been on the short list for the PRO job and he and several others had to appear before a final board. They had been warned that they would have to make a short speech as part of the test, and a great deal would depend on its clarity and delivery. About two minutes before he was due to go before the board Mr Attock dashed off to the loo. While he was spending a penny he decided to take out his false teeth and give them an extra clean so as to give a good impression. Unfortunately he was so nervous that he dropped them down the loo. With now only a minute to go, what would you have done, chum? Remember you had to make a speech which was to be judged on its clarity. I cannot tell you what Mr Attock did. All I can tell you is that he got the job!

There was a well-equipped theatre in Warminster Barracks where

Brigade HQ was situated, and Alfred Shaughnessy, now a TV script-writer, and I put on a few shows. I did my usual cross-talk act, this time with my storeman as my stooge. We also had a first-class tenor, a young Irishman called Tom O'Brien, who really had a superb voice. But in one show his big scene was completely ruined. He was supposed to be a homesick prisoner of war in a realistic prison exercise yard with a strand of barbed-wire across the front. This was very difficult to put up as it had to be uncoiled from the side of the stage in a blackout after a sketch. On the night in question Tom took up his position and the pit band struck up the opening bars of *Shine through my dreams* a song which normally brought tears to the eyes of the audience and received a tremendous ovation at the end.

But when the curtain rose it was obvious that any tears that night would be tears from laughter. Pinned to the barbed-wire was the figure of an officer dressed in mess kit – an unlikely sight in a prison camp. It was in fact one of our own officers Hugh Burge who had been in the audience at the start but had at the last moment volunteered to stand in for an absent stagehand. He had had no time to rehearse but was just told by the stage manager to feed the barbed-wire out on to the stage. Unfortunately he got caught in it and could only stand there looking helpless throughout the song. The audience roared their heads off and there were shouts of 'good old Hugh', 'why are you so stuck up', etc. It was more of a nightmare than a dream for poor Tom O'Brien that night.

The next two years we spent training with our tanks. From Warminster we went to Norfolk and trained in the battle area which was later used by *Dad's Army* for all the action scenes in their TV series. It was there that we received our first Sherman tanks with which we were later to fight.

General Paget, the C.-in-C. Home Forces came to inspect us and very smart he looked in breeches and highly polished riding-boots – but definitely not the correct gear to wear if you intend to inspect a tank. With great difficulty he climbed up on to one of the Shermans and inevitably slipped and slid right down the side of the tank. Highly undignified and very painful.

It was here in Norfolk that the first steps in my BBC career were unknowingly taken.

I was sitting in our mess one day when a great friend in our 1st

Battalion, Nigel Baker, telephoned to say he had a chap from the BBC staying in his mess. He was a Canadian called Stewart Macpherson who was attached to them to gain experience as a war reporter ready for when the second front came. Nigel asked whether they could come over to dinner and also bring another BBC reporter who was attached to the Irish Guards for the same purpose.

Of course I said yes and we had an hilarious evening, which was not surprising because the second reporter was that effervescent Welshman, Wynford Vaughan-Thomas. I saw a lot of them during the next few weeks and though I did not know it at the time, this chance meeting with these two famous broadcasters was to change my whole life.

From Norfolk we went to Yorkshire and took part in a number of exercises involving many miles in the tanks and nights out in the open even though it was still winter. We bought three white hens which we used to take out with us in a tool box on top of the cab of the store truck. They laid quite a few eggs and we had plenty of 'fry-ups' in the back of the truck.

In the spring Mr Churchill paid us a visit and insisted on going for a ride in one of our tanks across country. This could be very rough going but he seemed to revel in it. Wearing his black 'Derby' hat, halfway between a top-hat and a bowler, he stuck his head out of the turret and tapped the driver on the head urging him to go faster. What a man.

My job in 'action' was to travel in my scout car with the Battalion Headquarter tanks. I was in radio communication with all the squadrons and if they had a breakdown it was my task to direct one of three recovery tanks to their assistance or even go there myself if it was only a minor fault. We were kept pretty busy, especially with tanks losing their tracks.

I had a skilled signwriter on my staff and I got him to paint a small man with two fingers raised in a Harvey Smith V sign on the front of my scout car. He also painted on the name which I had chosen for it which was FUJIAR. These letters stood for a wellknown army expression '. . . you Jack I'm all right'. Fujiar soon became famous throughout the division, and was to be my mobile home throughout all the fighting in Europe. It never broke down and was still going strong at the end of the war.

As spring advanced and preparations for 'D' day gathered pace Monty began to tour the country to visit as many of the 21st Army

Group as possible. He liked to gather the troops all around him and give them an informal pep talk. In his 8th Army beret and battle dress he was received with tremendous enthusiasm wherever he went, and always departed with the cheers of the soldiers ringing in his ears.

Except, unfortunately, when he visited the Guards Armoured Division, where his reception both before and after his talk was noticeably cool. This was not Monty's fault, though he was obviously a bit shaken by the lack of the usual reaction. But his kind of hearty man to man approach was foreign to all guards' training. To them a general was a general and they expected him to behave like their idea of one.

In addition they had been waiting kicking their heels for about three hours at the airdrome where the parade was due to take place at 11 am. But due to typical army panic at the thought of being late on parade most of the Division had arrived soon after eight o'clock. Monty's staff had started the ball rolling by announcing that Monty would arrive at 11 am. Corps HQ just to make sure gave orders for the division to be drawn up ready by 10.30 am. Division told the brigades 10 am, they told the battalions 9 am, and the commanding officers told their squadrons 8.30 am. And so we ended up by having a 5.30 am reveille, and a ridiculously early breakfast. No wonder we were all browned off and even Raquel Welch would have received a cool reception in these circumstances.

Early in May we moved down the length of England to Hove where our first job was to waterproof all our vehicles. This was to protect all their essential parts, including the engine, in case they had to be driven through the sea when landing in France. There was a big build up of tension and the whole of southern England was one large armed camp, full of troops and vehicles getting ready for 'D' day, which was obviously fast approaching.

The people of Hove and Brighton were most friendly and hospitable in spite of the way our tanks damaged their roads and pavements. We found time to play some cricket on the Hove County Ground and actually won a one-wicket victory against a team from the Royal Navy.

We normally worked till late in the evening and then our Adjutant – Charles Sheepshanks – and myself used to retire each night to the Norfolk Hotel where a bottle of Perrier Jouet 1928 was always waiting for us in an ice bucket. We all had the feeling that for some of us this would be the last time we should ever see England and decided to enjoy ourselves while we could.

13

War and peace

On 6 June came John Snagge's announcement on the BBC that the invasion had started. From then on we were on permanent standby. We reluctantly gave away our three white hens but had two buckets of pickled eggs to take with us in case food was short in France. After the initial landings, bad weather slowed down the build-up of tanks and it was nearly three weeks before we received our orders to move.

One morning the people of Hove woke up to find we had gone, though I suspect the roar and rumbling of our tanks must have disturbed their sleep that night. We moved to near Portsmouth where we loaded our tanks and vehicles on to landing-craft and crossed over to Arromanches in a large convoy. After nearly three years of training and learning to be tank men we were about to be put to the test. At last we were genuinely at war.

Things got off to a bad start. First some of the guardsmen on our landing-craft mistook the washbasins sticking out from the wall for something else and used them accordingly, much to the indignation of the sailors. From then on they referred to the guardsmen as 'those pissing pongos'. So much for inter-service relations!

Then we had a calamity with our pickled eggs. We had hung the buckets from the roof of the store truck thinking the landing-craft would deposit it right up the beach. But the weather was still rough and our vehicles had to be unloaded quite a way out to sea. This meant driving down a deep ramp into the water. Our driver did his best but when his front wheels hit the bottom the buckets swung about all over the place and the eggs flew in every direction. We managed to salvage a few from the bottom of the buckets and were soon eating our first fried eggs on French soil in an orchard near Bayeux. This was enclosed farming country known as *bocage* and was quite unsuitable for tanks, which operate best in open country.

There were a few minor actions and skirmishes but everyone became very frustrated at our apparent immobility. We discovered later that Monty was deliberately using us as a sitting target to draw the fire and attention of as much of the German army as possible. This was to enable the Americans under Patton to break out from the west right across France and so trap the German 7th army in the famous Falaise Gap.

It was not much fun just sitting there being shelled every day, but even that was better than the Division's first big battle on 18 July. This was a bloody and chaotic affair fought for much of the time in clouds of black dust churned up by our tanks. The first I saw of my very first battle was hordes of bombers going over us at dawn as we lay in the fields waiting to advance.

There were two thousand of them and they were meant to soften up the opposition with their blanket bombing. It looked as if they had succeeded because as we advanced slowly through the dust thousands of bedraggled German prisoners passed us marching disconsolately back to our prisoner of war cages. But we were soon to meet tough opposition from some strategically placed Tiger tanks which with their big guns knocked out nine of our tanks. Most of them blew up and we suffered the inevitable casualties, many through burning. For us this was our first taste of real war and it was not much fun.

I am not going to attempt to give you a round by round commentary on what we did from then on. I was only the Technical Adjutant and although from my own point of view I was often too damn close I was not one of those actually fighting the battles in the tanks. They are the people best qualified to tell the tale. But I am never likely to forget those hot summer days from June to October.

The heat and the dust, the flattened corn fields, the 'liberated' villages which were just piles of rubble, the refugees, the stench of dead cows, our first shelling, real fear, the first casualties, friends wounded or killed, men with whom one had laughed and joked the evening before, lying burnt beside their knocked out tank. No, war is NOT fun, though as years go by, one tends to remember only the good things. The changes are so sudden. One moment boredom or laughter, the next, action and death. So it was with us.

From the frustrations of Normandy with the Americans getting all
the headlines and glory, we were suddenly given the green light to
'go'. We made a mad dash across France and Belgium and actually
advanced 395 miles in seven days, with a final spurt of 93 miles in one
day on 3 September to liberate Brussels. It was exhilarating and
thrilling and our good old Sherman tanks performed wonders as
they tore up miles and miles of French and Belgium roads with hardly
a breakdown.

The scenes of welcome and enthusiasm were unforgettable and the
cheering crowds in the towns and the villages often held up our progress as they thrust flowers, fruit and eggs on to the passing vehicles.
Better still, the pretty mademoiselles showered kisses on anyone they
could reach – even the Technical Adjutant. But it was not roses all the
way. Parts of the country were still held by the retreating Germans and
hard fighting took place here and there. After passing through one
cheering village with the pavements lined with women and children,
and gay flags and bunting, we rounded a corner and came upon one of
our tanks knocked out, with two of its crew lying dead beside it. So
all along the route as we raced towards Brussels, joy and sorrow went
hand in hand.

Brussels really went wild as our tanks roared into the city late in the
evening of 3 September. Everyone was delirious, the hospitality was
fantastic and there was no sleep for anyone that night. Unfortunately
for us it was short-lived as we left the next afternoon following hard on
the heels of the Germans. They had left Brussels by one end as we
entered it at the other and so had had no time to blow up bridges or
burn important papers.

More important from our point of view was a secret store full of
Krug Vintage champagne to which a friendly Belgian led us. It had
been left by the Germans and we distributed a bottle apiece to the
tanks there and then, and put the rest on to one of our petrol lorries,
which for the next few weeks went up to the tanks at night with the
petrol convoy, but carried bottles instead of jerry cans.

A fortnight later our tanks made another dash – this time across
Holland – to capture Nijmegen Bridge. The idea was to link up with
the airborne forces who had 'dropped' at Arnhem across the River
Waal. As we approached the town of Nijmegen we were met by the
officer commanding all the airborne troops some of whom, like
himself, had glided in on our side of the Waal.

It was my cousin 'Boy' Browning – now a Lieutenant General. It was a dramatic moment for him as he greeted his old 2nd Battalion which he had commanded in its infantry days just before the war. After a desperate struggle a troop of our tanks under the present Lord Carrington captured the huge Nijmegen Bridge, but alas the planned link-up with Arnhem never took place. If this was a history of war I would try to explain why. But luckily it isn't. But had the plan succeeded the war would probably have been over by Christmas.

As it was we had a cold and unpleasant winter digging our tanks out of mud and snow. It was not until the end of March that we finally crossed the Rhine and fought our way up through Germany. Although it was obvious that the war was nearing its end the Germans on our front, many of them from the navy, put up a fanatical resistance and we suffered many casualties in the last few weeks. It was a terrible time for the men in our tanks. They knew that both victory or death were just around the corner but which would it be? For some sadly, as I've said, it was death.

On the lighter side, I actually captured three German prisoners all off my own bat. At about 5 pm one evening I was going up in Fujiar to some tanks of ours in a burning village which a squadron had just taken. It was nearly dark and we were travelling very slowly when all of a sudden three grey figures rose up out of a ditch and ran towards my scout car. I had visions of hand grenades and quickly pulled down my armoured hatch.

There were loud bangings on the side of the car and I peeped out through the visor at the side. To my relief I saw six arms in the air and heard voices shouting, 'Kamerad'. Quickly I stuck my head out of the hatch and became every inch a true Grenadier!

With signs, I ordered the Germans to clamber on to the car and we bore them back in triumph to Battalion Headquarters where I was treated as a bit of a hero until I owned up as to what had really happened.

By the last week in April the Division was on the outskirts of Bremen and Hamburg, and they fell to us on 26 April and 2 May. The next day General Sir Brian Horrocks our Corps Commander paid us a visit and seemed far less enthusiastic than usual. He suggested to our Commanding Officer that we should take things quietly for a day or two and not attempt to advance any further. He said he wanted to review the situation. But of course as he told us afterwards he knew that the armistice was about to be signed any day, and he wished to avoid any unnecessary loss of life in the last few hours of the war. Still, at the time, I must admit that we thought he was getting senile and losing his drive.

We actually heard the good news on the radio on 5 May and it was amazing how calmly everyone took it. Peace. We just could not believe it. So far as I remember I went and sat on the loo out of relief. We had a few celebrations in the mess tent that night and I had a few drinks with my own boys. But the greatest treat was not having to 'stand to' at dawn for the first time since arriving in Europe. Reveille was actually put back to 7 am. What luxury!

It seemed strange to be at peace again but after several moves we finally settled down at Sieburg near Bad Godesburg, with our officers' mess in a large and luxurious castle or *schloss*. As we travelled across Germany and drove through cities like Cologne we realised what a terrible hammering Germany had received from our bombers. The whole Ruhr was a mass of rubble and the population appeared to be in a state of shock, which was hardly surprising considering what they had been through.

Whether they were Nazis or not, the death of Hitler in his bunker, the capture or death of the prominent Nazi leaders and the total collapse of their country must have been shattering to a people who had been told they were invincible. They were mostly in a poor state physically and would do anything for a cigarette. But it was difficult to feel sorry for them, at any rate the grown-ups, especially after we had liberated one of the smaller concentration camps. I only looked in from the outside but what I saw was sufficient. Fellow officers who had to go inside were physically sick. I shall never understand how human beings could have descended to such animal depths.

But it was a lovely summer and our *schloss* was very comfortable and situated high up in beautiful grounds. We relaxed and enjoyed ourselves and soon began to play cricket again, mostly on matting, though we did teach the Germans to prepare one very good grass pitch.

As soon as the war was over we had been told that we were going to be turned back into infantry. This meant saying goodbye to our tanks, which we did in a giant parade in front of Monty on Rotenberg airfield on 9 June. In true Guards' fashion the tank crews cleaned, painted and polished their tanks and burnished their guns.

Over three hundred tanks were formed up in one long line and they dipped their guns in salute as Monty stepped out of his aeroplane. He then made an extremely complimentary speech – '. . . I want to say here and now that in the sphere of armoured warfare you have set a standard that it would be difficult for those that come after to reach. . . . You have achieved great results. . . . You will long be remembered for your prowess in armoured warfare.' Not bad coming from Monty, especially after that cool reception which we had given him before 'D' day. It made our three years of training all seem worthwhile.

In return the armour did him proud. As they filed past the saluting base each tank traversed its gun towards him and once again dipped in salute. The tanks then accelerated and disappeared over the top of the hill out of sight. As they were lost to view and the roar of the tank engines faded away, the sound of a band could be heard. From over the top of the hill now came several hundred marching guardsmen as a symbol that the Guards had once again assumed their time-honoured role as infantry.

I ceased to be Technical Adjutant after what must be a record four years and was promoted to be a major in command of the HQ Company, with special responsibility for welfare. We soon set about preparing a revue which we called *The eyes have it* (the insignia of the Guards Armoured Division had been an ever-open eye).

We staged the revue in a well-equipped theatre in Bad Godesburg where it played to packed houses for a week. We then spent much of the remainder of the summer touring with it round all the units of the Division. It was quite an ambitious production with a pit orchestra, professional sets and lighting. We even imported two girls from Brussels.

I am afraid many of the jokes would not pass the BBC censors even with today's liberated outlook. Two samples: A man and girl riding a tandem bicycle came to the bottom of a hill. Said the man: 'Get off. We are going to push it up here.' Replied the girl: 'Suits me but what shall we do with the bike?'

Or, a honeymoon couple were having a very late breakfast in their hotel bedroom. The bride rang the bell and ordered bacon and eggs for two and lettuce for one. 'What's the lettuce for?' asked the groom. 'I want to see if you also *eat* like a rabbit' said the bride. See what I mean?

The autumn became a series of leaving parties as wartime only officers and men were gradually being demobbed. In November it was my turn and Hugh Burge (of the barbed-wire) and I gave a big party in the *schloss*, with band, cabaret and lashings of champagne. Tom O'Brien sang *We'll gather lilacs* which brought tears to the eyes, and to the same tune Hugh and I sang a song which gained a few drunken laughs. We wrote the words ourselves and here they are with only one (Kenneth Tynan) word changed.

> *We'll go to England when our Age Group goes*
> *We'll change our battle dress for civvy clothes*
> *What we'll do then the Lord God only knows*
> *When we come home again.*

> *One thing is certain, there'll be no more drill*
> *We'll hold COs orders in the Berkeley Grill*
> *We'll stay at Claridge's and blast the bill*
> *When we come home again.*

> *We'll say goodbye to all our bits of frat*
> *Thank God our wives don't know what we've been at*
> *We'll don again that famous bowler hat*
> *When we come home again.*

> *Between the hours of ten and half past three*
> *It's in the City we shall be*
> *With that blonde typist back upon our knee*
> *When we come home again.*

> *We're glad to go, but there must be regrets*
> *For back in England no-one ever gets*
> *400 marks for 50 cigarettes*
> *When we come home again.*

> *And when we go to bed and try to doss*
> *We'll get no sleep, but simply turn and toss*
> *Dreaming of 9-course dinners at the Schloss*
> *When we come home again.*

We'd like to tell you in our last refrain
If our address you can't obtain
There is one place where we will meet again
When we come home once more.

And as the gentle light of dawning pales
There's one address that never fails
It's 'C/o Millie at the "Bag of Nails" '
When we come home again.

14

I meet 'Auntie'

Pleased as I was to be going back to civilian life, it was also with great regret that I said my goodbyes to all my friends in the Guards – both officers and men. For five years they had given me their friendship and in spite of all the unpleasant things we went through together, it is the fun and laughter that I always try to remember. I still keep up with many of them and at Christmas I still receive at least ten cards from various members of my technical staff.

I nicknamed my scout car driver Hengist. He always had a smile on his face and was a tremendously hard worker. His favourite expression was 'way oop' and each year I get a card without any Christmas greeting on it. It simply reads: Way oop – Hengist. That is the sort of thing which made it all worth while.

And about ten years ago I received another bonus. I was motoring through Leicester and in the Midlands and the North many of the policemen are old Grenadiers. I accidently drove up a one-way street and as they generally do, all the drivers of the oncoming cars started to hoot and wave their arms. I went very red and stopped and my heart sank as I saw a very tall policeman walking slowly towards my car. I could sense the drivers' feeling of pleasure that this twerp who had driven up the wrong way and was delaying them, was about to be dealt with by the law. I put my head out of my window as the police-man approached and started to say: 'Sorry, officer . . .' when he suddenly stopped, sprang to attention and gave me a terrific salute. He was one of my old guardsmen and had recognised me. My long nose is useful in this respect!

He then bent down and for a minute or so we discussed Fujiar, army food and how brave we had both been, completely ignoring the waiting drivers. He then stepped back, saluted again and directed me *up* the one-way street. I must say I felt a bit smug as I drove past the other drivers champing at the bit in their cars. Up the Guards!

And so I returned to England, drew my blue pin-stripe demob suit from Olympia, and went down to my mother's cottage to sort myself out and decide exactly what I was going to do with my future.

Now that I had time to sit back and think I was more determined than ever to do something in the entertainment world. But I realised only too well all my limitations and how inexperienced I was. I had a slick way of telling a story and by now could put over a cross-talk act. But that was about all and if I wanted to become an actor it would mean learning the business from the bottom either in repertory or in drama school. I was now aged thirty-three and felt that it was too late in life to start. So I decided to try for the management or production side of the business.

I came up to London and stayed in the Guards Club which was then in Brooks Street. First of all I went to the office to say goodbye to everyone and to thank Arthur Whitworth for all he had done to help me and apologise for leaving them in the lurch. I then set about seeing some theatrical managers and producers who were all very kind and sympathetic. But it soon became obvious that they had nothing to offer me, which was not really surprising, because I really had nothing in the way of experience or ability to offer them.

I trailed around for about a fortnight and began to get very depressed. What *was* I going to do? And then luck – of which I freely admit I have had more than my fair share – came to my aid. I was sitting rather gloomily reading a paper in the Guards Club when an old officer friend asked me whether I would like to have dinner and help entertain two BBC types whom he gathered I already knew. They were of course Stewart Macpherson and Wynford Vaughan-Thomas and it was this second dinner party with them that was to decide my future.

During conversation I casually mentioned that I was looking for a job in the entertainment world, but could not think of exactly what to do. At that time I never gave a thought to the BBC which I regarded with a mixture of respect and tolerant amusement at its 'Auntie image'.

Stewart said nothing that evening but next day rang to say that there was a vacancy in the Outside Broadcast Department and would I like to come up to their office in Portland Place for an interview with the Head of 'OBs' Seymour de Lotbinière. Even then I was only mildly enthusiastic but had the sense and good manners to say thank you and yes of course I would come.

I vaguely knew de Lotbinière or Lobby, as he was always called, from before the war. He was an old Etonian, about 6 ft 8 in. tall and had been a keen member of Toc H. Tubby Clayton used to tell how he had once been staying with the Provost of Eton, and was going up to bed when a tall figure opened a bedroom door to put his shoes out to be cleaned. (I believe it is considered terribly non-U to do this in a private house and of course is a waste of time nowadays in an hotel.) Tubby did not know who it was but in typical fashion said: 'Good evening. And what do you know about Toc H?' To which the tall figure replied: 'Nothing, thank God,' and slammed the door. Tubby was never defeated however and it was not long before he had converted Lobby, and he later said of him, 'Lobby came to us as proud as Lucifer but we made him scrub floors.'

So I went to see Lobby without honestly thinking there was much in it for me. His secretary had told me the wrong time for the interview, so although I arrived in true Guards' fashion five minutes early for parade, I nearly missed it altogether. In the time available Lobby quizzed me about my knowledge of entertainment and sport, and seemed particularly keen to discover whether I was interested in people. At the end of the interview he said he would give me two tests and if I passed them he could then offer me a job. It might only be temporary and in any case would be pretty poorly paid. I told him that neither of these things worried me as I did not expect to make broadcasting my career and I still had a bit of my army gratuity left.

Nothing like being honest! Anyway I said I would like to have a crack at the tests. The first was to go down to Piccadilly Circus and write a five-minute report on what I saw there – just as if I was going to give a radio talk. And here again luck or fate took a hand. As I was walking down Regent Street wondering what on earth I was going to say I passed one of those shops where you can record a birthday or Christmas greeting. 'Why not record your message?' it said in gold letters in the window and that's just what I decided to do. I went to Piccadilly Circus, made some notes and then went back to the shop to record my five-minute message. I played it back and it sounded ghastly. It was the first time I had heard my voice recorded and like most people in similar circumstances I could not believe that it was my voice. It sounded far too low. Anyhow the nice girl in the shop was very sweet and said it sounded 'smashing', and I left the record at Broadcasting House for Lobby to hear. He was I learnt later, surprised and moderately impressed at finding a record instead of a piece of paper, so that my chance look into the record shop turned out to be a lucky one.

The other test was more difficult. Wynford was due to do some street interviews outside the old Monseigneur News Theatre in Oxford Street in a programme called *Saturday Night Out*. His interviews would be 'live' but when he had finished I was to record some interviews of my own with passers-by.

I must admit I was scared stiff as I was now beginning to be bitten by the broadcasting bug, fired by the obvious enthusiasm and happiness of those working in OBs. Wynford was a great help and gave me tips on how and how not to do an interview. First and foremost, if you have the time make friends with your 'victims' before hand and gain their confidence. Chat them up in fact. Never start (as so many people do these days) 'Now tell me . . .' Never frame a question so that the only answer left is yes or no. Always *listen* to the answers in case you can follow them up. Many interviewers are so busy thinking of their next question that they often fail to do this. Unless the answer is not clear or is inaudible never repeat it. Be courteous, don't hector, don't lose your temper. But if the answer is evasive press on politely until you get something definite.

Finally, always remember that you are only the link between the listener and the person being interviewed. They want to hear him or her, not you. So keep your own opinions to yourself, your questions as short as possible, and try not to swamp your victim with your personality. These and many other tips Wynford passed on to me and they have proved a valuable basis to work on throughout my broadcasting career. They do not apply of course to the type of hard political interview which you hear so often nowadays on television or on radio programmes like *World at One*. But thank goodness I have never been caught up in those.

On this occasion I watched Wynford's technique carefully while he was doing his interviews, then with butterflies in my stomach stepped out on to the pavement to do mine. I asked passers-by what they thought of the present rations and as you can imagine got quite a few earthy replies. But I got through it somehow and as Wynford said afterwards at least I kept going and did not dry up, an invaluable asset in a broadcaster.

Lobby must have thought roughly the same, as after I had waited anxiously for a few days, his secretary rang to say that I had 'passed' and that I was to report to OBs on 13 January 1946. So I was in the BBC, although I had been warned it might only be temporary. When as frequently happens, people ask me, 'How *does* one get into the BBC?' I can truthfully answer that in my case it was largely due to luck. I *happened* to meet Stew and Wynford during the war. I *happened* to be demobilised early when the BBC was short of staff. I *happened* to be in the club to receive that dinner invitation to meet Stew and Wynford again. I *happened* to have looked up as I passed that record shop. And I suppose I ought to add in fairness that I *happened* to have been born with the gift of the gab.

Once started it had all happened very quickly and I only had a few days in which to find myself some rooms before I was due to report to the BBC. I found some in Gloucester Place which was very handy being only ten minutes' walk away from Portland Place. Neither before the war nor since have I ever commuted to work. I have always felt it an awful waste of two hours or so a day to spend them dashing to and from stations and sitting or standing in trains. What I have done with the time saved I am not sure but at least I have been spared the strain and tension of having to catch the 8.14 am train each morning or the 6.11 pm in the evening. In my job at the BBC it would in fact have been doubly difficult as I often worked up to late hours at the theatres or had to come in early for programmes such as *Today*. Later when I became BBC Cricket Correspondent I was frequently rung up at my home in St John's Wood at all hours of the day and sometimes at night, asking me to pop in to Broadcasting House to do a two-minute report on some cricket news such as the announcement of a Test team or death of a famous cricketer. Had I not lived near my work this would have been impossible.

I was to be in rooms on my own as I had lost touch with William Douglas-Home for the time being. He had had rather an unhappy war ending up in prison after being court-martialled for disobeying an order on active service. This sounds bad and at the time we all felt indignant and unsympathetic about it, and thought it served him right. There were we fighting the Germans not approving of it nor enjoying it any more than he did. But if everyone had behaved like him Hitler would presumably have won the war and then what would have happened to our families and homes and our way of life in England.

That's what we thought at the time but when it was all over and everyone had cooled down it was easier to see his side of the whole thing. At heart he had always been a conscientious objector or a pacifist in the sense of wanting to abolish war – we are all of us pacifists in its other sense of liking peace. He had started the war in the fire service and when conscripted accepted without protest but with the proviso that he would not make a very good soldier. He went to the Buffs as a private and was then sent to the OCTU at Sandhurst from where he passed out as an officer. Then comes the incredible part.

He was posted back to the same battalion to command men with whom he had served as a private. On one rifle inspection he told a man his rifle was dirty. 'Not half as dirty as yours used to be, Bill,' was the retort. An impossible position, especially as William was still loud in his criticism of the war and the way it was being run, and even stood in a by-election at Windsor as an anti-Churchill candidate.

Then came the invasion of Europe and the Buffs were part of a force ordered to take the port of Le Havre, which in spite of repeated demands the Germans refused to surrender, although it was full of civilians, mostly women and children. The only way left to take it was by shelling and it was at this point that William told his Commanding Officer that he could not obey an order to attack which meant endangering the lives of these women and children. His Commanding Officer knew and liked William and understood how strongly he felt. He overlooked this refusal to fight and gave William instead a more non-combative job with the transport. But William also refused this and wrote a letter to the local paper in Maidenhead where the Buffs had been stationed explaining exactly what had happened. Now that it was public, the Commanding Officer was left with no alternative but to put him in close arrest and have him court-martialled.

William was sentenced to a year's imprisonment which he spent in

Wormwood Scrubs and Wakefield, serving eight months of his sentence. Needless to say he was visited by Lord Home. At the end of the visit Lady Home was sitting in the taxi outside the prison gates when she saw Lord Home going down the street to another entrance. She called out to him that the taxi was waiting for him. 'I know,' he said, 'but I must just go and thank the Governor for having dear Willie!'

Based on his experiences in prison, William wrote his first really successful play called *Now Barrabas*. I attended the first night and in the audience were some of his old prison friends, with whom of course he had been extremely popular. At the reception afterwards Lord Home greeted them and chatted as if they had been fellow peers at some Scottish gathering.

From all this you will have gathered that I had got in touch with William again. I have gone into his case in some detail because I have always felt guilty and ashamed that at a time when he was in trouble I had been too proud or superior to try to help him or even to write to him. My only excuse is that war seemed to make one intolerant of anyone who did not conform. But I am still deeply sorry that I behaved as I did.

Some years later his second brother Henry was gaoled for a short time for some motoring offence. William wanted to go to see him but could not get permission. So he asked his brother Alec if he could use his influence to arrange a visit. Alec refused, so William went and called on the Governor of the prison where Henry was. He asked for and was given permission to see Henry. In triumph he went back and told Alec how he had managed to get in to see Henry. Alec said, 'All I can say is, that it must have been Old Boys' Day!'

15

My OB apprenticeship

The Outside Broadcast Department or OBs as they are always called is responsible for all broadcasts which take place outside a studio. These include all sport, ceremonials, relays from the opera and theatre, church services and events from places like the Albert Hall.

During and just after the war most of the now famous commentators were on the staff, but by the time I arrived some of them were beginning to become freelances. The basic difference here is that on the staff you get a fixed salary and of course a pension. You get paid the same no matter how many or how few broadcasts you may do. The freelance on the other hand is paid for each broadcast so that his income depends on the amount of work he does. With some of the freelances the BBC gives a short-term contract of three or five years. This guarantees them a fixed amount but also leaves them free to do other outside work as well.

The BBC has always been very generous in allowing staff to accept outside work so long as it does not interfere with BBC duties. For instance for years I have given talks at dinners or luncheon clubs, or done commentaries for films, but always with the rider that if a BBC job crops up at the last moment it must have preference. This has worked very well, though of course I was never able to do any advertising for commercials while on the staff.

Every Monday, Lobby used to hold a meeting to discuss past programmes and to plan future ones. At my first meeting I felt very much the new boy as I sat down to join such household names as Raymond Glendenning, Stewart Macpherson, Freddy Grisewood, Rex Alston, Audrey Russell, Wynford Vaughan-Thomas, John Ellison and even Gilbert Harding before he left the department.

My confidence was soon restored as I saw these famous broadcasters waiting humbly for Lobby's verdict on their particular efforts of the week before. Lobby was a perfectionist and the architect of all commentary technique which remains basically unchanged today (or should do if it is a good commentary).

He tried to listen to every OB and had a little black notebook in which he jotted down all the good and bad things in a broadcast. He was extremely fair but never over-fulsome with his praise. 'Not bad' or 'On the whole a brave effort' meant you had done pretty well. But if he began to beat his clenched right hand into the palm of his left, and say: 'Brian, I was a bit puzzled . . .' you could be sure that your commentary was about to be pulled to bits. But no one ever resented it, and at these weekly meetings we all used to chip in and say exactly what we thought of each others' efforts. No holds were barred. It was always perfectly friendly and the helpful criticism kept everyone up to the mark.

For as long as he was Head of OBs most of us used to ring Lobby up at home after every broadcast, and ask anxiously for his verdict. It was quite a tense moment as one waited to hear if that fist would start beating, something incidentally which he seemed able to do with a telephone receiver in his hand.

The OB Department was divided into various sections such as events and ceremonials, sport, and entertainment, and I was allotted to poor John Ellison as his assistant in the latter. I could not have wished for a better person to teach me my job. He had been in the BBC for six years after being invalided out of the RAF as the result of a car accident. He had also been an actor in repertory and the West End and knew everyone in the entertainment world, both performers and management.

At that time there were a lot of live relays from theatres and music halls and we had to go and vet all the West End shows to see if they were suitable for broadcasting. Normally we did a half-hour excerpt usually from a musical or a farce. Straight comedies or dramas were too visual and difficult to understand. Once we had found a suitable show we had to check whether the management wanted a broadcast. If the show was doing well they usually preferred to wait, but if it was at all shaky they leapt at the chance of getting it on the air.

They all remembered the famous example of *Me and my girl* which had been doing badly at the Victoria Palace. By chance a programme fell through and at the last moment an OB from *Me and my girl* was hurriedly arranged. There were some bright tunes in it by Noel Gay, and though the knockabout humour of Lupino Lane was largely visual, the radio listeners heard the theatre audience roaring their heads off with laughter.

Even before the broadcast was over the box office telephone began to ring and *Me and my girl* was saved. It ran for another three and a half years, and proved what a wonderful shop-window radio could be.

So long as the music was good and there were plenty of laughs the listener at home would then pay to go and *see* the show. John and I had to choose the best bits to broadcast and if necessary had to persuade the management to change the running order about a little in order to include a particular hit song or a strong piece of comedy in our excerpt. They usually agreed to do this so long as it did not interfere with the story line. But in one pantomime both the management and we slipped up badly. We had brought forward into the broadcast a dramatic scene in which the Wicked Robbers were finally killed off. After the broadcast we were watching the rest of the show when to our horror and to the puzzlement of the audience, the Robbers came back live and well in a scene which normally preceded the one in which they had been killed.

The most important thing we had to do was to write and speak the linking commentary from one of the boxes. We had to fill in all the visual gaps, describe the scenery and action and explain the story up to date, also mentioning the names of the actors and actresses playing the various parts. We had to be as unobtrusive as possible so as not to interfere with what was going on on the stage. It required perfect timing and crisp, clean delivery. To get everything right we had to see the show two or three times before the broadcast, not only to perfect our commentary but to give our engineers a chance to place the microphones in the right places.

So there I was, slap in the middle of the entertainment world to which I had so badly wanted to belong. I was meeting all the stars and leading players and what was more important, was working with them. I was also seeing all the shows in the West End free! We broadcast such shows as *Song of Norway, Oklahoma, South Pacific, Annie get your gun, Carousel, The King and I*, plus a lot of farces. I know I saw *Carousel* fifteen times because we did separate broadcasts from it – and I cried each time! You will notice the absence of *My Fair Lady*. Due to some copyright trouble we could never get the management's permission to do it. I had certainly fallen on my feet.

Another chore – and a very pleasant one was a weekly half-hour broadcast called *Round the halls*, which came from one of the many music halls which then existed all over the country. So I was back with my old love – variety – and visited all the big music halls to choose suitable acts. On the day of the broadcast I would then rehearse and time the three acts chosen, usually made up of a singer or singers, a stand-up comic or cross-talk act, and some sort of speciality which would make good radio. This could be an impressionist, instrumentalist or animal impersonator.

The timing was difficult because the broadcast took place direct from the theatre during one of the two evening performances. The running order often had to be adjusted to include our three acts, who in turn had to adapt their own timing and material for the radio. What went well at the New Cross Empire was not always suitable for the front parlour in a spinster's home in Bournemouth!

First of all the whole broadcast had to last a maximum of twenty-nine minutes to allow time for the studio announcements. Singers and instrumentalists were easy – if they were any good their songs or pieces which they played lasted exactly the same time at each perform-ance. But comics were more difficult. One had to gauge the amount of time to allow for the laughs which varied from audience to audience. Also if they knew they had a hidden audience of several millions they used to try to 'milk' the laughs with a lot of extra visual effects so that people at home would say, 'He *must* be funny. We must go and see him.'

And then of course there was censorship. In those days the BBC was very strict and there was a long list of things that could not be the basis of a joke – sex (naturally), physical disabilities, politics, religion and of course any innuendos. Even mother-in-law jokes were frowned on as they might be embarrassing to a family sitting at home with ma-in-law present. It's difficult to believe now but I was given a rocket for passing the following:

'Have you seen the PT instructress?'

'Oh yes, she's stripped for gym.'

'Lucky Jim.'

Just think what gets by today! It was not always easy to make some comics cut their material. After some outrageous *double entendre* they would look at you with great big innocent eyes and say: 'What's filthy about that? It's all in your mind.' Or they would say: 'Oh, I did that one in *Henry Hall's Guest Night* last week and he did not object.'

But we soon got to know the form and most of them played ball, though occasionally one would slip a joke in which we had taken out. One of these was a 'drunk' comic who took a drink out of a glass on the table and spat it out with the words, 'I'll kill that ruddy cat.' Note too the word ruddy which was just allowed, whereas bloody was definitely out. The BBC's solution to any joke was: 'If in doubt – out,' which did not make the comedian's job any easier. It was a wonder that they had anything left to be funny about.

But they were fabulous people to meet and I was made welcome in all their dressing-rooms. They were all extremely kind to me and there was a wonderful feeling of *camaradarie* back-stage. For the first time I met and made friends with people like Arthur Askey, Ted Ray, Tommy Trinder, Hutch, Terry Thomas, Jimmy Edwards and two promising newcomers whom I first met when they were unknowns in a Jack Payne show in 1947 – Frankie Howerd and Max Bygraves.

In the summer *Round the halls* was given a rest and instead we used to broadcast concert parties from the sea-side. What fun they were! Some were in the open air, some in Winter Gardens or Floral Halls. There was always a lovely holiday atmosphere with everyone out to enjoy themselves. If the weather was fine I must admit that John and I sometimes took more time than we should have done to rehearse and broadcast the shows. By this time we knew pretty well every gag in the business and when a comic started a story or a joke we used to have a competition to see who knew the finish. In the end if we thought a concert party needed a bit more humour we would suggest gags ourselves. We 'sold' one to an outdoor concert party at Eastbourne and were rewarded by hearing the roar of laughter from the audience in their deck-chairs. It was as corny as they come.

Comic I was walking along the beach here the other day and saw a girl bathing, and she was calling for help as she slowly drifted out to sea.

Stooge Really. What did you do? Dive in and save her?

Comic Nothing of the sort. I threw her a cake of soap.

Stooge Whatever for?

Comic To wash her back of course.

There was one famous producer who used to star in his own show and after every broadcast used to write and tell us what a wonderful reaction he had had from the listeners – 'hundreds of telegrams of appreciation old boy'. John and I suspected he sent these telegrams to himself and were proved right after one broadcast which due to a technical hitch had not gone out over the air. We did not know this until the end of the show and went round behind to break the news to our friend. But before we could get a word in edgeways he greeted us at the door of his dressing-room with: 'Wonderful broadcast. It's gone over a treat. The telephone hasn't stopped ringing with people from all over the country sending their congratulations.' We hadn't got the heart to tell him the truth.

I was also made responsible for an amateur show which had started in the war and carried on for a few years afterwards. It was called *Work's Wonders* and was a variety show put on by workers of a factory with their own talent. I used to go down and audition them, choose the best (or least worst!) and then produce and introduce the show. Some were quite good but naturally lacked the professional touch. One exception was certainly George Martin the casual comedian, who at that time was working in an ordnance factory in Aldershot.

We sometimes used professionals to entertain the audiences before the shows began and two young comics who were especially popular were called Bob Monkhouse and Benny Hill.

The other celebrity of today whom I met in very different guise was the chairman of an RAF Old Tyme Music Hall which we broadcast from the RAF station at Henlow. He was tall and very funny and spoke with a slight lisp and a drawl. He kept his RAF audience in fits of laughter and was down in the programme as Aircraftsman Frank Muir.

But my very first broadcast for the BBC had nothing to do with entertainment.

Early in 1946 the authorities drained the lake in St James' Park so that the sappers could blow up an unexploded bomb that lay on the bottom. At the last moment it was decided to do a 'live' broadcast of the blowing up and Lobby thought he would throw me in the deep end without any preparation or warning. He kindly came down to hold my hand and we took up our position with a microphone on one of the bridges. But the police told us that this was too dangerous and advised us to go inside the near-by ladies' lavatory. By standing on one of the loo seats I managed to look out of one of the small windows and could just see enough of what was going on to give my first commentary. I described the explosion and its after-effects and Lobby has told me since that I got very excited and finished the broadcast by promising the listeners to bring them a bigger and better bomb next week! All I know is that I was very nervous and came out of that ladies' loo looking very flushed!

In spite of the fact that we all seemed to work very long hours there was plenty of time for fun and games in the office. There was a marvellously happy spirit in the department and it was a great joy to be working in it. At our weekly meetings we used to play a game with the OB Manager Frank Anderson. He was a dear person who pretended to be crotchety and we nicknamed him 'the crusty old faggot'.

One of his jobs was to see that billings of programmes for *Radio Times* were handed in to his office in good time for publication. If any of us were late in sending them in he used to read out our names from a book when requested to do so by Lobby. He loved to catch us out but his book was not always up to date. So we played it like tennis, everyone shouting out the score after each announcement. If he was right he would start fifteen love and then if we could prove him wrong the next time we would call out fifteen all, and so on. Just before one meeting John and I realised that we had not sent a billing for *Round the halls* to his office, so as we entered the meeting we slipped it into his pocket without him knowing.

There were a lot of entries in his book that day, some right, some wrong and the score had reached advantage in his favour, and he only needed one more success for game. With a gleam of triumph in his eye he announced that Ellison and Johnston had failed to give him the billing which was due for Lewisham Hippodrome. 'Oh no we haven't,' we shouted, 'what's that sticking out of your pocket?' Frank sheepishly put his hand in his pocket and withdrew our billing. 'Deuce,' roared the meeting. Childish but great fun.

We also used to ring each other up pretending to be someone else and it got so bad that no one was ever quite certain whether any call was genuine or not. It all started soon after I had joined when at the weekly meeting Geoffrey Peck brought up the question of commentators for Wimbledon in the summer of 1946. He explained that he had written to Borotra to see if he would be interested in being one of the summarisers. Since then, however, our European Service had heard about it and were not entirely happy. At that time evidently there were some queries about Borotra's co-operation with the

Germans, though these were subsequently satisfactorily cleared up. But meanwhile the European Service felt he should not be used.

Geoffrey asked Lobby what he should do and was advised to write to Borotra and regretfully cancel his offer without giving any reason. After the meeting I went round to my room and dialled Geoffrey's number and when his secretary answered I said in a very phoney French accent that I was Borotra and could I speak to Mr Peck. Geoffrey came on and began to say that he was just about to write to me. But I did not let him get any further and went on to say how much I was looking forward to broadcasting at Wimbledon, how much it would mean to me after six years of war and how nice it would be to meet all my old English tennis friends again.

I then let Geoffrey get a word in, as he had been spluttering in the background for sometime, trying to interrupt. He just managed to say that he was very sorry but his offer was cancelled and then I let fly, pretending to be very excited and angry. I called him an 'English pig-dog' and that I would make 'the big sue' of the BBC for breaking a contract, etc, and demand 'ze big money' in compensation. I could hear Geoffrey saying 'Please, please Mr Borotra, let me explain'. But after a few more expletives I rang off.

I then wandered out of my office and saw Geoffrey looking very harassed and upset as he rushed round to Lobby's room. I gave them a minute or so and then walked in to hear Lobby saying that he had better telephone the BBC solicitor at once to warn him what might happen. I let Lobby ask for the number and then quickly started off at Geoffrey in my phoney accent: 'Ah, you English pig-dog, you make to ring *your* solicitor . . .' Lobby slowly put down the receiver and a look of doubt came into his eyes. Had he been right after all to give this chap a job?

On another occasion I had Frank Anderson rushing off to meet the Dean of Westminster in the Crypt of the Abbey as a result of a fake call from me complaining about some BBC broadcast of one of the services from there. I managed to stop him as he was going down in the lift. But not all my leg-pulls were so successful. We had a marvellous little man called Spud Moody who was the number two in charge of engineering in the department. We had been playing around and I locked him up in his room. I returned to my desk and after a few minutes looked up as a shadow fell on the desk from the window. There to my horror was Spud. He had walked along a narrow ledge of about two feet and our offices were six storeys up. Had he slipped or fallen backwards he would have plunged sixty feet or so to his death. I hurriedly opened the window and let him in and never locked anyone else in their office again.

John and I had a big office without any carpet on the floor. In those days one's status at the BBC was reflected by the amount of carpet one was entitled to. The top people had wall-to-wall carpeting, and the lower down the scale you were the smaller was your carpet. So you can see how highly we were rated!

We decided one day that our bare floor would make an ideal cricket pitch and invented a new game of office cricket. We had one of those miniature cricket bats, a squash ball and the waste-paper basket as the wicket. There was just room for three a side, and it was four if the ball hit the wall, six if it hit the ceiling full pitch. For the sake of those underneath we decided against running up and down the pitch so the only scoring was by boundaries. The batsman could be caught off either the ceiling or the wall or if the ball landed in the 'in' or 'out' tray. (We also had an lbw tray – Let the Blighters Wait.)

The bowling had to be under-arm and not too fast, but as it was possible to get terrific spin on the ball, scoring was none too easy. The official scorer was our secretary Polly Polden whose desk was at square leg and she was also called on to umpire. We used to play during the lunch hour or at odd moments when things were slack. I must admit that once or twice the telephone rang and the caller was asked to hang on until the end of the over, a somewhat puzzling request to most callers. The fame of this game soon spread and we had many visiting players to our room, such as Denis Compton, Bill Edrich and the Bedser twins.

Our own regular opponents were Stew, Wynford and Geoffrey Peck who earned the nickname of 'Slasher' by his occasional brilliant bouts of hitting. When he was really in form Polly Polden would duck behind her typewriter and Stew, who wore glasses, retired behind my desk which was in the gully. To start with Stew was scornful of the game comparing it unfavourably with baseball. But he soon caught the bug and introduced a certain ruthlessness into the gentle game of cricket. He could not understand the lbw law and kept both his legs permanently in front of the waste-paper basket.

Stew was also prone to dispute Polly Polden's decisions. John was the most consistent bat and Wynford used to bowl from half-way down the wicket and so was the most successful bowler. I was rather inconsistent as I used to practice commentating at the same time as batting and found it rather difficult to do either.

From time to time, we would be interrupted by Lobby and as soon as we heard his footsteps used to hide the bat and ball, stand in front of the wicket and pretend we were having a conference. I doubt if he was taken in because we were all in our shirt sleeves and if in the middle of an exciting game were all rather hot and out of breath. Still Lobby was very patient and tolerant and it was not until two years later when I returned from my honeymoon that I found, sadly, that John and I had each been given a tiny office apiece, our beloved cricket pitch was covered with a carpet, and our room given to a senior member of the department, Henry Riddell, as his office.

16
Start of a long innings

Soon after I had joined, the department was a bit short of soccer commentators and we were all encouraged to have a test to see if we were any good. Geoffrey Peck and I thought we might as well have a go. He was the producer in charge of sports like racing, boxing and football so knew something about it. I knew very little except what I had learnt from watching the Arsenal.

Anyway we went down with a recording car to Loftus Road where Queen's Park Rangers were playing a mid-week fixture. We read up all that we could about the two teams and found that the QPR centre-forward McGibbon had scored three goals on the previous Saturday. The Press had labelled him '3 Goal McGibbon' and there he was No. 9 in the programme. During our tests of about fifteen minutes each we both gave him the full treatment with phrases like 'There goes "3-goal" again, a typical dribble, would recognise his style anywhere, easy to pick out with his balding head, anyone could see that he's an England prospect, etc, etc.'

It was not until we read the evening papers that we discovered McGibbon had withdrawn at the last moment and that the No. 9 whom we had been praising was a substitute. That was my first and *last* soccer commentary!

But my wonderful luck held, so far as cricket was concerned. When I joined the department there was no mention of cricket and it never entered my head that I would ever get the chance to be a commentator. There was already Rex Alston, a promising newcomer with a burry Hampshire accent called John Arlott, and Jim Swanton recently returned from being a prisoner of war under the Japs.

So I just could not believe my luck when my telephone rang one day and the voice at the other end was Ian Orr-Ewing recently out of the RAF and now Head of Outside Broadcasts Television. He and I had played a lot of cricket together before the war, and he knew how much I loved it and perhaps gave me some credit for knowing something about it, too. Anyway he said that television was starting up again after the war and would be doing some cricket matches from Lord's and the Oval during the summer. Would I like to have a shot at doing the commentary?

You can guess what my answer was though I had no idea of how to do a television commentary. Luckily, so far as cricket was concerned, no one else knew much either. There had only been four Tests ever televised, two in 1938 and two in 1939, so everyone including producers, commentators and cameramen would be learners. But once again fortune had been very kind to me. I *happened* to have played cricket with Ian Orr-Ewing who *happened* to be the man chosen to restart cricket on TV after the war. By such a small turn of fate was I destined to do the television cricket commentaries for the next twenty-four years.

The 1946 cricket season was excellent training for a new commentator. First of all, it was a wet summer, so right from the start I learnt to live with the frustrations of 'bad light stopped play' or 'no play today because of rain'. Cricket commentating must be one of the few arts which can be so interrupted. Imagine an actor having to stop in the middle of Hamlet's soliloquy because of bad light from one of the spots. Or a concert pianist being prevented from completing a concerto because of a leak from the roof on to his piano.

People often ask what commentators do when rain has stopped play.

I don't know why, but unlike most of the players we don't play cards. Some have their writing to do for newspapers, so get on with that. Others help sort out the hundreds of letters which we receive during every Test. On radio we now have a fixed spot for answering these during the lunch interval on Saturdays. But sometimes if there is a long delay we have an unscheduled answering session to fill in the time, though those who have sent in questions may of course not be listening. Otherwise we do what all cricketers do when two or three are gathered together – just talk cricket.

The touring team came from India, the first tourists since the West Indies in 1939. Asians are usually very difficult to tell apart so this offered quite a challenge to a new commentator. When a touring team first arrives, we usually meet them at dinners or receptions and get to know them personally, so that we can recognise them easily by sight. But of course it's much harder once they take the field, especially if they are wearing caps with big peaks, or worse still the now fashionable floppy white hats. These completely obscure their faces, so I personally have always tried to study the walks and mannerisms of every cricketer.

Sometimes, if a ball is hit to the far corner of the ground and the fieldsman is running away from you, the only way to tell who it is is by the way he runs, the slope of his shoulders or perhaps even by the size of his bottom! It is the same with batsmen at the wicket, who from a distance, if they are both wearing caps, often look alike until they start to make their strokes. Mike Denness and Brian Luckhurst are a case in point. So one looks for their particular habits, such as the way they prod the pitch or touch the peak of their cap when waiting for the bowler.

One can usually recognise a batsman also by his stance at the wicket, and I nearly got into trouble with this once. I was commentating on the radio at Hove where Sussex were playing Hampshire. Henry Horton came in to bat and he had a most peculiar stance, crouching low and sticking his bottom out. I thought it would be a good idea to describe it to the listeners. So I said, 'Henry Horton has got a funny sort of stance. It looks as if . . .' At this point I meant to say 'he is sitting on a shooting stick' but I got it the wrong way round! I may say that my scorer Michael Fordham gave a loud snort and collapsed with laughter. Luckily for me I managed to control myself and carried straight on as if nothing had happened.

This is the golden rule for any broadcaster who has said something outrageous by mistake. Never stop, nor apologise, nor try to explain what you *meant* to say. This can be fatal. Just carry on and the listeners will probably think that they have heard wrongly. A famous example of how an attempted explanation only makes matters worse was the American golf commentator talking about Arnold Palmer's wife. He was saying how very superstitious she was and that 'before every championship match she used to take Arnold's balls in her hand and kiss them'. All might have been well had he not realised what he had said and hastily added . . . 'his golf balls of course I mean'. It is sadly but not surprisingly reported that he got the sack!

The other difficulty with Asian sides is the formation and pronunciation of their names, more so with the Pakistanis than the Indians. It is quite possible to have a Mohammad Ali and an Ali Mohammad in the same side. The second time Pakistan toured England in 1962 Rex Alston got into an awful mess over one of their names. They had a player called Afaq – try to pronounce it at your peril! We were all naturally very nervous about it and dreaded having to commentate when he was playing. Luckily he was not much good and was seldom selected.

When the Pakistanis were playing MCC at Lord's I was doing the television commentary and Rex as usual was on the radio. I walked into the radio box during one of the intervals and said to Rex, 'Thank goodness this chap Afaq is not playing.' 'For goodness sake,' replied Rex, 'don't mention his name or I shall get it into my head.' So somewhat mischievously I murmured Afaq, Afaq, Afaq and left the box. Alan Gibson was the other commentator and swears that about an hour later it was obvious from consultations going on out on the field that there was to be a change of bowling. Barry Knight was the batsman waiting to take strike and Rex presumably as a result of my visit said: 'I think there is going to be a change of bowling. We are about to see Afaq to Knight at the Nursery End.' He quickly realised what he had said and added: 'Oh, what am I saying – he's not even playing.' I felt a bit of a cad when told about it afterwards but I am glad to say that none of our bosses spotted it.

In 1946 and 1947 my fellow TV commentators – all new boys like myself – included Aidan Crawley, Percy Fender, Walter Franklin and R. C. (Crusoe) Robertson-Glasgow. Our first task was to learn to live with the 'dirty talk-back'. Let me explain.

On TV the commentators use a lip microphone which has to be held close to the mouth and is specially designed to cut out all noise except the commentator's voice. This means that in the TV box everyone can talk in a normal voice to each other so long as the commentator is either speaking into the mike or has his hand over the business end of it if he is not talking. (The noise of ball on bat and the applause of the crowd is picked up on an effects mike outside the box.)

Each commentator also wears headphones through which the producer can talk to him from his control van or scanner parked somewhere behind the pavilion. The producer gives instructions such as when to start or return to the studio; or he may want to report that one of the cameras is temporarily out of action; or suggest that the score should be given at the end of the over, or perhaps that he has a good picture of the three slips talking to each other and that he will be showing it after the next ball.

All the time, remember, the commentator may be commentating on what is going on out in the middle or worse still be trying to give a summary of what has happened so far. At the same time he must learn to take in what the producer is saying. One of the hardest things for a beginner to avoid is acknowledging the producer's instructions or making a counter-suggestion if he does not agree. Viewers may sometimes have been puzzled to hear in the middle of a commentary a commentator say something like: 'Right ho, thanks,' or 'I've only just given the score.'

In addition to talking to the commentator the producer can also be heard giving instructions to his three or four cameramen about what pictures he wants or possibly discussing some technical detail such as the light or quality of the picture. You cannot become a TV commentator or introduce a programme until you have learnt the art of simultaneously talking *and* listening.

You will notice that 'front' men like David Coleman and Robin Day all have a small ear-piece behind their ear like a hearing aid. While talking to you they are getting instructions such as what to do next or a warning that the next piece of film is not yet ready.

All this was of course new to us and naturally we all reacted differently. Once Percy Fender was reminiscing about Tom Hayward the old Surrey batsman, and so missed something going on out on the field. 'Stick to the play, Percy, and keep that sort of chat for between the overs,' said the producer into his headphones. This irritated Percy, who put his hand over his microphone (thank goodness he remembered), turned to me and said: 'If he thinks he can do any better why doesn't he come up here and do it himself?' A natural reaction you might think. So was Crusoe's when just after he had given the score, he heard the producer say: 'I think it's about time we had the score, Crusoe.' To which Crusoe with slight venom in his voice said over the air: 'For those of you who were not paying attention when I gave the score just now, may I repeat . . .'

Crusoe was a great wit and my favourite writer about cricket. He was a large friendly person and a wonderful companion both on and off the field. After making a joke or telling a story he used to slap his thigh and let out a maniacal laugh. While up at Oxford I was privileged to hear him recite the whole of *Eskimo Nell* after a Trinity dinner and it really was a privilege. Unfortunately his voice sounded a bit pontifical so his great sense of humour never really came over on the TV or radio as it should have done.

Percy Fender was never really happy as a commentator but with all his knowledge of the game – especially of captaincy – he would have made a perfect summariser between the overs. On one occasion the sound engineer in the control scanner told Percy through his headphones that they were not getting enough voice from him. I looked across and saw that Percy was holding the lip mike some way from his mouth when it should have been right up against it. This obviously occurred to the engineer who went on to say: 'Hold the mike a bit closer so that it's touching the end of your nose.' Percy whispered angrily to me: 'I *am*.' And he was right – he was. But his nose was nearly as long as mine so that the mike was still too far away from his mouth!

We televised three matches that year, MCC *v*. Indians at Lord's, and the two Tests at Lord's and the Oval. We could not do the other one at Old Trafford because the transmitters only covered the London area. It was not in fact until 1950 that we were able to televise Tests from Trent Bridge and Edgbaston and 1952 before we were able to go to Old Trafford and Headingley.

There was nothing remarkable about the 1946 season except the rain. England won the first Test, and the other two were drawn, thanks to bad weather. Players were still flexing their muscles and trying to regain their form after the long lay-off during the war. Even so seven batsmen scored over two thousand runs including Washbrook and Compton, while Hammond sat proudly at the top of the averages, making 1,783 runs in only twenty-six innings for an average of 84.90.

Although aged forty-three, Hammond seemed to be batting as well as ever and scored seven hundreds all for Gloucestershire. This made his failure in Australia the following winter all the more sad and surprising. But I expect the truth is that the standard of English bowling in 1946 was pretty low compared with that in Australia. Bowlers like batsmen get rusty, though the old pre-war stalwarts such as Goddard, Hollies, Wright, Wellard and J. C. Clay all took a lot of wickets. The one new star was A. V. Bedser, already aged twenty-eight. He bowled brilliantly in the Tests taking twenty-four wickets in the short series and finished with 128 wickets in his first season.

The year 1947 was a complete contrast to 1946. This was the golden summer for cricket when the sun and Denis Compton both shone consistently and brilliantly throughout the season. The crowds – so long starved of first-class cricket – flocked to the grounds to bask in the sun and enjoy the sparkling cricket. Many of them were just out of the forces with their gratuities and with so few goods in the shops there was little to spend their money on. So cricket benefited and the players gave the huge crowds their money's worth. Nearly three million people paid to watch cricket that summer. The South Africans led by Alan Melville were the visitors, but good a side as they were, they found a revived England too much for them and lost the series 0–3. How they must have cursed the Middlesex twins Edrich and Compton who scored 1,305 runs between them in the Tests and then went on to help Middlesex win the County Championship. The debonair Compton, especially, played cavalier cricket and danced his way down the pitches of England to make eighteen hundreds and score 3,816 runs in the season. Both are still records and likely to remain so, now that the number of county championship matches have been cut to twenty.

I shared all the TV commentaries except for the last afternoon of the Oval Test when I went off to the show-jumping at the White City to commentate for radio on the King George V Cup. I had never done it before and never understood why I was chosen. Possibly word had got around about my success (?) on Tiptop and they must have thought that I knew something about horses. But they were dead wrong. However, I soon learnt about double-oxers, five-bar gates and triple bars, and had as my expert alongside me the announcer Lionel Marson, an old cavalry officer who did know what he was talking about. He was very horsey and used to commentate in a bowler-hat. He loved horses and got terribly emotional. When Foxhunter won the King George V cup for the third time tears streamed down his cheeks. I'm not saying that I did not have a lump in my throat – there was something special about that horse.

This dual loyalty between TV and radio became quite a problem in the years ahead, and in the early days there were one or two clashes. But we came to an amicable agreement which existed right into the late sixties. TV had complete priority over me for cricket, radio for everything else. Although I was always administered by radio OBs and had my office there, TV paid a percentage of my salary and everyone seemed happy. It was nice to be wanted! But I got no more money over and above my salary for appearing on TV – only a minute dress allowance of about £25 a year for appearing in front of the cameras.

However in those early days cricket occupied only a small percentage of my time. I was chiefly involved in broadcasts from theatres and music halls. My very first broadcast from a theatre was from the *Song of Norway* at the Palace Theatre presented by that king of pantomimes Emile Littler. We made quite a big OB out of it, including some back-stage interviews.

My first theatre commentary was from *Under the counter*, the first of many such broadcasts with that wonderful couple Cis Courtneidge and Jack Hulbert. Looking through my 1946 and 1947 diaries I am amazed at the number of famous names that figured in our relays from Variety Theatres.

What a marvellous music-hall bill they would make up, though alas some of them are no longer with us. But their names make one's mouth water in these days of largely synthetic entertainment. Here are some of them: Arthur Askey, Max Bacon, Max Bygraves, Clapham and Dwyer, Peter Cavanagh, G. H. Elliott, Cyril Fletcher, Frankie Howerd, Hutch, Nosmo King, Charlie Kunz, Murray and Mooney, Cavan O'Connor, Ted Ray, Terry Thomas, Nellie Wallace, Robb Wilton, Anona Winn.

There was also a husband and wife team – Ted and Barbara Andrews. He was a tenor and she played the piano and they had just begun to include in their act their ten-year-old daughter. She sang quite beautifully with a wonderful top note. We all thought it wrong at the time, thinking it would damage her young voice. But it didn't

seem to do any harm and as Julie Andrews she is still singing as beautifully as ever.

Behind the scenes I met all the people who make the entertainment
world tick – the impresarios, producers, agents and so on. Lew and
Leslie Grade, and Bernard Delfont – those three astonishingly successful
brothers were just starting in those days. John Ellison and I often used
to ring them up to arrange our broadcasts and agree on the three acts
for *Round the halls*. They are probably all millionaires today and it's
amusing to think that they used to concern themselves personally with
finding us an impressionist who could fill a six and a half minute spot
in our broadcast.

The secret of their success is hard work and Lew and Leslie were
always at their desks an hour or so before any of us had had breakfast,
and would often be visiting theatres in the West End or suburbs up
to late at night. Lew and Leslie soon became the largest and most
powerful agents with numerous artists on their books. There's a good
story of Lew Grade spotting a promising young artist at one of the
outlying music halls. He went round to see him afterwards and
suggested he should handle him in future. Lew said he would get the
young man X pounds a week more than he was getting now. Was he
tied up with another agent, if so what was his name? 'Lew Grade,' was
the surprising reply. The young artist was already on their books!

One of the most amusing men was Charlie Henry, Chief of Pro-
ductions at Moss Empires. He was a great variety director and first
under George Black and then Val Parnell, was the power behind the
scenes at the London Palladium and was really responsible for staging
many of the Royal Variety Shows.

Charlie's special forte was comedy and for the whole of their life he
directed and advised the Crazy Gang in all their comedy routines. He
had a marvellous sense of humour and pulled everyone's leg with a
deadpan face, but was a martinet when it came to producing a show.
He demanded the best and got it, because he knew the business backwards and was respected and loved by artists and stage staff alike.
During the war he lived in Brighton and came up to London each day
by train. He occupied the time by writing scripts or working out
complicated stage routines for new shows. One day a man sitting next
to him kept looking over his shoulder and reading what Charlie was
putting on paper. Charlie put up with this for a time but then got fed up
and the next time he felt the man was looking over his shoulder he

wrote across a blank piece of paper: 'Mind your own bloody business!' For the rest of the journey there was no more trouble from Mr Nosey Parker.

Charlie had been a song and dance man himself and was full of stories of funny things that had happened on stage. One of my favourites was of the two actors in a repertory company who were acting a scene together when the telephone on stage started to ring and went on ringing. There was no call for this to happen in the script and obviously someone back-stage had accidentally pushed the wrong button. Neither actor wanted to answer the phone as it would have meant improvising an imaginary conversation quite out of context from the plot of the play. But as they manfully tried to carry on their conversation the bell went on ringing and ringing. Obviously something had to be done as the audience were beginning to roar with laughter, and there were a few shouts of 'you're wanted on the phone' from the back of the stalls. So one of the actors got up from the sofa where they were sitting, picked up the receiver and said 'Hello.' He paused for a few seconds, then put his hand over the mouth piece and shouted across to his colleague 'It's for you!'

I have always been a glutton for theatrical stories and Dulcie Gray told me one once which she swears was true. It happened when she was with the open-air theatre in Regent's Park in the days of Robert Atkins. When the weather was fine the audience used to sit outside in deck-chairs and watch the performance on the open stage. In the event of wet weather there was a large marquee with another stage. If it was wet the performance would start there, or if rain began during the play then actors and audience would hurriedly repair to the marquee. The snag of the marquee was that it became stiflingly hot and not only were the seats hard and upright but there were not as many of them as there were deck-chairs. So if it was a full house outside and it started to rain conditions inside the marquee became hopelessly overcrowded and the heat unbearable.

It was during a heatwave, and the outside auditorium was packed at every performance with the audiences lounging comfortably in their deck-chairs under the hot sun. Robert Atkins had had occasion to sack a young actor for some reason at short notice and the afternoon matinée was to be his last performance. It was blazing hot and there was a full house. The actor only had a few lines to say such as: 'His majesty requires your presence, sir' and would then normally have made his exit. But he was determined to get his own back for what he must have considered to have been an unjust dismissal. So with the temperature in the eighties, and glorious blue sky overhead, the young man walked down to the front of the stage and said in an authoritative voice: 'In view of the inclement weather this performance will now be continued inside the marquee!'

Dulcie swears that the audience, typically British and obedient to any order from authority, quietly rose from their deck-chairs, gathered up their things and disappeared into the marquee before the damage could be repaired.

I was also lucky enough to meet Ivor Novello but not because of any broadcast. He was appearing in *Perchance to dream* and one evening I went along to see it with Nico Llewelyn-Davies, one of J. M. Barrie's wards. He was an ex-Grenadier and had been with me in our revue *The eyes have it*, in which he did a lifelike impersonation of Ted Lewis, singing *On the sunny side of the street*.

Nico and I were friends of Zena Dare's daughter Angela Thornton. We went with her and her husband to see the show and she arranged for us to meet Ivor at supper afterwards in the Savoy Grill. We were naturally thrilled to meet him and he was as charming and friendly as we had been led to expect. What is more, he appeared to listen and be interested in everything we said, not a very usual trait in a great artist. Naturally we told him how much we had enjoyed the show but were audacious or cheeky enough to offer a slight criticism – and even then he went on listening.

Our complaint was that the hit song of the show, that lovely number *We'll gather lilacs* had been largely wasted in the show. You could not have a much more romantic song and it cried aloud for a duet between a handsome young tenor and a beautiful young girl. But in the show, so far as I remember, Ivor as a composer, said to some ladies at a party, 'Have you heard my new song? Would you like to sing it?' Olive Gilbert and Muriel Barron then picked up the music, stood by the piano and sang a duet between a contralto and a soprano. They sang it beautifully of course, but it largely lost its impact being sung by two ladies. This worried me right to the end of the show. I felt the song had been thrown away. So I had the audacity to suggest to Ivor that he had a reprise just before the final curtain.

As the show stood, Ivor was sitting playing some chords at the piano as Roma Beaumont walked slowly up the stairs. Just before she disappeared from our sight, she turned and blew Ivor a kiss and the curtain slowly fell on this quiet and rather sad note. Why, I suggested, could Ivor not be playing *We'll gather lilacs* and when Roma Beaumont reached halfway up the stairs could she not turn and softly sing to him the words of the song, disappearing as the last note died away. Ivor said nothing at the time but I must say took it very well from two inexperienced strangers. But to my surprise and delight about a fortnight later the change was made and from then on *Perchance to dream* ended with the lovely melody of *We'll gather lilacs*.

I was soon to learn that not every broadcast is a success. A gentleman from Czechoslovakia persuaded Lobby that he had telepathic powers and Lobby invited him up to the office to prove it. He made us write something on a piece of paper, seal it up in an envelope and then hand it to him. He claimed he could tell us what we had written or at least the sense of it. He put up a terrific performance pacing up and down the room, screwing the envelope round and round in his hands and every now and again saying something like: 'I can see a journey' or 'I can feel unhappiness here', etc. After every statement he would look at us, hoping I suppose to gather something from our reactions. Anyhow he got near enough to what we had written to encourage Lobby to fix up a broadcast a week or so later.

Stuart Hibberd and John Snagge were placed in one studio where they wrote their pieces and put them into sealed envelopes. These were then taken along the corridor to another studio where the Czech went through his performance. But, possibly because he could not see the facial expressions of the writers, he made an awful mess of it and got everything hopelessly wrong. It was all rather embarrassing and we had to apologise to the listeners. We promptly christened him 'the original dud Czech'!

17

Climbing the ladder

1948 was one of the most eventful years of my life. I got engaged and married, I was auditioned for and offered my first film part, I commentated for the first time at an England *v.* Australia Test Match, and I started my series *Let's go somewhere* in *In town tonight* which was to be my big breakthrough in radio. I will take them in order.

It all started on Monday, 1 December 1947 when the telephone in my office rang and a girl's attractive voice said, 'This is Pauline Tozer. I am working in the photographic section of the BBC and my brother Gordon told me to give you a ring.' I immediately realised who she was, as Gordon Tozer had been my Assistant Technical Adjutant in the Grenadiers from 1942 to 1945.

My normal reaction would have been rather a cool one as I was quite happy leading a gay bachelor life plus working long and varied hours in the BBC. As a result I had not had much time or inclination for the opposite sex. In fact I learned later from Pauline that Gordon had told her that I would not be interested in her but that I might introduce her to some of my younger BBC colleagues. Certainly at that time most of my friends looked on me as a confirmed bachelor or thought that no woman would ever be brave enough to take me on. But there must have been something in that voice. Anyway I whipped out my diary and asked her to lunch with me two days later.

I went to pick Pauline up at her department in the old Langham Hotel and to my delight found that she was a very attractive blonde with blue eyes. We then had lunch in the Bolivar restaurant, now the BBC club. We got on well and laughed a lot, and the next night I took her along to the Chelsea Palace where I was doing a broadcast of a variety show. When I introduced her to Dorothy Squires and Billy Reid, Dorothy asked: 'Are you two engaged?'

We weren't then, but ten days after our first meeting I proposed.

Pauline played for time a bit before giving her answer and I don't blame her. However, she finally accepted me on 6 January, just over a month since we had first met. My mother was delighted and the Tozers, though slightly taken aback by the speed of the whole thing, seemed quite happy and gave their approval. I did the old-fashioned thing of asking her father Colonel Tozer for his permission.

I invited myself to lunch with the Colonel in the City and was so nervous that I talked about everything except the engagement. He knew exactly why I had come and was as relieved as I was when after the cheese and biscuits I plucked up courage to introduce the subject. Afterwards he told me that Mrs Tozer was waiting for him by the telephone to hear the result of the lunch. They wanted us to get married in June but I pointed out that this might mean me missing the Lord's Test against Australia. So in the end we were married at St Paul's, Knightsbridge on 22 April. As a wedding present the OB department recorded the whole ceremony and some interviews by Stewart, Wynford and Raymond as we emerged from the church under an archway of microphones.

The first week of our honeymoon we spent at the Grand Hotel, Eastbourne. It was an old haunt of mine from my schooldays at Temple Grove. My parents used to take me there for lunch and we listened to Leslie Jefferies and his Orchestra – the original orchestra from the radio programme *Grand Hotel*, still going as strong as ever, and which used to be broadcast from the lounge in the hotel. There was one amusing coincidence. We had shared the cost of the flowers with another couple called Tetley who were being married at St Paul's on the morning of the 22nd. We had never met them though I knew he had been at Sandhurst with me during the war. When we staggered down to lunch on the first day there was a couple sitting at the next table to ours, and I recognised him. It was the Tetleys!

After a very happy week we flew off to Locarno to stay at a small hotel by the lake for a fortnight. But this was not a success, due to my catching some kind of barber's rash on my face. I could not shave so grew a beard and had to go to a doctor who prescribed a course of injections. These had to be administered twice a day by Pauline in my bottom. Luckily she had been a naval VAD in the war so handled a pretty nifty needle. But it was not exactly romantic, and the injections made me feel very low and dispirited.

Furthermore, in those days we were only allowed £25 of currency each and with the extra cost of the injections on top of the hotel charges we had no money to spend on ourselves. All we did was to sit around the hotel and wait for the 4 pm steamer which took us across the lake to a tea-house. We were just able to afford one meringue each a day, oozing with cream, an unheard-of luxury in England in 1948.

When we came back to London, we set up in a small flat in Bayswater which was singularly devoid of furniture. I had my beard shaved off and returned to work, while Pauline set about finding us a home. I left it entirely to her, with only one stipulation. It must be in St John's Wood, near Lord's.

In the month before our marriage I had been asked by film director Terence Young whether I would like to appear in a film he had written about the Guard's Armoured Division. He had been one of the intelligence officers and the film was to be called *They were not divided*. Some of his characters were based on officers whom he had known in the Division. He had the idea of getting them to play themselves in the film. He had written a part for me and for some reason, I can't think why, the character was nicknamed Nosey! With one or two other officers I went down to Denham studios to do a film test. We were made up, put into battle-dress and had to wear one of those awful berets again.

The test took place in a hay-loft as we were meant to be hiding from the Germans. All went well and I was offered the part at £50 a day whenever I was needed, with an option on my services of up to six weeks. The BBC had agreed to give me leave without salary but I was suspicious of film-makers, and suspected that the six weeks would stretch into several months, and that I would have to make myself available if this were so. It would mean that I would definitely miss the Lord's Test. So to make it worth my while I decided to ask for £100 a day.

Somewhat naturally perhaps, the casting director who was a lady turned down this demand from an unknown 'actor'. So I said 'right that's it' and somewhat relieved rang Terence to tell him the sad news and also to thank him for having given me the opportunity in the first place. He seemed disappointed and tried to get me to change my mind, saying he might be able to get me the extra money. But by now I had realised how much BBC work I would be missing, so regretfully but definitely said no. My part was then slightly rewritten and given to

David Niven's friend Michael Trubshawe with the mutton-chop whiskers. Nosey became Bushy and as it turned out the filming did take far longer than six weeks. But it was a jolly good film and I saw it again recently on TV.

In the cricket world there was great excitement at the arrival of Don Bradman's Australian team. It was exactly ten years since the last Australian tour, which had ended so disastrously for them in the 5th Test at the Oval, when England made a record 903–7 declared and Len Hutton his 364. This 1948 team was probably the best team Australia has ever sent to England. It had everything and was full of great and exciting cricketers. There was Bradman himself, Arthur Morris, Sid Barnes, Ray Lindwall, Keith Miller, Don Tallon and Neil Harvey. England were still recovering from the war years and except for Alec Bedser were woefully weak in bowling, and had to rely too much on Hutton and Compton for the batting.

With their powerful attack of fast bowlers Australia also gained a tremendous advantage from the current law of a new ball after only fifty-five overs. The tour was full of drama and excitement, and more important still the big crowds saw some splendid cricket. Don Bradman made his usual hundred at Worcester and in spite of being in his fortieth year still looked the master batsman except for a certain fallibility against Bedser's in-swinger. On three occasions he was caught at short leg, by Hutton.

Lindwall and Miller provided one of the fiercest and fastest opening attacks in the history of cricket, and this made Compton's two hundreds against them an even greater achievement. His 184 at Trent Bridge only ended when he trod on his wicket defending himself from a Miller bouncer, and his 145 at Old Trafford was a gallant effort after being carried off with a nasty cut over his eye. In this match too, Sid Barnes fielding very close at short leg was hit full in the stomach from a hefty pull from Dick Pollard, and was carried off.

Then there was that incredible Australian victory at Headingley where they scored 404 to win on the last day in the fourth innings. Unfortunately TV could not be there but I remember listening on the radio to Alston, Arlott and McGilvray as first Morris and then Bradman thrashed the England bowlers all over the ground. And then the final drama of Bradman's last Test innings at the Oval, after England had been dismissed for a miserable fifty-two. He only had to make four runs to average exactly 100 for all his Test innings and was cheered all the way to the wicket by the huge crowd who stood up as he made his usual slow way to the wicket.

As he approached the square, Norman Yardley called for three cheers from the England side. This was the best cricket moment on TV so far, and there was a complete hush as he played his first ball from Hollies. But the next ball was fatal. It was Hollie's googly, Bradman pushed slowly and uncharacteristically forward, missed it and was bowled. Possibly he had been affected by the emotional reception which he had received. Anyway once again the crowd rose and applauded him all the way back until he finally disappeared into the pavilion and out of Test cricket for ever, but with a batting average of only 99.94! A great moment both for TV and cricket.

It was about the Headingley Test that one of cricket's best-ever stories was told. It was probably apocryphal but I hope not. The England team had assembled at the Queen's Hotel in Leeds on the Wednesday afternoon before the match, but Alec Bedser and Jack Crapp were late arriving. Surrey had been playing Gloucestershire and they had travelled up to Leeds together. Jack went into the hotel first ahead of Alec and approached the girl receptionist, who did not recognise him as one of the England team.

'Bed sir?', she said.

'No, Crapp,' replied Jack, thinking she had mistaken him for Alec.

'Second door on the left,' said the receptionist as she returned to her books.

One of the luckiest breaks of my career came in March 1948. For some time John Ellison had taken over the outside interview spot every Saturday in *In town tonight* on the Home Service. It had originally started with Michael Standing's *Standing on the corner* and then became *Man in the street* with Harold Warrender and Stewart Macpherson as the interviewers. John took over from them and changed the spot to *On the job* where he went and talked to people at their work.

One Saturday in March he was to interview an air-hostess in a BOAC plane on its flight from London to Prestwick. In case the ground-to-air contact failed, he asked me to stand by with another air-hostess at London Airport. Once again I was lucky. The engineers could not contact John in his plane, so I did my interview instead. Peter Duncan the producer of *In town tonight* must have thought it

In demob suit and shirt introducing one of my first *Works Wonders* from a factory.

A day I shall never forget! Underneath the microphones at St Paul's, Knightsbridge, 22 April 1948. On left, Stewart Macpherson, Raymond Glendenning, Geoffrey Peck. On right, Wynford Vaughan-Thomas, John Ellison, Frank Anderson.

(*Top*) My first *Let's Go Somewhere* – from the Chamber of Horrors at Madame Tussaud's in October 1948. I am the one with the mike! The other 'horror' is Count Fieschi in an iron mask being slowly roasted to death.
(*Bottom*) The result of my 'shave and shampoo' by the Crazy Gang at the Victoria Palace.

(*Top*) Rustler pins me to the ground with his teeth embedded in my padded arm. Trevor Hill comes to the rescue (page 133).
(*Bottom*) Waiting apprehensively to be sawn in half by Robert Harbin.

Help! No brakes! I am rescued by two of the crowd at the end of my ride on a Penny Farthing round the Herne Hill Cycle Track.

(*Top*) Through the wall of barrels at 50 mph. My helmet can just be seen as I crouch on the pillion behind Mad Johnny Davies (pages 134–5).
(*Bottom*) Two of Mad Johnny's stunt team take a 'running jump' as I describe my feelings into the mike.

(*Top*) Treading water in the channel five miles off Folkestone as Sam Rockett feeds me with a grape.
(*Bottom*) Don't forget the diver! Just before going down to broadcast from the bottom of a diving tank.

I fly through the air with the greatest of ease as one of the 'birds' in the Flying Ballet at the Empress Hall Ice Pantomime (page 148).

was not too bad. At any rate a few weeks later John became the studio interviewer and I was asked to take over *On the job*. This was just another instance of how lucky I have been throughout my career at being in the right place at the right time.

Except for a break for my honeymoon I did *On the job* throughout the spring and summer but somehow it did not seem to amount to very much. It was all talk and too similar to what was taking place in the studio. Peter Duncan thought the same and asked Lobby and me whether it would be possible to do something with more movement and excitement and even with the occasional bit of humour – in complete contrast to the scripted interviews in the studio. So we decided to revive a feature called *Let's go somewhere* which John Snagge had done in the thirties.

Let's go somewhere was to start in October and we immediately set about thinking up some ideas. Little did I think then that I would do 150 of these broadcasts, and that except for the summer break which *In town tonight* always took, Saturday nights would not be my own for the next four years.

I could never have done the series without the help and skill of our engineers in OBs. Spud Moody, a dynamic little grey-haired man, was to be my 'Svengali'. He was responsible for many of the ideas, and worked out how they could be done technically. This was not always easy if I was riding a horse round a circus ring or being rescued from the sea by a helicopter. Without his cheerful support I could never have gone on week after week. People of course sent in ideas but many of them were impossible to do and others I just did not fancy. Like the listener who suggested that I jump off Nelson's Column with an open umbrella as a parachute!

The spot was always 'live', not recorded, and lasted from three and a half to four minutes. This meant that each Saturday became a 'first night' and one either got it right or wrong. There could be no re-takes. As a result we had our failures and I hope our successes. But it was always hit or miss. I had no producer to help me and I even had to carry and keep an eye on my own stopwatch, no matter what I was doing. My team just consisted of myself and our engineer Nogs Newman, who with occasional relief from Oggie Lomas, gave up all his Saturday nights. He never complained and remained cheerful wet or fine, failure or success. I owe these backroom boys a deep debt of gratitude for all their skill and loyalty. But like me they seemed to enjoy it. It was a

challenge with plenty of variety and the skills required by both engineers and commentator in order to produce a good broadcast, were
really what broadcasting is all about.

18

Let's go somewhere

I won't bore you with a complete list of all the things I did during the
course of our show, but will select a few from each category – exciting,
funnies, musical, theatrical and so on.

The very first came from the Chamber of Horrors in Madame
Tussauds. There was a story going about that they would pay £100 to
anyone who would spend the night there alone. It was rumoured that
one or two people had tried and had gone off their heads. We checked
with Tussaud's PRO Reg Edds who denied the story completely. He
added that no member of the public had in fact ever been there alone
after the section closed at 7 pm. He offered to let me be the first person
to do this and that after *In town tonight* I could stay on until eleven
o'clock for a later broadcast but definitely *not* all night.

I was secretly very relieved at this and we agreed to do *Let's go
somewhere* at about 7.30 pm and then a later broadcast before the Home
Service closed down at 11 pm. Just before 7 pm I somewhat apprehensively went down the twisty stone staircase into the Chamber, and
through the iron gate which clanged shut behind me. Nogs had left a
microphone and a pair of headphones by a chair under the only light
in the Chamber – a very dim bulb rather like those in a wartime railway
carriage. The leads from the mike disappeared through the iron gate,
and were my only link with the outside world.

Reg had had the chair placed in front of a group of murderers consisting of Crippen, Smith of the brides in the bath, and Mahon the
Eastbourne trunk murderer. These figures were tremendously life-like
and were dressed in the actual clothes they had worn when alive –
Madame Tussauds used to buy them off the widows. In addition to all

the murderers, there were instruments of torture like the rack, a guillotine and the actual bath used by Smith. Definitely not a place for the squeamish. I had brought the evening papers with me and while waiting sat down to read the football results. I had the uncanny feeling that Crippen was looking over my shoulder to see how Arsenal had got on.

Then I tried walking round the dark chamber. But it was too eerie and I felt that all the staring eyes of the figures were following me around. So I hurried back to my chair and something soft brushed against my head – it was the noose of a hangman's rope! Even worse when I sat down, there was a low rumbling noise and all the figures began to sway slightly. It shook me for a moment but I then remembered we were directly over the Bakerloo line and that this must be the trains passing by underneath.

I was in quite a state by the time I put on my headphones to get my cue from John Ellison, and my voice was unusually shaky as I greeted listeners for my first *Let's go somewhere*. I described the Chamber to them and tried to give a picture of what it was like down there alone in the semi-dark with all those terrible people. I said goodbye with great reluctance when my time was up, as it was the last time I would be speaking to anyone for the next three and a half hours. Home Service were to come back before they closed down to check up if I was still sane.

I must say it seemed a very long wait. Pauline had provided me with some food but when I took my first bite at an apple it echoed round and round the Chamber. I did not dare walk round again so just sat and got colder and stiffer. And for those of you who, like me, are interested in that sort of thing, I can reveal that there was a bucket available should the call of nature make it necessary. But in fact it wasn't. Anyway I was extremely relieved when Home Service called me up just before 11 pm and Reg Edds unlocked the iron gate to let me out. It was not an experience I want to go through again, and although I think I just managed to keep my sanity, I have never been down there since.

As a boy I had often read thrillers in which the hero was trapped on the railway, and had to lie down between the rails and let the express roar over him. He always emerged none the worse for the experience, so we thought we would try it in real life.

Southern Region gave me permission to do the broadcast from a

stretch of line about a mile out of Victoria Station. It was not as dangerous as it sounds, as at that spot there was a deepish pit between the lines
where it was possible to crouch as the trains roared by overhead. We
ran out the microphone cable under the lines but had to be very careful
as they were of course electrified and my heart was in my mouth
each step I took over one. A man from the SR and myself took up our
position in the pit and it was hoped to time my broadcast to coincide
with the arrival of the Golden Arrow. Unfortunately it was late and
when they cued over to me I had to make do with an electric train. It
was quite a frightening sight as it thundered towards me in the dark,
sparks flying everywhere. When it was about thirty yards away I
ducked down and I must say got a terrific shaking as it sped over me.
It made quite an exciting broadcast with my build-up of the approaching train and the sound effects when it finally arrived.

The SR man told me to stay where I was as the Golden Arrow was
now due on the same line and when it had passed we should have
more time to negotiate the live rails in the dark. It was jolly lucky we
were not on the air when the Golden Arrow did eventually come –
as when it passed over me someone was washing their hands – at least
I hope they were! I got absolutely soused and my subsequent language
would not have enhanced my BBC career had it gone out over the air.

One Christmas I went to the circus at Harringay Arena and tried
my hand at riding bareback (the horse not me!) round the ring during
a performance before a packed audience. This involved some rather
tricky technical arrangements as I was suspended on the end of a
pulley so that if I fell off I would be landed gently into the middle of
the ring. The idea was to canter round once or twice in the normal
position, then try kneeling and finally standing up.

I just managed the kneeling part but as soon as I tried to stand up
lost my balance and was swung across the ring. I breathlessly described
my efforts into the microphone tied across my chest. But for good fun
I had added one extra ingredient. One of the clowns lent me his 'quick-
release' trousers and as I felt myself falling I pulled a tape and the
trousers fell down to my ankles as I landed with a plop in the middle of
the ring. The audience had been told that I was broadcasting in *In
town tonight* and the sight of 'the man from Auntie' with no trousers
brought the house down.

There was a sequel to this. A few weeks later a friend of mine went
to the same circus when my clown friend came on disguised as a

member of the audience to try his hand at riding the horse. He always did this at the end after everyone else had tried, and in fact I had filled his spot. He did what I had done, though of course far more skilfully and at the end down came his trousers. Two people sitting behind my friend said: 'What a shame. He must have been listening to *In town tonight* and he has pinched Brian Johnston's idea.'

Something rather more frightening was when we decided to see how effective a police or guard dog could be in chasing and catching a criminal. A broadcaster called Trevor Hill owned an Alsatian called Rustler who was trained to do almost anything and had in fact played himself in a TV series *Riders of the range*. I was given a special coat with heavy padding on the left arm and was assured that Rustler had been trained to go for this, and no other part of me. For the broadcast I got Pauline to walk across the BBC cricket ground and I crept up behind her and snatched her bag, and ran off. As rehearsed, she let out a piercing scream and Trevor was soon on the scene with Rustler on a lead. After hearing Pauline's explanation of what had happened he released Rustler and ordered him to 'get' me. By this time I had gone about eighty yards and was quite out of breath trying to talk and run at the same time.

I could hear Rustler padding up behind me and it reminded me of the Hound of the Baskervilles, as he got closer and closer. When he reached me he leaped through the air and seized me by my padded left arm, and his weight knocked me to the ground. I could just feel his teeth through the padding, but as soon as I was down he let go and stood on guard wagging his tail as he waited for Trevor to arrive. But when I tried to get up and escape he bared his teeth and seized me once again. So I thought it wiser to lie still until Trevor arrived and put him on his lead. It had been an impressive performance and I hope acted as a deterrent to any potential bag-snatcher who happened to be listening – especially as they would not have the benefit of the padded arm.

I was several times challenged to be the target for a knife-throwing act but always refused, making the excuse that there was bound to be an element of risk of serious injury and that it would not be fair to Pauline. Actually of course I was scared stiff at the prospect. I reckoned that even knife-throwers are human and can make mistakes, just as a great batsman is clean bowled or an expert shot misses the bull's-eye.

But I did accept a similar challenge and looking back, I was a fool even to do that. There was a darts champion called Joe Hitchcock who in his spare time used to visit pubs and give demonstrations of nail throwing in aid of charity. He had a stooge who stood sideways about ten feet away and Joe would then throw four-inch nails with specially sharpened points. The stooge would start with a cigarette in his mouth. Joe would knock this out with a nail. The cigarette was then replaced with a matchstick, with the same result. The stooge then turned his back on Joe and stuck a cigarette in each ear and whizz would come the nails and knock them out – usually but not always first throw. Then the stooge would again stand sideways, fling his head back and balance a penny on the end of his nose. This time Joe took one or two 'sighters' but always just above the penny not under, as otherwise the nail would have gone slap through the stooge's nose.

Then, as if that were not enough, came the climax. The penny was replaced by a pin of all things, and once again Joe knocked that off. I felt an awful coward but all I would agree to Joe doing was the cigarette stuck in the mouth and ears. Even so I was frightened and let the listeners hear the pounding of my heart as I held my mike over it. It was a horrid moment waiting for those nails realising that the slightest mistake and one of my eardrums could be punctured. He missed once or twice – deliberately I am sure to build up the tension – and each time the nails whizzed by my head. That was a broadcast I did not enjoy. About two years later I had another challenge from Joe. He said he was now doing the act blindfolded! You can guess what my answer was!

Equally frightening was riding on the pillion of a motor-bike through a wall of empty beer barrels. This was a stunt done by a character called Mad Johnny Davies. He also used to ride through burning hoops or even through a sheet of glass. He did this stripped to the waist and afterwards had to pluck bits of glass splinters out of his body. I decided to play safe and chose the barrels as being the least dangerous. But in all these stunts I always made sure first of the skill and safety record of those with whom I was working. In the same way that Joe Hitchcock's stooge was apparently unharmed, Johnny Davies was still in one piece.

So I strapped a mike to my chest, got on the pillion and prepared to take a two-hundred yards run at the barrels which were piled high in a pyramid fifteen feet high. We were on a large recreation ground and it was a bit greasy from rain. But we soon got up speed and by the time we reached the barrels were going at a good 50 mph. I really was scared at what lay ahead but I tried to keep talking as we roared across the ground. I must confess that I was hugging Johnny as if he had been my girl friend. I had worked it out that I would be the third thing to hit the barrels, first the front wheel of the bike, then Johnny, then me.

There was a terrific bang as we hit the barrels, piles of debris shot into the air and the bike slithered and skidded all over the place. But Johnny managed to keep it upright and we came to a welcome halt. Except for the impact as the bike struck the barrels I had not felt anything except a few bits of barrel landing on my head. But it's not a way I would like to earn my living.

Another test of my nerves was when I lay on a table on the ice rink at the Empress Hall and was jumped over by a speed skater. Once again I made sure he was an expert but even so the flash of the skates as they passed inches over my body were a fairly forbidding sight. Some years later on TV I was jumped over by four horses as I sat drinking a cup of tea at an army trestle table. This was during a rehearsal for a Military Tattoo and I think that I preferred the skates to those hooves. Just suppose one of the horses had made a mistake and landed on the tea-table or me.

At the start of the series we had been asked to get some movement into the programme and we did our best to carry out our brief. I piloted a light aircraft, drove a steam train, launched a lifeboat, rode on the Big Dipper, and tried to keep talking as I was hurled round and round the Rotor at the Olympia side-shows. I also challenged the Brighton police to catch me in my car after doing a smash and grab and needless to say I lost.

One of the coldest jobs was when I went out in a boat five miles off Folkestone with Sam Rockett the channel swimmer. We wanted to see what it was like for a swimmer to be fed while in the water. I trod water by the boat as Sam lent out and fed me with nuts, dates and grapes and gave me orange juice to drink. This I understand was the staple diet for such occasions but I found it almost impossible to talk and eat and avoid swallowing oceans of sea water. It was also freezing cold so far out and I was frozen and exhausted when lifted back into the boat. I had only been in the water for about five minutes. Channel swimmers stay in for fourteen hours or more. Rather them than me.

One of the most painful things I did was to try out the ejector seat which pilots use to escape from the cockpits of jet planes. In the old days a pilot could clamber over the side and drop with his parachute. But now the jets go so fast that if a pilot stuck his head out it would be like hitting it against a brick wall at 500 mph. So now he slides back the canopy of his cockpit and pulls a small canvas screen over his face. This fires two charges which eject the seat at great speed, sixty feet into the air clear of the plane. The seat has its own little parachute which opens and gives the pilot time to get out of the seat, drop off and open his own individual parachute.

The purpose of the screen over the face is to prevent burning and blast on the face when it meets the air at speed. It also pulls the head and neck down. Otherwise they might be thrown back and the neck possibly broken. The seat was invented by Sir Martin Baker and is made at a factory at Denham where they have a test seat which shoots sixty feet up a vertical tower and is halted when it reaches the top. I broadcast from this seat and had a nasty few seconds before pulling the face screen down. I shot up into the night. The acceleration was phenomenal and I had no time to say a word before I reached the top. It is a wonderful invention and has saved hundreds of lives all over the world. The only snag from my point of view was that I had a terrible pain up my backside for a few days, as a result of the tremendous boost when the charges went off. I wonder if other people who have ejected have experienced the same thing.

Just before Christmas 1950 we did the first ever 'live' broadcast from the actual face of a coal-mine. It was at Snowdon Colliery in Kent, one of the deepest mines in the country. We went down over three thousand feet in a cage at what seemed a terrific pace. I believe it was 40 mph but we got the impression of greater speed as we shot down through the hot, dust-laden air which blew up the shaft. At the bottom we walked a few hundred yards and then travelled over a mile in a paddy – the miners' name for an underground truck. Finally we had to crawl on our hands and knees along the coal face, only three feet high. I broadcast, half kneeling, half lying, in a temperature of 90°F. trying to hew some coal with a pick. It was back-aching and nearly impossible and I only managed to loosen a few measly lumps. I was only at the face for half an hour and down the mine altogether for about two hours, but it seemed a lifetime to me. I felt trapped, shut in and completely at the mercy of nature.

I couldn't help thinking of the three thousand feet which lay between me and the surface. It seemed that the only things which prevented the coal above from crushing us were the wooden pit props. These have been replaced in some pits I believe by aluminium props. But the miners told me that they preferred wood as they could tell by their creaks when danger was near.

After this experience, I have always believed that miners were entitled to a special high wage. I certainly won't take any criticism of them from people who have not been down a mine, as they can have no idea what the job is like. The long journey to the coal face, working in cramped conditions for hours on end, the dust and the heat. No smoking, no telephoning girl friends, no popping out to get a haircut or a breath of fresh air. Plus of course the ever-present sense of danger.

At the end of a long and monotonous day there is the journey out of the heat into the cold above and the task of cleaning up before going home. Whatever our jobs, most of us are lucky just to be able to breathe fresh air. It does not smell so good three thousand feet below the earth.

Two of our broadcasts brought Piccadilly Circus to a standstill, one intentionally, the other not. The first was on a date many Londoners will remember – 2 April 1949. This was the night that all the signs and neon lights came on again in Piccadilly Circus, after nearly ten years of darkness. By arrangement with the authorities and the police it was timed to coincide with *In town tonight*.

I was on a balcony overlooking the huge crowd below and they could hear all that was happening through a public address system. In the broadcast I interviewed Hubert Gregg who during the war had written the song so many of us sang – *I'm going to get lit up when the lights come on in London*. Then Zoe Gail, the girl who had made the song famous in the show at the Prince of Wales Theatre, came out on to the balcony, dressed in top-hat, white tie and tails. A spotlight was on her and the crowd cheered and wolf-whistled as she shouted: 'Abracadabra – Lights up', and pressed a switch. As if by magic up came all the lights and Zoe then sang the song to the crowds below who all joined in. It was quite a moving moment after ten long years and I expect many people did get lit up in London that night.

The other occasion was the one which became known in the BBC as 'the Piccadilly incident' and which for some reason – probably shortage of news – caused quite a sensation in Fleet Street. At least five Sunday papers had columns about it and *The People* went so far as to splash across their front page in one-inch type: BBC STUNT STARTS A GIRL STAMPEDE IN PICCADILLY. Headlines in other papers included, 'Cruel Hoax', and 'Broadcast in worst possible taste'. With the coming of television and the sort of things that are now broadcast there would have been no fuss at all if it had happened today.

Our idea was to discover whether people ever read the Agony Columns in the newspapers and if so did they act on them. The editor of *The Evening News* was a friend of mine so I swore him to secrecy and asked him to insert the following in his personal column in all the editions on Friday: 'Well set-up young gentleman with honourable intentions invites young ladies seeking adventure to meet him on the steps of the Criterion Restaurant, Lower Regent Street 7.15 pm Saturday, 19 May. Identified by red carnation and blue and white spotted scarf. Code word "How's your uncle?" ' I inserted a password as I could not believe that we would get any reaction, and as I always had to fill a minimum of three and a half minutes I thought I might be left on the steps talking to myself. At least with a password I could challenge a few passers-by with 'How's your uncle?' and their re-actions might have made a jolly good broadcast.

On the Saturday I was doing a TV commentary at Lord's and then dashed off by taxi down to Piccadilly Circus. As we approached the bottom of Regent Street we made very slow progress. There was a traffic jam ahead and large crowds were milling round. I paid off the taxi and fought my way through to the front entrance of the Criterion, and once inside rushed round to the swing doors in Lower Regent Street. My heart sank. The street was packed solid, with a row of policemen with arms linked trying to prevent the crowd from pushing up the steps. No traffic could possibly get through and the police told me later that there were four or five thousand in the crowd. There were hundreds of girls and middle-aged ladies, some pretty, some not, and never say that modern youth is not an opportunist – dotted among the crowd were several young men sporting blue and white spotted scarfs and red carnations.

I kept out of sight until John Ellison cued over to me and then I hurriedly explained to the listeners that there would be complete chaos and told them why. I then stepped out through the swing doors and hundreds of voices greeted me with 'How's your uncle?'

Amidst all the uproar and noise I managed to talk to some of the girls as they rushed up the steps past the police barrier, but I doubt if the listeners heard much. Most of the girls said that they had read the advertisement or had had it pointed out by friends and had come along to see what the adventure would be. None of them seemed disappointed that I was neither well set-up (whatever that means) nor young, and appeared to be enjoying themselves. I found no one who knew that it was a BBC stunt beforehand, though once I had come out on the steps with a microphone many in the crowd recognised me from TV and realised what was up.

The police as usual were wonderful but a somewhat annoyed inspector told me to ask the crowd to disperse as quickly as possible after my interviews. This I did, thanking them all for coming and apologising if they thought they had been cheated. They shouted good-bye and I grabbed some of those I had interviewed and took them with me inside the Criterion for a drink. I certainly needed one.

After the adverse reaction of the Sunday critics, the weeklies had time for reflection and were kinder to me. One went so far as to say: 'Praise to Variety boss Michael Standing for ignoring stuffy criticism of Brian Johnston's Blind Date episode for Saturday's *In town tonight*. The stunt was original and it had a purpose – to see what response the "agonies" get. Let us defend the right of the BBC to be free.' Michael's department ran *In town tonight* and he and Lobby were wonderful in the way they supported me in spite of some pressure from above. They took the view that the BBC were always being criticised for being stuffy and stuck up, and having no new ideas. Now as soon as they tried something original and made an effort to get away from the 'Auntie' image, the critics were still complaining. One man who did NOT complain was my friend the editor. He now knew that his readers did read the personal column.

I have said that the police were wonderful. They were at the time. But our good relations were nearly wrecked on the Monday morning. I had a long discussion with Lobby about the broadcast, and he supported me one hundred per cent, with one slight reservation. He thought we should have asked the permission of the police beforehand. I agreed with him but pointed out that had we done so they would not have given it. A few minutes after I had left Lobby's room his telephone rang and the conversation went something like this.

Voice This is Inspector —— of —— Police station speaking. I am ringing about the affair in Piccadilly Circus on Saturday night.

Lobby Quite good, Brian, but not quite good enough. That's not the sort of voice a police inspector would use.

Voice What do you mean? This *is* Inspector —— speaking.

Lobby I don't believe it. It's you, Brian so please ring off. I'm busy.

Voice Well, if you *don't* believe me ring this police station at REG . . . and check.

Lobby (*with a sigh*) All right, I will.

He did and it was of course the real Inspector, who was naturally very annoyed by now. Lobby calmed him down and tactfully explained that I had this strange habit of ringing people up pretending to be someone else. The Inspector, though obviously puzzled at such goings-on in the BBC, was mollified and said they would take no further action in the matter. But he extracted a promise from Lobby that in future, for any similar type of broadcast we would always get their permission first. So I got away with it – just.

One Saturday I became a fireman with the London Fire Brigade. In uniform and helmet I sat playing cards with the crew at Chiltern Street Station as we waited for the alarm to go. Peter Duncan had organised a fire on some waste ground behind B.H. and then dialled 999 during the programme. When the alarm rang in the station we made a dash for the hole in the floor and slid down the shining steel pole to the ground twenty feet below. Within twelve seconds the doors had been flung open, the engine started up and we had all scrambled aboard. The Station Commander shouted where to go as we shot out into the street.

It was a tremendous thrill to commentate as we raced through the streets, bell clanging and cars and people dashing for safety. These drivers really are terrific and are allowed to go through red lights and pass the wrong side of traffic islands. But if they have an accident they are treated like any other motorist. As David Frost would say – they do a grand job.

One broadcast which I hope did some good was when I became a blood donor (for the first time). In those days people knew very little about it except from that very funny record by Tony Hancock. As a result everyone – including myself – was a bit scared of giving their blood. But while on the air I was able to describe the actual insertion of the needle and the blood running off into the bottle. Except for a slight wince when the needle went into the vein, I hope I made it all sound as easy and painless as it undoubtedly is, and possibly secured some badly-needed recruits for the Blood Transfusion Service.

But I certainly did not help the medical profession when I was hypnotised on the air. Some thought it one of the funniest things they had heard on the radio, others were shocked and frightened. We originally got the idea from Cicely Courtneidge's famous record in which she accidentally inhales some laughing gas and becomes hysterical with laughter. We thought I might be given some of this gas and see what happened. But we discovered that laughing gas is the same as that used by dentists which when administered in a certain way can produce laughter. So we discarded that idea, as it might make people lose confidence in their dentists if they felt they made fools of themselves when under gas. So we then thought of hypnotism.

We had read how stage hypnotists could put a whole audience to sleep or make them all cry or laugh. Here surely was something which would give us our laughter on the radio and at the same time prove whether this kind of hypnotism was genuine or not. We got in touch with an ex-RAF officer called David Stewart, who was practising as a professional hypnotist, both privately and with stage shows. He had been badly shot up in the leg during the war, and while lying in pain in hospital had found he could hypnotise himself into believing there was no pain. So successful was he that the surgeons were actually able to perform a lengthy operation on his leg without even a local anaesthetic.

David came to visit me in my office, an impressive-looking man with flashing eyes, big black bushy eye-brows, and handle-bar moustache. I told him what we wanted and asked him to try and see if he could make me laugh. I had three of my colleagues in the room with me as witnesses to prove it was all genuine, because I made it quite plain to him that this broadcast was not going to be faked. If he did not hypnotise me into laughter then I would say so on the air and would not laugh. As I have said, we wanted to see whether this type of hypnotism worked in addition to getting the laughs.

His technique was fascinating. There were none of the staring eyes and pointed fingers that one had always heard about. Quite the opposite. The first thing he did was to ask me if I was willing to be hypnotised. He explained that no one who was *not* willing could be hypnotised against his will. A comforting thought, which I for one had not known before.

He then started to 'work' on me. He sat me in a chair and told me to relax completely and close my eyes. For about five minutes he then kept up a continuous drone of talk in a quiet rather monotonous voice which somehow gave me complete confidence. He seemed to ooze kindness and understanding. I felt myself trusting him completely.

I began to find myself breathing slowly and more heavily while in the background I could hear: '. . . you're relaxed completely, you're feeling tired and sleepy, you've got no worries, in a few moments you will do just as I tell you, but you will be quite happy to do it, just relax, don't worry, you're feeling fine. You've got a tingling sensation running up your legs and arms . . .' And so it went on in this soft, soothing voice, and I felt a tingling in my arms and legs. He gradually began to make me do various physical things such as getting up out of the chair and falling back completely stiff into his arms.

Or again he said my arms would slowly leave my sides and rise very gradually until they met above my head. I could hear him telling me all these things, and just felt I wanted to do them. I made no effort to get out of the chair, nor to raise my arms above my head. They seemed to float ever so slowly upwards. My witnesses told me afterwards that they could hardly see them moving, they went so slowly. After another five minutes he tried to get me to go back to my childhood and speak and write as I did then. This was not very successful, so I was told afterwards. He then started on the laughter. He made me relax in the chair again and began to drone again: 'You're just going to hear the funniest thing you've ever heard in your life. When you hear it you will laugh and laugh as you've never laughed before. You won't be able to stop until I snap my fingers and tell you to. Listen, this is very, very funny. Just picture a policeman directing the traffic in bathing trunks and a policeman's helmet. Nothing else. It is very funny . . .'

About here I began to feel my stomach muscles move, and my whole body began to shake like a jelly. A chuckle which seemed to come from the depth of my stomach crept up and up until it reached my mouth and grew into a laugh. A steady cackle at first, getting quicker and shriller, ending up in a peal of high-pitched laughter. All this I learnt afterwards from my friends who were watching. All I knew was that I was laughing.

Suddenly I heard him say: 'I am now going to snap my fingers and when I do so you will stop laughing. Before I snap my fingers I am going to try a little pre-hypnosis. When you come round you will be quite normal. You will feel fine and talk quite naturally to me. I will then point to Vic Moody who is standing in a corner and when you look at him you will go straight off into your laughter again.'

He snapped his fingers and said: 'Stop laughing now, it's no longer funny,' and my cackles slowly stopped like a gramophone running down. I sat there still with my eyes closed but quite quiet and composed. He said to me: 'Before you open your eyes I just want to say this – no one, not even myself, can ever hypnotise you again unless you yourself wish it. Now open your eyes.'

I had heard all he said, and felt compelled to open my eyes. I looked in front of me and saw the amazed look on my colleagues' faces. I talked normally to David, who asked me how I was and whether I felt any ill-effects. I said 'no' truthfully, because I was feeling fine. He said: 'Just look behind you.' I did so, and there in the corner was Vic Moody. I remember pointing my finger at him and going off into shrieks of laughter again until David stopped me by another snap of the fingers.

And so our experiment ended. It had obviously been a success. I had laughed, and hypnotism had worked. There could be no question of a fake – no one could pretend to laugh like that for such a long stretch. I give you my word it was genuine, I just could not help myself. And so we decided to put it on the air. David explained to me that as he had already 'worked' on me, so long as I was willing again, he would now only have to walk into a room and he could get me laughing in under a minute. We took one important precaution. His voice at the moment of hypnotising me must not be heard on the air. It might affect people listening, and some lonely spinster sitting alone in her room might be sent off into peals of laughter, with no David Stewart there to snap his fingers at the end.

So at the beginning of *In town tonight* they came over to me in one of our offices and I told the listeners what was going to happen. They then went back to the studio for another short interview, during which time David hypnotised me into the early state of complete relaxation and semi-coma.

At the end of the studio interview, they cued back to Henry Riddell, who was in the office with a microphone and he was able to tell listeners what David had done and then let them hear David actually making me laugh. It went just the same as it had in the original experiment, except this time when I came round I pointed my finger and laughed at Henry Riddell. Rather bad luck on him in front of millions of listeners. They must have begun to think he really looked funny. And so the broadcast ended as they faded out to the sound of my laughter.

The next two days were pretty hectic. As I have said, the reaction was fairly well divided between those who had thought it very funny, and those who had found it frankly horrifying. I listened to the recordings and was inclined to agree with the latter. The laughter sounded terrifying, at times even maniacal, as someone put it in a letter: 'It was as if your soul had gone into another world.' We kept the item in the repeat of *In town tonight*, but cut down the laughter.

We had proved to a lot of sceptical people that hypnotism worked, but we had also brought pain to others. Inadvertently, too, we may have frightened people away from hypnotism as a new force in the medical world, especially in its growing use in cases of childbirth. We had chosen laughter because we thought it would be funny and also because almost anything else could be faked. If David had made me do something like standing on my head, or reciting Shakespeare, the listener would have had no proof that I was hypnotised. I could have pretended to be by just doing the things he told me. But in all the many letters which we received for and against the broadcast, not one suggested that I was 'putting on' the laughter, for it was too hysterical for that. And so although we had done what we set out to do, had we been able to listen to it on a recording beforehand, I feel sure we would never have put it out on the air. As soon as I heard it I swore that I would never be hypnotised again.

I have always been fond of music, mostly of the sort you can whistle or hum. I had had piano lessons up to the age of sixteen and then rather stupidly gave them up as I was not allowed to learn what would now be called pop. But as a result I am able to read sheet music of popular numbers, though my rhythm is not much good. I had always envied the cinema organist as the spotlight turned on him and he slowly rose up on the consol of the organ from the depth of the orchestra pit.

So one Saturday night I went along to the Granada Tooting to try out my skill on the mighty organ in front of a full house. A notice was flashed on the screen saying that Brian Johnston the famous BBC organist would be broadcasting a short recital on the organ. On my cue from John I pressed a button and slowly ascended as I played a few chords. As the organ reached the top I swung round and bowed to the applauding audience. They must have thought that they were in for something good. I announced in a serious voice that for my first piece I would play part of Tchaikovsky's Piano Concerto in B Flat Minor.

There was a murmur of approval as I turned round and pulled out some of the stops which Johnny Madin, the regular organist had shown me. I started to play and after a few notes there was a roar of laughter, and no wonder. Instead of Tchaikovsky I was playing the Harry Lime theme, and then went straight into *We'll gather lilacs*, interrupted by sounds of trains, birds and galloping horses which it was possible to produce by pulling out various stops. The audience had a good laugh and I had achieved one of my ambitions.

A few months later I achieved something which I would never have believed possible. I played a street piano in a side street near the Victoria Palace and, wait for it, I actually sang *Underneath the arches* with Bud Flanagan. When I had first heard Bud and Ches sing it together in the early thirties, little did I think I would ever have the honour of actually taking Ches' place. But Bud was a real friend of mine, and to help in my spot, came out of the Victoria Palace, placed his hand on my shoulder and sang just as beautifully as if he were appearing in a Royal Variety Performance. What a lovely man he was. This really was one of the great moments in my broadcasting life.

I achieved one or two other musical ambitions. I played a barrel organ in Camden Town and disguised myself as a French siffleur with a little pointed beard and sang at the Allegro Bar just off Jermyn Street. I was even allowed to conduct an orchestra at the Royal Academy of Music to see what would happen if they *did* follow my baton. The result was foreseeable – a ghastly cacophony of sounds ending in a tremendous race to the finish.

But I did earn some money from one of my musical broadcasts, when I sang disguised as a tramp in the Strand. I had always felt sorry for street musicians and singers and wondered what they felt like – ashamed, embarrassed, or scornful of those who either slipped them the odd penny or sixpence or pretended not to notice them as they passed by.

I put on a dirty old macintosh and hat and the oldest pair of trousers and shoes that I could find. I dirtied my face and my hands and with a microphone hidden under my scarf shuffled out into the street from under an archway where I had been waiting. I carried a small tin with some matchboxes on it and started to sing *Tipperary* in a very shaky voice. It was extremely embarrassing singing in a public street – you try it sometime and see how you feel. I had to force myself to do it and tried not to look at the various passers-by, most of whom were trying to avoid me. However, in my three and a half minutes I did collect nearly a shilling, though twopence of this was given by one of our engineers *pour encourager les autres.*

He also threw in a halfpenny at the end as a signal that my time was up, as a tramp would obviously not have a stop-watch. I was immensely relieved when it was all over and ever since then if I pass one of these singers I always try to give something – however small. I know exactly how they are feeling.

I must have tried out twenty or thirty jobs during *Lets go somewhere* and among these were a cowman, RAC Scout, Wheel Tapper, Bell-ringer, Town Crier, Ice-Hockey Goal-Keeper, Salesman on an exhibition stand, a recruit in a drill squad and a toastmaster. The man who coached me in toast-mastering was himself one of the best known in the West End. He was telling me of some of the times when things had gone wrong. He was once announcing the guests at an important function when he was suddenly called away by the organiser of the banquet who wished to discuss arrangements for the speakers. He had chosen a quiet moment when most of the guests seemed to have arrived. Unfortunately during the minute or so that he was away a guest called Sir William Orfe came up the stairs and seeing no toastmaster announced himself to his host and hostess.

'I'm Orfe', he said, shaking hands.

'Oh I'm so sorry', replied his hostess, 'the party has only just begun'!

19
Let's go to the theatre

With my love of the stage I made sure that quite a few of my broadcasts came from theatres. For instance, during a performance of the pantomime *Puss in boots* at the Palladium I came on as the donkey in place of the usual man. I played a short scene with Tommy Trinder but found it unbearably hot inside the skin and very difficult to breathe with the microphone inside the donkey's mouth. But as Tommy rode off on my back I could at least claim that I had 'played' the Palladium.

Another time I was challenged by a Strong Woman to see if she could lift me up and turn me upside down. Her name was Joan Rhodes and she was a young attractive blonde in a beautiful evening gown. Somewhere underneath must have been hidden some rippling muscles, but on the surface her figure was super. In her act at the Shepherd's Bush Empire she tore telephone directories in half and bent nails and iron bars. When I went up on to the stage to accept her challenge she lifted me up like a child and then held me head downwards until all the money fell out of my pocket and one of my braces burst. She got a great hand from the audience and I must admit it was a remarkable performance as I weighed 14½ stone at the time.

I once sawed a woman in half and was also sawn in half myself by Robert Harbin. It was an extraordinary feeling watching the saw apparently sawing right through my stomach. But I must not reveal how it was done. The secret of a mental telepathy act in which I took part was on the other hand a little easier to fathom. I was blindfolded on the stage while my partner held up various articles which he borrowed from the audience.

Partner I have an article here. Tell me what it is. Take your time.

Me A watch.

Partner Quite right. And now I have a visiting card from a gentleman. Can you tell me his name. He is of Jewish extraction.

Me Is he?

Partner That's right.

That's how we did it, but I am assured that some of these acts really do pass thoughts to each other. I wonder.

I had always wanted to test out the theory that if you suck a lemon in front of a brass band they will all dry up. So one Saturday I went on stage at the Adelphi Theatre and by prearrangement interrupted Jimmy Edwards in the middle of his trombone act. I challenged him to play as I sucked. I had a very juicy lemon and as he started to play I began to suck it right in front of his face. For about half a minute he struggled bravely but what had started as *presto agitato* rapidly became *andante*. He got slower and slower and began to drool at the mouth. In the end he was just pushing the rod of his trombone backwards and forwards, and all that came out were a few phut phuts of air. He gave up and burst out laughing. He claims it had nothing to do with the lemon but that it was the sight of my face, coupled with the laughter from the audience. So I never really discovered for certain whether my theory was right or wrong.

I had always been an admirer of the way Peter Pan and the fairies in pantomimes flew unconcernedly about the stage. I was therefore delighted when I was invited to be a member of the Flying Ballet during a performance of the Ice Pantomime at the Empress Hall. I was disguised as a fantastic-looking bird, feather wings and a large yellow beak and so on. They fastened a belt round my middle on to which were attached two very thin wires hanging down from the roof. They had to be small to be invisible to the audience but I was assured they would bear the weight of a twenty-two stone man, so I decided to take the risk. There were about six other 'birds' in the ballet and as the orchestra struck up we were hoisted into the air high above the glistening black ice fifty feet below. I did not know the steps of the ballet or whatever they are called in the air – but I flapped my wings and then held them spread out as if swooping like a bird. It was terrifying looking down at the upturned faces of the audience and realising that I was only being suspended by the two thin wires. That ice looked horribly hard. After being swung three times up and down the length of the arena I was slowly lowered on to the ice. I can understand birds enjoying flying through the air. It was a very pleasant sensation. But they don't have to worry about two thin bits of wire. And I never did discover how they knew the wires would take up to a twenty-two stone man. Had they tried a twenty-three stoner and had the wires broken? If so, that's one job I would not like – a flying ballet wire tester.

One of the most uproarious and chaotic of the broadcasts was when I was shaved and shampooed by the Crazy Gang during their show *Together again* at the Victoria Palace. They had a barber's shop sketch and I took the place of the man who twice nightly was given the full treatment. They lent me some old clothes, a macintosh, wig and all I had to do was to sit in the chair and try to keep talking into the microphone. As soon as I sat down they pulled off the wig and poured bottles of coloured shampoo all over my real hair and face – green, yellow, red, any colour you can think of. They had an enormous brush, dipped it into some white lather and 'shaved' me. The lather went into my mouth and up my nose and as I tried to talk they stuffed the brush into my mouth. They were having the time of their lives, and so were the audience. Teddy Knox and Jimmy Nervo were the chief culprits, and I finished up on the floor as they poured water down my trousers and tickled me in the tummy.

It must have sounded chaotic to listeners at home. All they could have heard was my screams and the roars of the audience. But it was surprising how many people told me afterwards how much they had enjoyed it. That's one of the great things about radio. It encourages the use of one's imagination. I took over an hour to clean up and get all the colours out of my hair and skin. As I left the theatre one man came up and shook me by the hand. It was the actor who normally sat in the chair – I had spared him the ordeal for at least one performance.

The Crazy Gang were wonderful people, always friendly and cheerful, and I did quite a few broadcasts with them. They were tremendous practical jokers and I was warned never to leave my overcoat in Bud Flanagan's dressing-room. People who had done so found sewn inside a notice: 'This coat has been pinched from Bud Flanagan. Please inform the police.' Very awkward, if the owner at some posh function hands it in to a cloakroom attendant who then spots the notice.

The Gang would go to any lengths to make a successful joke. At one time Jack Hylton used to leave his best suit in one of their dressing-rooms so that when he came up from a day at the races, he could change into something more suitable for the theatre. The Gang hired a tailor to come in each day and take about an eighth of an inch off the bottom of the trousers and then sew it up again. For the first few times Jack did not seem to notice anything. But after a bit he began to let out his braces and could not understand why the trousers were creeping higher and higher up his legs. In the end his braces would not let out any further and he became suspicious, and finally found out. But showman that he was, he appreciated the trouble that they had taken to produce a laugh.

One of the most unusual places from which I broadcast was from inside a letter-box at Oxford. It was Christmas time and the idea was to see how people were helping the Post Office by writing clearly, putting the town in block letters, and sticking on the right stamp when posting their Christmas cards.

We went to Oxford as this was the only box the Post Office could find large enough to contain me. I crouched inside with my microphone and as the letters and cards dropped in I reported on the things that had been done right or wrong. All went well but as usual I was tempted and went a little too far. No one had any idea that I was

inside so to finish I put my hand up to the slit through which the letters
are posted and when a lady came up to post her card I put my hand out
and took the letter. There was a loud scream and I gather she nearly
fainted. You can hardly blame her. You don't expect to see a hand
emerging from a letter box and grip your letter. It was a rotten trick
to play.

I also made a speech from Speakers Corner which was not at all
easy to do. It takes quite a bit of courage to get up on a soap-box and
start talking about nothing in particular in front of a crowd made up
largely of regulars. It is undoubtedly the best free entertainment in
London and the repartee of the crowd is usually far better value than
the speakers. I remember once an old favourite there called Charlie
denouncing capitalists and 'their superfluous profits'. 'Was Moses
one?' came immediately from the crowd.

During my broadcast one of them asked me: 'Why, with the present
food shortage does the BBC waste so much tripe on the air?' It wasn't
a bad question! All I could rather feebly reply on the spur of the moment
was: 'Because they know their onions.'

One date in 1950 was too good to miss. 1 April happened to fall on a
Saturday, so, although one is not supposed to operate after 12 noon,
we decided to make an April Fool of John Ellison. I told him that I was
going to do street interviews that night about 1 April. Secretly we had
tried out various impersonators to see if they could copy my voice.

Funnily enough, only one of them could, and he got my rather
stupid giggle off to perfection. It was Peter Sellers. On that night I hid
in the studio and John quite unsuspicious cued over to Peter, thinking
it was me. Peter did perfectly and I must say sounded just like me.
After a few hilarious interviews he pretended he was feeling ill and
that the crowd was pressing against him, so cued suddenly back to
John in the studio. Peter Duncan in the control panel signalled John
in the studio to take over. John, quite nonplussed said: 'We're sorry.
Brian is obviously not feeling too well, so we will go on to the next
item.' (He told me afterwards that he thought I was drunk!) As he
said this I crept from behind a screen, went up behind him, tapped him
on the shoulder and said: 'April Fool.' He turned round and looked
amazed, but was decent enough to admit that we had caught him fair
and square.

On two occasions I did on the radio what would have been impossible to do on the TV (in those days, anyway). I broadcast lying starkers

on the slab of a Turkish Bath, with all the slaps and grunts, and another time when actually having a bath in my own house. I did this because I had been going to talk to the crews after the Boat Race, but it never took place as Oxford sank. So I had to think of something at the last moment and had a boat race all of my own with some of my young son's boats in the bath. It was not one of my most exciting broadcasts!

One day late in 1950 I was sitting at my desk thinking out future stunts when I suddenly realised that I must be nearing my hundredth 'performance'. I checked up and found that all being well I would reach it on Saturday, 24 February. I puzzled my brain as to how best I could celebrate it. I thought of one or two really sensational things I might do, but discarded them pretty quickly. I did not want it to be my hundredth-and-last *Let's go somewhere*. So I hit on another idea.

Why not get Peter Duncan to allow me to do something I had always wanted to do on the air but which I would obviously never do in the ordinary course of broadcasting? In fact as a birthday treat I asked for 'the freedom of the air' to do what I wanted. It was not an outrageous request, and Peter agreed to it straight away. For three and a half minutes on 24 February I could try and be a cross-talk comedian! I was lucky with my straight man. Ever since I had shared an office with John Ellison we used to try out gag routines, many of them picked up in music-halls where we used to go for *Round the halls*. So we arranged that we would do the 'act' in front of the *In town tonight* audience in the studio.

We spent days preparing a suitable script, and some of my most treasured gags had to go – victims of the blue pencil. But this time I was censoring myself, and however good the gag, if it was at all 'blue' I would not let myself be influenced by myself. It was out! Finally the script was ready – all taken from my file and as you can imagine as old and corny a collection of jokes as were ever heard on the BBC – and that is saying something! Our only hope was that they were so old that the younger generation of listeners might never have heard of them. We also decided to sing (rather *à la* Flanagan and Allen) the usual treacly sentimental song with which so many comics finish their acts.

We rehearsed for days as we wanted the act to go with real punch and speed – we could not afford to dawdle with some of those jokes! We eventually managed to get it off slickly enough, and the studio audience were very kind and laughed quite loud and often. And –

an unheard-of thing in the somewhat austere atmosphere of the *In town tonight* studio – they even applauded at the end of the act. So I had my birthday wish and I think got away with it. There was an amusing sequel.

On the following Monday a well-known radio comic was walking up Shaftesbury Avenue when he was stopped by the 'funny' man of a radio cross-talk act. The conversation went as follows:

'I say, Ted, did you hear Brian Johnston in *In town tonight* on Saturday? He pinched all my gags from my act and I don't know what to do now. I've got *Henry Hall's Guest Night* tomorrow.'

And we thought the gags were old and corny! So that you can judge for yourself, here is the script as we did it that night. I hope you have not heard them all before, and that you get at least one laugh out of it.

> J.E.   Ladies and gentlemen, tonight I am going to give you a serious
>   monologue entitled *The Orphan's Return* –
>   *'Twas a dark cold night in December*
>   *And the snow was falling fast,*
>   *Little Nell lay in the gutter –*
>   *And the rich folk by her passed.*
>   *You may ask me . . .*
> B.J.   I say, I say!
> J.E.   Yes, yes, what is it?
> B.J.   I've just seen forty men under one umbrella, and not one of
>   them got wet.
> J.E.   Forty men under one umbrella and not one of them got wet – it
>   must have been a very large umbrella!
> B.J.   Certainly not, it wasn't raining.
> J.E.   (*Indignant and exasperated*) What d'you mean by coming on
>   here and interrupting me while I'm reciting – now go away.
>   I'm sorry, ladies and gentlemen, I'll begin again –
>   'Twas a . . .
> B.J.   It's in all the papers tonight.
> J.E.   What is?
> B.J.   Fish and chips. We don't w ant London Bridge any longer.
> J.E.   Why not?
> B.J.   It's long enough already. D'you know who's in the Navy?
> J.E.   No, who?
> B.J.   Sailors. I've got a goat with no nose.

J.E. Really? How does it smell?

B.J. Terrible.

J.E. I don't want to know about that. Will you go away!

B.J. I've got a letter here. If I post it tonight, do you think it will get to Glasgow by Wednesday?

J.E. My dear fellow, of course it will.

B.J. Well, I bet it won't.

J.E. How's that?

B.J. It's addressed to Shoreditch.

J.E. It seems to me you're next door to a blithering idiot.

B.J. Well, move over and give me a chance. By the way, I *nearly* saw your brother the other day.

J.E. How do you mean, you *nearly* saw my brother?

B.J. Well, isn't your brother a policeman?

J.E. That's quite correct – he is a policeman.

B.J. Isn't he P.C. 49?

J.E. That's quite right – he is P.C. 49.

B.J. Well, I met P.C. 48.

J.E. You met P.C. 48 . . . Well, you may think you're very very clever, but let me tell you I've got a brother who even though he was on the dole, always managed to live above his income.

B.J. That's impossible, he couldn't be on the dole and live above his income.

J.E. Oh! yes, he did. He had a flat over the Labour Exchange. By the way, what's *your* brother doing these days?

B.J. Nothing!

J.E. Nothing? I thought he applied for that job as producer of *In town tonight*?

B.J. Yes, he got the job. They call him Button B, you know.

J.E. Button B, why on earth do they call him that?

B.J. Well, he's always pressed for money.

J.E. Well, I must say I don't know what your wife thinks about all this.

B.J. That reminds me, here's a letter from her.

J.E. (*Reading letter*) But there's nothing written on it.

B.J. No, we're not on speaking terms. Not that it matters, I've just got six months for rocking her to sleep.

J.E. You can't get six months for rocking your wife to sleep.

B.J. Oh yes I can, you should have seen the size of the rock.

J.E. I'm sick of this, let's go into this restaurant and get something
to eat. Waiter, do you serve lobsters here?

B.J. Yes, sir – sit down, we serve anybody.

J.E. I see you've got frog's legs.

B.J. Yes, sir – it's the walking about that does it.

J.E. How long will the spaghetti be?

B.J. I don't know, sir, we never measure it.

J.E. I think I'll have some soup.

B.J. Right, sir – here it is.

J.E. I say, waiter, there's a fly in my soup.

B.J. All right, sir, don't shout – all the others will want one.

J.E. Have you got any eggs?

B.J. Yes, sir.

J.E. Are they fresh?

B.J. Don't ask me, sir, I only lay the tables.

J.E. Oh! This is hopeless. I think I'll have a drink. What d'you
suggest?

B.J. I'd have a mother-in-law, sir.

J.E. Mother-in-law, what's that?

B.J. Stout and bitter. Terrible weather, isn't it, sir?

J.E. Yes, terrible.

B.J. I call it Madam Butterfly weather, sir.

J.E. Madam Butterfly weather?

B.J. Yes, sir, *One fine day*. But cheer up – just around the corner
may be sunshine for you . . .

Brian Johnston and John Ellison into song

Just around the corner may be sunshine for you,
Just around the corner skies above may be blue –
Even tho' it's dark and cloudy
Mister Sun will soon say 'How-dy'
Just around the corner from you –
We'll see you later,
Just around the corner from you.

I did my final *Let's go somewhere* on 17 May 1952 when I was winched
out of a boat in the Solent by a Royal Naval helicopter. It was not an
easy operation as the back-stream from the chopper blew the boat
backwards and forwards. But of course in the safe and skilful hands of
the Royal Navy it was perfectly safe and an everyday job for them.
It was, however, with a sense of relief that I was safely pulled aboard

the hovering helicopter and was able to say a final goodbye to the listeners of *Let's go somewhere*.

I would not like to be so immodest as to say I went out at the top. But I was determined to stop before everyone began to get bored with me. During the next few years people often asked me why I had stopped and could I not do some more. If I had continued they might have begun to ask why I didn't stop. As it was I was able to declare the innings closed with a final score of 150 not out.

20

A mixed bag

There is no doubt that at the end of *Let's go somewhere* I was intolerably swollen-headed. This is an occupational hazard for all broadcasters and TV personalities. They wield tremendous power because they have such a vast audience listening to what they say. You can try as hard as you like but it is not easy to hide your personal opinion about any subject being discussed. The inflection of the voice or the way of phrasing a question can reveal which side the broadcaster is on. This gives a sometimes unconscious feeling of power which is further increased by the minor flatteries, recognition and extra attention a broadcaster receives at the hands of the public.

It only requires a few appearances on the telly for people to start staring in the street. Some will greet the personality without thinking because they recognise the face and feel that he is an old friend. Others just want to be friendly and start up a conversation about the particular programme in which you have been appearing or the subject on which you are meant to be an expert. For years I have been greeted with such remarks as: 'What, no cricket today Brian?' or 'Do you think we shall beat the Australians?'

This recognition can be a great help in public places and restaurants. It's also no use denying that it is immensely satisfying to be greeted by the Immigration Authority on arriving back at London Airport with a 'Had a good trip, Mr Johnston?' All this contributes to the swollen head.

But luckily, there are antidotes. I often used to be made to look small in front of my friends. Someone would rush up to me and say: 'Oh, we do enjoy your programmes. We always listen to you.' Then as the modest smile began to play on my lips the person would go on: 'And what's in box 13 tonight, Michael?' I evidently had a certain likeness to the late Michael Miles of *Take your pick* fame and every-time this happened I was suitably deflated.

Even better was the occasion when I had finished doing *Let's go somewhere* and was staying one winter's week-end down in Surrey with John Ellison. He was still introducing the programme and on the Saturday he left me by the roaring log fire and set off in his car for London. It was snowing hard and after he had gone a mile or two he skidded into a ditch full of snow. He was well and truly stuck. So he went up to a near-by cottage and knocked on the door. A man answered and John asked him if he had a spade as his car was in a ditch. The man recognised John and said: 'It's John Ellison, isn't it? Of course I'll help.'

He went off, got a spade and started to dig like mad to free the car. After about ten minutes he had not got very far so John asked if he could use his telephone to ring up a friend for help. 'Of course Mr Ellison. You use my telephone. Anything you like. Meanwhile I'll go on digging.' He could not have been more affable. John rang me up and asked me to bring my Ford Pilot and a towing rope to pull him out, and so reluctantly I left the warm fire. John told me later that as he saw me approaching he thought he would encourage the chap who was still digging hard. 'This friend of mine coming along in the car. You'll know him. He used to do all those stunts in *In town tonight* – it's Brian Johnston.'

The name worked like magic on our affable friend. He put his spade down in the snow and said: 'Brian Johnston. Yap, yap, yap, yap. Can never understand a bloody word he says.' And so saying he stalked off to his cottage, leaving us to get on with it as best we could. I must say this had a very salutary effect on me, and took me down a peg or two. To think that anyone could feel so strongly about me!

During the four years of *Let's go somewhere* I had become involved in a variety of programmes. It was a great experience and training ground for me but I fear the poor listeners must have suffered. They were getting as their guide a jack of all trades who knew very little about any of them. For instance in 1949 it was decided to have an extra commentator on the Boat Race at Hammersmith Bridge and possibly because my father had been a Blue, I was chosen. It luckily only involved describing the two crews shooting the bridge and estimating the distance between them. I did not dare to ape John Snagge and risk any 'in-outs', though I have done so more recently when I have been at the finish at Chiswick Bridge.

Again it was assumed that because of my military past I would make the ideal commentator for Trooping the Colour. It was true that I had been in the Brigade of Guards but, as you have probably gathered, the one thing which I had managed to escape during the war was drill parades. My knowledge was therefore extremely sketchy and it was quite an ordeal commentating on such an important occasion. I knew that the slightest mistake would bring a shoal of letters from ex-Guards colonels listening with pens poised. By doing a lot of homework and with the help of the officers from London District I just about got by. I think my most serious crime was to say that the companies were 'wheeling' instead of 'forming'.

But it was a difficult broadcast to do. It required expert explanation of what was going on, and plenty of extra titbits to fill in during some fairly lengthy pauses. But the commentator also has to let the listeners hear the music of the massed bands and irate letters pour in if he speaks too much over the music. The best by far at striking the right balance is Robert Hudson, who year after year gives an impeccable commentary, a model for every budding commentator.

It was also inevitable that I should be allotted the El Alamein Reunion, although I had never been in the desert war. I did the commentary for a number of years and it was fun having a yearly meeting with Monty. The first time we met I reminded him of the Parkstone sidelights incident and he tactfully pretended to remember. He was always extremely helpful and co-operative, and at rehearsals the BBC were given priority over everyone else to make sure the broadcast was a success.

Sometimes Monty was there himself and would ask exactly what we wanted, and gave us the timing of his speech to which he always stuck. When he was not there we used to read aloud the copy of his speech for timing purposes, trying hard to imitate the staccato voice with the short crisp sentences. We had to make a generous allowance for applause and laughter, for he always got plenty of both. Monty was the perfect example of a world figure who knew the value of good publicity and realised that the best way to get it was to do what he was asked by the BBC – within reason!

We continued doing our late night birdsong programmes but moved from the Surrey wood to Hever Castle in Kent. Henry Douglas-Home, Percy Edwards and myself spent many happy May evenings year after year, wandering round the woods and persuading the nightingales to sing. Lady Violet Astor was very kind to us and before the broadcasts we were invited into the Castle for drinks, though we were never suitably dressed for the luxurious surroundings of her beautiful home. One year we got so carried away by her hospitality that we lost count of time, and failed to notice that her house guests kept leaving the room and reappearing in evening dress, until the butler was forced to announce that 'Dinner was served', and we made our way back to the woods, feeling somewhat ashamed. We had held up the Castle dinner by half an hour.

Among the guests, Henry pointed out to me a peer of the realm whom he said had suffered very severe shock when he had fallen off his pony as a boy. He had been so badly shocked that for the rest of his life whenever he saw a horse he started to neigh! Henry assured me that there had been complete chaos one summer at Ascot. The peer had strolled towards the paddock and on spotting the horses started to neigh loudly. All the horses parading round the ring then joined in and the peer had to be escorted hurriedly away before peace could be restored!

Cricket continued its postwar popularity in 1949. It was a fine summer and the New Zealanders under Walter Hadlee were the tourists. They were determined to show that they deserved more than only three-day Tests and succeeded in drawing all four Tests played to prove the point. They were able to do this thanks to the magnificent form of those two fine left-handers – Bert Sutcliffe and Martin Donnelly, both high on the list of Test batsmen. Of the established England stars Len Hutton had a wonderful season, scoring 3,429 runs and a new star – eighteen-year-old Brian Close – became not only the youngest player ever to play for England but also the youngest to do the double of 1,000 runs and 100 wickets in a season.

1949 was an important year for Pauline and me. We had found our house in St John's Wood, 1A Cavendish Avenue, just about 100 yards from the Nursery End at Lord's. It was possible on big match days to hear the applause and the oohs and the aahs of the crowd, and I became quite expert in guessing whether it was the fall of a wicket, a boundary or a dropped catch. Just after midnight on Easter Sunday 17 April our eldest son Barry was born in the Lindo Wing of St Mary's Hospital, Paddington. He arrived a fortnight early and I am ashamed to say that I failed to carry out the traditional fathers' role of pacing up and down the corridors of the hospital. I was fast asleep at home and was woken by the telephone with the good news. Pauline still thinks that I should have been there by her side and I am sure she is right. I did better with the other four!

Television had still been confined to the Lord's and Oval Tests but in 1950 the Sutton Coldfield Transmitter was opened and we were able to televise the Trent Bridge Test as well. It was a cold and wet summer and there was a decline in the standard of cricket played in the County Championship. But the season was saved by the brilliance and exuberance of John Goddard's West Indian touring side. They won the Test series 3–1 and won their first-ever Test in England at Lord's. This was followed by scenes of wild enthusiasm, the crowds rushing across the ground to the front of the pavilion where 'Lord' Kitchener sang a Calypso especially composed for the occasion. There must have been much subterranean activity that day in the churchyards of England as old MCC members turned in their graves. A Calypso on the hallowed turf of Lord's. By gad, sir!

The tour was made memorable by the superb batting of 'the three W's', Worrell, Weekes and Walcott and the spin bowling of that remarkable pair Ramadhin and Valentine. Ramadhin had only played in two first-class matches before the tour started and had a mystery leg break which our batsmen found very difficult to detect. He bowled in a cap which is unusual for a bowler. I remember that Ronald Colman did so in the cricket match in the film of *Raffles*, and Wally Hammond used to do so on occasions. Clarrie Grimmett also hid his bald pate under an Australian green cap. But it was a rare thing to do.

With sleeves rolled down Ramadhin brought his arm over quickly and his stock ball was one which turned slightly from the off. The difficulty was to spot the one that straightened or turned from the leg to off. We got very excited on the television at Trent Bridge as we thought we had discovered the secret of how Ramadhin let Walcott behind the stumps know when the leg break was coming. We noticed that on occasions after getting back to his mark before starting his run he ran his left hand down the back of his cap. Every time he did it we checked and so far as we could see at least no ball ever turned in from the off after he had done it.

We told the England Captain Norman Yardley of our theory but I am not sure whether the England batsmen ever had sufficient faith in us to play for the leg break whenever they saw him touch his cap. After the match we challenged John Goddard about it in an interview on television but not surprisingly he denied it completely.

There was an amusing incident on the television in this Trent Bridge match. Worrell and Weekes put on 283 for the fourth wicket and on the Friday evening were hitting the England bowling all over the field. We were getting a bit tired of showing four after four, so to vary things I said I wondered what Norman Yardley was going to do to separate the two batsmen. The camera obediently panned round on to Norman at mid-on but unfortunately we caught him scratching himself in a very awkward place. As he was in close-up on the screen I had to think of something to say to cover up quickly and the best I could do was: 'Obviously a very ticklish problem!' Incidentally Norman got a terrible rocket from his wife Tony who had been watching on the telly at home. She said that in future she would prefer him *not* to come up to scratch!

In addition to the television I was now beginning to do some radio commentary on county matches and the first one with which I was entrusted was Middlesex *v*. Yorkshire at Lord's. Not a bad starter!

During the summer we also did a radio programme about the Hythe and Dymchurch Miniature Railway run by an enthusiast named Captain Tom Howey. On the day of our broadcast something or other was being opened by the Mayor of New Romney and as a sequel to the ceremony he was to be taken for a ride on one of the trains. In his Mayoral robes and chain of office he was placed in one of the small open carriages right at the rear of the train. The guard waved his flag and blew his whistle. The engine driver gave a toot, the Mayor raised his tricorne hat as he waved to the crowd on the platform and with a slow 'chug chug' the train started on its journey. But to everyone's horror, though to our delight, the Mayor's carriage was left stranded in the station as he continued to wave vigorously. They had forgotten to hook it on to the carriage in front!

At this time I began to make quite a few journeys to Alexandra Palace. First I stood in for Leslie Mitchell as stooge for Terry Thomas in his TV show *How do you view?* This was produced by Bill Ward, now one of the big nobs in ATV. How it ever got on the air I don't know. There were just two tiny studios for the whole of television output and the place was a mass of scenery, cables and cameras. There would be a newsreader or announcer in one corner and all the various scenes for Terry's show dotted around the place. It was all done 'live' and he had to dash from set to set changing as he went, while someone filled in with a song.

The spot I did was an interview with him disguised as a com-missionaire, lion-tamer (Captain Shaggers) or the man who hit the gong for Ranks. It was my job to put the questions and to try to keep a straight face. He had a terrible twinkle in his eye and was always trying to make me giggle. These shows were fun to do and Terry used to come and rehearse in our garden at Cavendish Avenue. Some years later he made an LP including two of these interviews and I was honoured to be chosen as the stooge. In those days the newsreaders and presenters still wore evening dress. During one of Terry's shows Macdonald Hobley who was reading the news that night, went home as he was not feeling too well. As luck would have it a news item came in unexpectedly which had to be read. Panic stations!

However, someone spotted me and persuaded Eric Robinson to lend me his dinner-jacket so that I could make the announcement, something to do with Mr Attlee at No. 10. They only showed my top half as I had a pair of check trousers on and had not got time to slip into Eric's trousers as well. Imagine that happening today with all the elaborate newsreading and presentation set-ups at Television Centre.

I also used to dub commentary on cricket film for *Television News Reel* which used to go out twice a week from Alexandra Palace. I worked from a script and was started and stopped by a chap sitting alongside me pinching my arm. He also used to produce the sound of ball on bat by actually knocking a ball against a bat into my micro-phone. He sometimes got it wrong and when a batsman was hit on the pad in the picture you could hear bat striking ball. This particular chap has gone quite far since then and for six years was Controller of BBC-1, before going to Yorkshire television. It was Paul Fox. The commentator for the newsreel was Ted Halliday the famous portrait painter. He lives just up the road from me and there's a marvellous story told about him. A rich society lady called on him and the conversation went as follows:

Lady Mr Halliday. Would you do me a great favour and paint me in the nude?
Ted (*After a pause*) Well, yes I will. But on one condition.
Lady What is it?
Ted I *must* keep my socks on, as I have to have somewhere to stick my brushes.

1950 was a repeat of 1949 so far as our family was concerned. Our daughter Clare was born on 14 September. This time I was present and correct which was more than our very nice gynaecologist! He arrived breathless in a morning coat and dashed up the stairs as the cries of the newborn babe came from the nursery. Pauline's mother had coped perfectly and all was well.

With two children life became even more hectic but we were lucky always to have a housekeeper who lived in our basement flat and also a nanny, or perhaps I ought to say a succession of them. They were mostly on the young side and generally quite nice. But somehow they appeared to come and go with fairly frequent regularity.

At any rate, Pauline still managed to come out on as many OBs as possible and we were also lucky in getting tickets for theatres which I had to vet. It was not only nice to have Pauline around, but being a Yorkshire girl she was very candid and always said what she thought. This meant I have always had some truthful criticism which has been an enormous help.

Before I married Pauline, her father warned me that she had a habit of putting her foot in it unintentionally, and we have had quite a few hilarious moments as a result of this. One example was when we went out to dinner with someone we did not know too well. We were all dressed up as we had been told it was evening dress. Our hostess opened the door of her flat and I must admit did not look too glamorous. 'Oh, I'm sorry,' said Pauline, looking at her, 'I thought we were going to change.' 'I have,' replied the hostess somewhat icily.

1951 brought us the South Africans, a rather dull series which England won 3–1, an undistinguished domestic season, and plenty of cold wet weather. One bright spot was the arrival of Peter May on the Test scene with a hundred in his first match. It was of course the Festival of Britain and we had many broadcasts to do in connection with this.

One of the most enjoyable was the play especially commissioned by BBC TV for the occasion. It was *The final test* by Terence Rattigan and

I was lucky enough to be given the part of one of the commentators, which did not take a lot of acting. It was produced by Royston Morley, a rabid cricket enthusiast, so between us we were able to see that all the cricket details were accurate. Patrick Barr played the lovable professional, a part which Jack Warner was to play in the film.

Patrick had got a rowing blue at Oxford but by the end of rehearsals he had been completely converted to cricket, as were several others in the cast. It was a most moving play and it was lucky that I was not in any of the closing scenes as in rehearsals and on the actual transmission I was blubbing!

Around this time I became involved in several other activities new to me. I entered the romantic world of dancing by commentating on the Star Ballroom Championships with the legendary Josephine Bradley as my expert guide. 'Jo' was the most graceful lady I have ever met – she carried herself magnificently. She was a champion herself many times over and was world-famous as a teacher. I enjoyed several years of broadcasting with her and shall always be grateful for her kindness and help and the way she held my hand in a world strange to me.

I also began to commentate on another yearly event – the Brass Band Championships at the Royal Albert Hall. Here again I had an expert at my side, Harry Mortimer, then a colleague at the BBC, but always in great demand as a conductor. He is still Mr Big of the Brass Band World and how I used to envy him his mop of hair, which fell about all over the place as he waved his baton feverishly in the air. I always felt terribly sorry for the judges who were shut up in a large box-like affair in the middle of the Hall. It had no windows but was air-conditioned so that they could only hear each band, not see them. They were usually rather elderly men and were locked in at about 10 o'clock in the morning and emerged looking slightly dazed around 4 pm. They were, I was assured, supplied with sandwiches, drink and a few buckets but even so it must have been quite an ordeal.

Another annual event in the Royal Albert Hall was the Burma Reunion for the 14th Army, with the emphasis on entertainment from the various stars who had entertained the troops in Burma. Special favourites were Stainless Stephen, Gert and Daisy and inevitably Vera Lynn. So far as the speeches were concerned I generally had to deal with Lord Mountbatten and as with Monty he appreciated the value of a good broadcast and was always most helpful.

At this time we were still doing *Postman's Knock* every Christmas morning. Nowadays everything is pre-recorded but for at least ten years I used to get up early every Christmas and go out to do a 'live' broadcast either with a postman delivering the post (there *was* one in those days on Christmas Day) or at some children's hospital, opening their parcels.

One year my colleague Henry Riddell was allocated a street and the idea was to knock on the door with the postman, wish whoever opened it a Happy Christmas and ask them to open some of their cards and tell us whom they were from. Looking back nowadays it all seems rather nosey. Anyway Henry wanted to make sure there was someone at home in the first house he was due to visit. So about ten minutes before the broadcast he went to the house and rang the bell. A lady answered who said she was Mrs Brown. Henry explained to her what it was all about and warned her he would be back in ten minutes. When the broadcast started he once again walked up to the door – this time with the postman and a microphone in his hand. He knocked and after a short pause the door opened and the same lady appeared. 'Happy Christmas madam,' said Henry, 'I am from the BBC and we have your Christmas Day mail. Could you tell me your name?' 'I'm Mrs Brown', she said, sounding rather annoyed, 'as I told you when you called round a few minutes' ago.' Collapse of Henry and the broadcast completely spoilt.

It was during this year that I received an unexpected telephone call which resulted in my taking part in my first and only film. The call came from Herbert Wilcox's secretary, asking whether I could go down at short notice the next day to Shepperton Studios. They were filming *Derby day* and had suddenly decided that they wanted an interview with Peter Graves on the 'racecourse'.

There would be no script, I was to bring my own morning dress and I was to report at some ghastly hour of the morning. Of course I accepted and on my arrival was greeted by Herbert who told me my part would last about one minute, that I could work out the dialogue with Peter but that there was one question he wanted asked at the end of the interview.

It all seemed delightfully casual and the cameramen and technicians were most friendly and helpful. Peter was great fun to work with, though he was a terrible giggler. We did one or two takes but I don't think we fluffed too badly.

Now I can understand why film-stars so dislike seeing their old films on TV. *Derby day* was re-shown on BBC-1 in 1972 and I watched horrified as a youthful-looking Johnston suddenly appeared on the screen. It was the first time I had seen the film and I was pleased to see that our interview had not been cut in any way. Herbert is now an old friend of mine and I have seldom felt more proud than when he recently introduced me to someone in Australia. 'This is Brian Johnston. He once played for me in one of my films.'

1952 was a year of great variety and quite a few 'firsts' for me. In January Max Robertson fell ill and I went at the last moment as co-driver and co-broadcaster with Richard Dimbleby on the Monte Carlo Rally. We were not competing, as Raymond Baxter used to do in later years, but we travelled in Richard's touring Allard and broadcast from the various report centres along the route.

We were always 'tail-end Charley' as our broadcasts were so timed that we could describe how everyone was doing at each stage of the Rally. To start with, the weather was fine but the further south we got the worse it became. First it rained, then it froze and the roads became like an ice-rink. Then it started to snow, and we bought some snow chains which promptly broke. We got miles behind the other competitors and failed to make Monte Carlo for the planned evening broadcast. We sent back a report from a hotel bedroom in Digne where we were forced to spend the night as the snowstorm made conditions impossible.

Richard had done most of the driving and was dog-tired. We had a steak for supper and as Richard put his fork into his mouth his head fell forward and there he was fast asleep with the fork in his mouth. We set off early next morning and on arrival in Monte Carlo found that only five of the original 362 starters had completed the route without loss of penalty points. We had a delightful few days on the Côte D'Azur and a leisurely drive back to England.

Richard was a marvellous companion and had a superb sense of humour. The jobs he was called upon to do may have made him appear rather pompous on occasions but he was anything but. I think to all broadcasters he was the greatest – a complete professional who was never at a loss for the right word. He was a tremendous hard worker and would work for days before a broadcast collecting what we call associative material about the subject he was to cover. He would then write this on to small cards which he would keep in front of him as he talked, ready for any emergency. He was thus able to keep talking throughout delays or changes of programme.

Perhaps the best example of this was after Princess Margaret's wedding, when she was an hour late arriving at Tower Bridge on the way to her honeymoon. Richard filled in as if nothing untoward was happening and regaled viewers with details about the Royal Yacht, the Tower, the River Thames – anything in fact which was in sight. He had done his homework and had filled those cards of his with all the information he might need in a crisis. And this – in a broadcasting sense – certainly was one.

It always distressed me that he was never knighted before he died so tragically of cancer. Everyone had known for two years at least that he had not long to live. It always amazed me how he bravely continued to broadcast almost to the end, often in terrible pain. I remember asking Edward Ford, then one of the Queen's secretaries, whether nothing could be done to get Richard honoured before he died. Unfortunately I believe the Palace thought that the move should come from Downing Street, but alas it never did. Richard so far has never been replaced, and there will certainly never be a better broadcaster. Nor a nicer, kinder or more generous man.

As a result of this Monte Carlo adventure with Richard I reported the Rally for radio for the next six years. Another example of how lucky I have been in my broadcasting career. It all happened just because I was available when Max suddenly could not go. It was a very pleasant annual excursion from the cold and fog of an English January to the sunshine and gaiety of Monte Carlo and although it was hard work, we managed to enjoy ourselves as well.

One year I was invited to dinner with Sir Bernard and Lady Docker on board their famous yacht *Shemara* in Cannes Harbour. It was an hilarious evening during which we played tiddly-winks and Lady Docker summoned the Captain to the dining saloon and sacked him on the spot! I must say he did not seem very concerned at the time, and afterwards I discovered it was an almost nightly performance.

One very special year was when Sheila Van Damm won the Ladies Prize, and the Sunbeam Team in which she was driving, the team prize. There had been quite a lot of argument with the Rally authorities over the marks before the cup was finally awarded to the team, and naturally enough the champagne corks popped in celebration. It was not perhaps the best time for them to do so, as the Rootes financial director had been sent down to see how economies could be made in the team's budget for the next year. However, he soon joined in the celebrations and it was lucky that he did because he had the unusual name of Goat and when someone said to me: 'I want to introduce our financial director Mr Goat', I replied inspired by the champagne, 'you must be kidding!'

A few weeks after my first Rally I shared another broadcast with Richard, this time on the television. It was the funeral of King George VI and we were to do the commentary along the route which the funeral procession took from Westminster to Paddington Station. This was the biggest challenge and opportunity which I had had since joining the BBC six years before and although there was very little time to prepare for it, I was determined to prove that I could do a serious job like this as well as the lighter ones with which viewers and listeners usually associated me.

In this type of broadcast you *have* to get everything right. You cannot correct a small mistake with a laugh or a joke as is possible on lighter occasions. So I thought I would make sure to get a good start. Richard was to be stationed in St James' Street and I was placed at Hyde Park Corner, and it was arranged that he would hand over to me just as the head of the procession came up the slope towards the Corner. I did my homework and discovered that at the head would be five mounted Metropolitan Policemen. I even found out from the PRO at Scotland Yard that they would be on white horses. So I wrote out an opening sentence – something I would never usually do. But I felt that if only I could get off on the right note all would be well.

On the few nights before the funeral I said to myself before I went to sleep: 'And here comes the procession now. Led by five Metro-politan Policemen mounted on white horses.' Not brilliant I agree, but at least it would be factual and get me going. From then on I felt I could cope. On the day I was sitting on our stand at Hyde Park Corner listening to Richard in my headphones describing the procession winding its way up St James' Street. Keith Rogers our producer told me to stand by and then I heard Richard cue to me with the words . . . 'The head of the procession should now be reaching Hyde Park Corner, so over now to our commentator there, Brian Johnston.'

At this moment I could just see the caps of the five policemen at the bottom of the slope as Keith Rogers said: 'Go ahead, Brian,' into my headphones. So off I went with my little prepared piece. 'Yes here comes the procession now led by five Metropolitan Policemen mounted on . . .' and then to my horror I realised that they were not on white horses but black. My mind went a complete blank. I had rehearsed and rehearsed 'white horses' so often that I panicked and could not think of any other colour. So what I said was . . . 'mounted on (pause) horseback'. This brought an immediate response from Keith Rogers in my headphones: 'What on earth do you think they are mounted on? Camels?' So my carefully prepared start had gone for a Burton and it took me quite a few minutes to recover. Never again did I learn a written piece beforehand.

I had one other nagging thought at the back of my mind as the cortège bearing the coffin approached. I had to keep saying to myself, don't say it, don't say it. It was a phrase often used by commentators doing this type of commentary, but which would have been disastrous on this occasion. It was: 'Here comes the main body of the procession'. Luckily I never said it! But as you can imagine this was not a broadcast I enjoyed doing, though I was naturally honoured to be chosen for such a big national occasion.

21

Many a slip . . .

1952 was a key year for television cricket, because the Holme Moss Transmitter was now open, which meant that for the first time we were able to televise the Old Trafford and Headingley Tests.

The Indians were the visitors and we went to Worcester to televise their first match. As usual it rained and we had to fill in time with interviews under umbrellas. The Indians had an amusing and volatile manager called Gupte, who spoke very quickly but perhaps did not understand English all that perfectly. Anyway I was interviewing him and asking him about the Indian team. 'What about your batsmen?' I asked. 'Oh, we've got seven very good batsmen indeed,' he replied.

'And your bowlers?' 'Oh, six very good bowlers indeed.' I thought we were not getting very far so switched my questions to him personally. 'What about yourself. Are you a selector?' 'No,' he replied. 'I'm a Christian'! I hurriedly changed the subject and asked him what he thought of our weather!

Television could not have wished for a better start to the Test series. The first Test was at Headingley and Len Hutton was captain of England – the first time ever that a professional had been chosen to captain England in this country. It was also the first Test appearance of a young twenty-one year old fast bowler from Yorkshire called Freddie Trueman. And to cap everything, in their second innings India were 0 for 4, Trueman taking three and Bedser one. So television's first appearance at Headingley was quite something, though the rest of the four Test series was disappointing, England winning easily 3–0. The new boy 'Fiery Fred' took twenty-nine wickets in only four Tests, with some really devastating fast bowling which the Indians understandably did not relish. Not a bad start to a Test career.

During my time as a cricket commentator I have become famous for some of the gaffes I have made on the air – all of them unintentional I assure you! During this summer I made what was probably the first of them when I was broadcasting for radio on the Hampshire *v.* Surrey match at Southampton. Rex Alston was up at Edgbaston covering one of Warwickshire's matches and close of play there was not until 7 pm.

At 6.30 pm at Southampton as the players left the field I said something like: 'Well that's close of play here with Hampshire 301 all out. But they go on playing till 7 o'clock at Edgbaston so over there now for some more balls from Rex Alston.' I really did not mean to say it and luckily none of my bosses seemed to notice. But Rex's wife Elspeth did, and she has not yet forgiven me.

Later that year, I appeared on a cricket quiz at Eton. This had become a regular annual event following the first one a few years earlier at which Sir Pelham Warner had been on the panel. I am told that he never really recovered from the very first question put to him by a small innocent-looking boy at the back of the hall. 'Please, sir,' he asked, 'was W. G. Grace a cheat?' I gather there was a deadly hush while Sir Pelham turned pale at the iniquity of the question.

Remembering some of the stories told about W.G. it was perhaps not such an unreasonable question to ask. But after the first shock Sir Pelham gallantly defended the G.O.M. of cricket. But some of the W.G. stories *do* need explaining away. Like the occasion when a ball from a fast bowler just flicked off W.G.'s off bail. W.G. stood his ground remarking to the umpire: 'Very windy today isn't it umpire?' 'Yes doctor it is', replied the umpire. 'And be careful it doesn't blow your cap off on the way back to the pavilion!'

In spite of doing so much cricket I still kept up with my contacts in the entertainment world. We continued to broadcast excerpts from the West End shows and during the summer started a new series – *Saturday night at the London Palladium*. This was at a time when they were featuring big American stars like Jack Benny, Bob Hope, Betty Hutton, Sophie Tucker and Schnozzle Durante. We used to broadcast their acts live at the second house to the Light Programme listeners, and it was great fun meeting all these great entertainers.

In addition we began to broadcast the Royal Variety Performance every year. We recorded it on the Monday night and I did a linking commentary for an edited version which went out the following Sunday. The great thing was that it meant that Pauline and I went along to the actual show, and in addition I attended all the rehearsals. With so much of my job now divided between cricket and the theatre I was on top of the world, and had to keep pinching myself to make sure it wasn't all a dream. I was being paid to do what I enjoyed doing most and realised that I was lucky enough to have a job in a million – the only one of its kind.

1952 finally taught me the danger of practical jokes. I played one on a friend which completely misfired and I hope and believe it taught me a lesson. In February I was doing a *Let's go somewhere* from a motor torpedo boat off Portsmouth. On the way down I passed the house of a friend called Cecil Fielden who lived in Hampshire.

At the time there were a number of burglaries from country houses by a ladder gang who got away with thousands of pounds worth of jewellery. I was staying with a friend of mine called James Whatman who lived a few miles from Guildford, and I took him along with me to the broadcast. I also had with me another BBC colleague – Douglas Fleming – who after being an announcer had just joined the OB department and wanted to see how an OB worked.

We did the programme and then returned with the naval boys to an hotel on the quayside. After a few drinks one of us – I'm sure it was *not* me! – remembered that we had passed the house of Cecil Fielden on the way down. Why not ring him up and pretend we were the ladder gang? It was no use James Whatman or myself doing it as our voices would be recognised, so we persuaded Douglas Fleming to do it. It was really a very silly thing to do as it was extremely unlikely that the ladder gang would ring someone up before burglaring them.

Anyway, Douglas rang up and in rather a sinister voice with a lot of heavy breathing said he was the ladder gang and that they were on the way to burgle the house. We just could not believe that anyone would be taken in. Unfortunately we did not know that Cecil Fielden was in bed with a high temperature so that the telephone was answered by a French governess whom they had.

After he had given the message Douglas rang off not realising the commotion he had caused in the house. The governess had hysterics, and Cecil rang the police from his bed. The call was traced to the hotel but luckily by then we had left. However, blissfully unconscious of the hue and cry we stopped at a callbox on the way back to Guildford and rang the house again to say we were on the way and it would not be long now. Again we could not believe that anyone would take it seriously.

We went back to James Whatman's house laughing at what we had thought was a good joke. We did not realise that the police had been called out and had waited in vain for us hidden in the garden of the Fielden house. Nor did we know until later that the French governess gave in her notice on the spot. This was extremely serious as she always acted as a sitter-in and so made it possible for Mrs Fielden to go on parties or on trips to London.

But we knew nothing of this at the time and thought no more about it until about a week later the local bobby walked up the drive of James Whatman's house and asked to speak to him: 'Certainly,' said James, 'come in and have a drink.' 'I am sorry sir, but I am on duty,' was the ominous reply! He then began to question James as to his whereabouts on the Saturday night in question, and in the end got a semi-confession out of him. He would not reveal, however, with whom he had been and also quite rightly denied that he had done any of the ringing up himself. We lived in suspense for quite a few weeks, dreading the knock on the front door. But luckily it never came.

I think what happened was that people talked at a party and Cecil Fielden heard James Whatman's name linked with the episode. He knew the Chief Constable and I suspect suggested he should send the bobby to interview James and give him a fright. If so, he certainly succeeded, but nothing further came of the affair. James I think later told Cecil the whole story and as a result since then the Fieldens and Johnstons have not been the closest friends!

Anyhow I learnt my lesson, though it was bad luck that Cecil was ill at the time so that the ladies had to deal with the calls. He was a tough character and would not have panicked, and would almost certainly have realised that it was a 'joke'.

On one occasion he went into his office where unknown to him an intruder had forced his way in. On hearing Cecil arrive he hid under the desk. Cecil quite unsuspecting sat down at the desk and as he stretched his legs out felt them contact a body. Most of us would have jumped up and shouted for help. Cecil just sat where he was, dialled 999 and after asking for the police calmly said: 'I have got an intruder under my desk. Could you please send someone round to arrest him?' You see what I mean. It was bad luck that he had been ill that night. He would certainly have told the ladder gang where to go in no uncertain terms.

1953 was not only Coronation Year but also the year in which England won back the Ashes after nineteen years. Lindsay Hassett led the popular Australian team and it was a splendidly fought series. The first four Tests were drawn, with England just saving the game at Lord's thanks to the defiant fifth wicket partnership of 163 between Willie Watson and Trevor Bailey on the last day.

It was a tense, thrilling struggle as they kept the Australian bowlers at bay for over four and a quarter hours in the heat. I shall always remember the look of intense agony on Bailey's face when he was finally out caught off the first real attacking stroke he had played in his entire innings. He also saved England from losing the 4th Test at Headingley when Australia got to within thirty runs of victory with six wickets still in hand. This was not such a worthy effort as his seventy-one at Lord's as he bowled six overs wide down the leg-side well out of reach of the batsmen in a successful attempt to stem their rate of scoring. In fact Graham Hole did manage to reach one ball which he swept high to Tom Graveney at deep square leg who caught it high above his head. Had he not done so, it would have been a six.

We covered this exciting match on television with Jim Swanton, Peter West and Jack Fingleton as my fellow commentators. During the match there was a mysterious happening which we never unravelled. Jim Swanton was commentating on the play when a man walked past our commentary point. He was carrying a ladder over his shoulder and round his neck was a lavatory seat! He caused quite a commotion in the crowd as he disappeared under one of the stands. Jim dealt with the situation with his usual aplomb and completely ignored the man, even though he had been picked up by our cameras. Instead Jim directed the viewers' attention to Lindwall's beautiful action out in the middle.

The sequence to this event came about ten minutes later when the man returned still with the ladder but minus the seat. What had he done with it and why if he had to fix it, did he need a ladder? Do they sit that high in Yorkshire? Jim was still the commentator and the viewers were not given any assessment of the situation by him. Perhaps it was just as well that I was not the commentator at the time!

The four draws built up to a wonderful climax at the Oval, and I was lucky enough to be commentating during the final stages, when Denis Compton joined Bill Edrich with England needing forty-four runs to win the match and the Ashes. When they were within nine runs of victory Hassett conceded victory by putting himself and Arthur Morris on to bowl. With four runs needed the tension and excitement became unbearable. The crowd, shouting their encouragement, had edged right up to the boundary ropes, ready to rush on to the field. Morris bowled one of his 'chinamen' (an off break from a left-arm bowler) outside the leg stump. This is it, I thought, as Compton played his famous sweep. The crowd started to creep over the ropes, but it was a false alarm. Alan Davidson had put out his great paw at backward short leg and stopped it.

The next ball was just the same and this time Compton made no mistake. He swept the ball for four down to the gas holders and bolted for the pavilion. Whether in fact the ball ever reached the boundary I don't think anyone ever knew. It was enveloped by the crowd as they surged on to the field. Edrich and Compton had to fight their way back holding their bats aloft just like submarine periscopes over the heads of the crowd. On television I'm afraid that I was overcome by excitement and emotion. As Compton swept the four for victory all I could do was shout into the microphone; 'It's the Ashes! It's the

Ashes!' It was certainly my greatest moment so far, as a TV commentator. It also made Arthur Morris the most televised Test Match bowler ever, as for several years this last over was used as a demonstration film sequence in all the TV shops.

For the Coronation I was again one of the TV commentators on the route of the procession.

This time I was in Hyde Park and shared the commentary there with Bernard Braden. It was a filthy day, and we all got horribly wet. We had had to get up at some unearthly hour in order to make sure of getting to our position, and then of course we had to wait for about six hours before anything happened. By the time the procession had reached us so far as I remember Sir Winston Churchill had 'fallen out' from the line of vehicles. But like everyone else we were enchanted by the friendly buxom figure of Queen Salote of Tonga in her open carriage. In spite of the pouring rain she sat there without even an umbrella waving and blowing kisses to the damp but cheering crowds. Alongside her, a small man was sitting; when asked who he was, Noël Coward is reputed to have said: 'Her lunch!'

Royal occasions have always been dangerous hazards to commentators and many of the most famous broadcasting gaffes have been made when describing royalty. Max Robertson said of the Queen of Norway as she arrived at the Guildhall for lunch – 'She is looking charming in an off-the-hat face'!

Audrey Russell once told her listeners that the Queen Mother was wearing dark black, and at the Lord's Test of 1969 when the New Zealand team were presented to the Queen in front of the pavilion Robert Hudson said: 'A tremendous occasion this for a touring side. It's a moment that they will always forget.'

Then there was the commentator who had to describe the departure of the King and Queen for Canada in 1939. They were to cross the Atlantic on HMS *Vanguard* and there was to be a twenty minute OB of the scenes at the quayside. The commentator had done his homework and filled in the time with describing the scene, the cheering crowds, the band of the Royal Marines, the decorations, details of the *Vanguard* and the programme of the tour in Canada. That should have been enough but unfortunately the tugs had difficulty in getting the huge ship away from the quay and it all took far longer than the BBC had bargained for.

Twenty minutes became twenty-five and the commentator was

getting desperate for something new to say. For the umpteenth time he mentioned that the King and Queen were waving from the bridge, and then suddenly noticed that the Queen was no longer there. Grateful for something new he said, 'I see now that the Queen has left the bridge and gone below for a moment.' He then got stuck and in desperation a few seconds later added . . . 'and I can see water coming through the side of the ship'!

There was also the Commonwealth commentator who at one of the Independence Day celebrations was talking about the late Duchess of Kent, then representing the Queen. As her carriage passed by he said: 'The Duchess is now going into the President's Palace to take off her clothes ready for the reception.' But of course none of these mistakes will equal that of the newspaper during the Jubilee celebrations in 1935. The reporter had written . . . 'Queen Mary then passed over Westminster Bridge.' Unfortunately the printer replaced the *a* in passed with an *i*!

I suppose the most amusing mistake on TV happened when Wynford Vaughan-Thomas was the commentator at the launching of the *Ark Royal* at Birkenhead by the Queen Mother. The producer Ray Lakeland told Wynford beforehand: 'Don't talk while the Queen Mother is breaking the bottle against the bows, and keep quiet as the ship slowly glides down the slipway. We shall be taking the cheering of the crowds and the music of the Band. Wait until the *Ark Royal* actually hits the water and then start talking to your heart's content.'

All went according to plan. No. 1 camera showed the Queen Mother making her short speech and breaking the bottle. No. 2 camera showed the ship as it gradually moved, and No. 3 had shots of the cheering crowd. Ray punched all these up in turn so that they came on to the screens of the viewers at home. Then just before the *Ark Royal* reached the water he noticed that No. 1 camera had got a marvellous picture of the Queen Mother smiling in that charming way she has.

Ray was so enchanted that he forgot all he had told Wynford and immediately pressed the button which filled the viewers' screens with the Queen Mother. This unfortunately coincided with the moment the *Ark Royal* entered the water. Wynford was watching this and not his screen, so remembering his instructions started to talk: 'There she is', he cried, 'the huge vast bulk of her'! He then looked at his monitor and to his horror saw the Queen Mother not the *Ark Royal*. Even this usually volatile Welshman was at a loss for words. But as you might expect when the Queen Mother was told about it afterwards she was delighted.

Another Royal occasion in the following year taught me the importance of learning the difference between radio and television commentary technique. On the radio the commentator is the eyes and ears of the listener. He must paint with words the picture of what he is seeing and hearing. In addition to having the gift of the gab he must therefore have good powers of description and an extensive vocabulary. But on TV the cameras become the viewers' eyes and the problem for the commentator is to know when to talk and when to shut up.

A golden rule is only to speak when you can add to the picture. I have always tried to imagine myself as a friend or expert guide sitting alongside someone at an event, and so think of myself as speaking to one particular viewer, not the millions who may be watching. It is my job to fill in all the details not obvious from the picture. I must try to identify people and things, give interesting and pertinent facts about them, and to explain the ceremony or event and what is its theme, purpose and traditions. In other words to dot the 'i's without being too intrusive and taking care not to describe the action of something the viewer can see for himself on his screen. In general it is always better to talk too little than too much.

In 1954 the Queen and Prince Philip visited Australia and on their return were to sail up to Tower Bridge in the Royal Yacht, and travel from there in a launch up to Westminster Bridge. There they were to get into an open carriage and drive up Whitehall and the Mall to Buckingham Palace. Television OB's were to cover this return journey, with Richard Dimbleby at Westminster Bridge, myself halfway up Whitehall and Berkeley Smith at Buckingham Palace.

In our conference beforehand it was decided that Richard should deal with all details of the reception at the pier. I was to cover the journey down Whitehall and give all the necessary information about the horses and the carriage and the escort of Household Cavalry with the Blues in front and the Life Guards in the rear. Berkeley Smith was to describe the arrival at Buckingham Palace. On the day it was foggy and the river was shrouded in mist. When the broadcast started I heard in my headphones Richard identifying all the people assembled to welcome the Queen or to be presented to her. There was the Queen Mother, Princess Margaret, various ministers, a Lord Lieutenant and a

Mayor, plus the Guard of Honour from the Queen's Company 1st Battalion Grenadier Guards.

Richard as usual was doing his job superbly with complete confidence and ease. He did, however, keep mentioning that the Royal launch was still not in sight and that it must have been delayed by the mist on the river. Soon even Richard began to run out of material and after a bit I heard him describing the carriage and giving the names of the Windsor Greys. How one was called Monty, another Eisenhower, and that they had been given by the Queen of Holland.

He then went on to give full details of the Escort, naming the officers, describing the uniforms, and adding a bit of regimental history. All this time I was crossing out the notes I had made until there was nothing left on my bits of paper. At last the Royal launch came into sight and Richard was able to describe the arrival and reception on the pier. Then when the Queen and Prince Philip had got into the carriage I heard him hand over to me halfway up Whitehall.

The next day, people congratulated me on my commentary and said it was one of the best I had ever done and that I even matched Dimbleby. Actually what I had said was something like: 'Yes the carriage is just turning out of Westminster Square into Whitehall.' I then watched it in silence as it passed down Whitehall and when I saw in my monitor that it had gone through the cheering crowds in Trafalgar Square and under Admiralty Arch into the Mall I said: 'And as the Queen and Prince Philip reach their home straight after their long journey, over to Berkeley Smith at Buckingham Palace.'

In other words I said precisely nothing because there was nothing to add to the picture. The viewers knew who were in the carriage, Richard had already filled in all the other details, so what *was* there left to say? It was a salutary lesson in the art of TV commentary.

I appeared on the *Twenty Questions* panel for the first time when Kenneth Horne was absent and Richard took over as Question Master. It was fun to do but in my eagerness I wasted quite a few questions and was not too popular with the regular members of the panel – Anona Winn, Jack Train and Joy Adamson. They had evolved a formula for finding out quickly if the object was animal, vegetable or mineral and then what sort of animal or mineral. But I didn't do too badly and at the end of one of their series I was asked to get up an OB team to take on the panel.

My team included Audrey Russell and Raymond Baxter and although we did not win, we did at least manage to draw. It was an amusing contest but I don't think there has ever been one since. First one team was in the studio and tried to guess the object. Then they went out and the other team came in and tried to guess the same object. The team which took the least number of guesses under twenty were the winners of that particular round.

I also became chairman of a regular quiz on radio called *What's it all about?* The panel included Kenneth Horne, Celia Johnson and Dilys Powell. I had to read out cards sent in by listeners relating some extraordinary incident which had happened to them. The panel then had to guess how and why it had happened. It was fairly childish but became quite popular. I also began to cover the Motor Show, a job I always found frustrating with so many wonderful cars well out of reach of my commentator's pocket.

Tommy Trinder used to tell of the very posh salesman in morning dress on the Rolls-Royce stand at the Motor Show. There he was alone on the roped-off stand leaning nonchalantly against a gleaming car costing goodness knows how much. The milling crowd looked enviously at the car and occasionally asked a few questions, knowing full well that a Rolls was really miles beyond their reach. One day a chap leaned over the ropes and asked the salesman the way to the gents. 'I'll show you myself,' said the salesman, and leaving the stand led the enquirer through the crowds to the other side of the hall. When they reached their target, the chap thanked the salesman for being so kind and asked him why he had taken so much trouble. 'Candidly, old boy,' said the salesman, 'your's was the first genuine enquiry I have had all week'!

Pauline and I once again had an increase in our family – this time another boy, Andrew. He started to arrive on the afternoon of Saturday, 27 March just as we were watching the Grand National on TV. I am glad to say we were able to see 'Royal Tan' win the race before rushing Pauline off to the nursing home in Avenue Road.

In the summer Pakistan made their first tour of England and caused a sensation by winning the fourth and final Test at the Oval. They thus squared the series 1–1, and became the only country to win a Test Match on their first visit to England. It was a nasty wet summer and my two outstanding memories are the superb bowling by Fazal Mahmood with his leg-cutters, and an astonishing innings of 278 by Denis Compton in the Trent Bridge Test. It was to be his highest

Test innings and only took him four hours fifty minutes. I have only seen one other innings with such an array of orthodox and unorthodox strokes in top-class cricket – Gary Sobers' 254 for the World XI at Melbourne in 1972.

During 1955 I continued to spread my wings in TV when I took part in a quiz series on children's TV called *Ask your dad*. I was provided with a 'family' of two and we competed against Ross Salmon and his 'family'. At this time he owned a ranch on Dartmoor and was billed as the TV Cowboy complete with all the gear – hat, ropes, revolver, chaps – the lot. I was also called on to introduce *Sportsview* on several occasions when Peter Dimmock was away.

This was in the early days of the tele-prompter which is now in regular use by news-readers and presenters. It's a gadget whereby you can read a revolving script by looking into the lens of the camera. It's all done by a complicated system of mirrors and nowadays is operated by remote control by a special operator. But when I first used it I had to control the speed at which the script revolved by pressing on a switch with my foot – rather like a dentist and his drill. It was a nerve-wracking operation, for if you pressed too hard the script would disappear out of sight on the roller before you had time to read it! You had to apply just the right pressure to keep the next line on a level with your eyes.

Jack Cheetham's South Africans were a magnificent fielding side and only narrowly lost the series 2–3, all five Tests producing a result. I have always thought that the 3rd Test at Old Trafford was one of the best I have ever seen, South Africa winning by three wickets with three minutes to spare after the fortunes of the two sides had swayed backwards and forwards. In this match Paul Winslow scored his first Test hundred reaching it with a six off Tony Lock which nearly smashed one of our TV cameras on our scaffolding. This was a time when England had to rely too much on their captain Peter May to make the runs, though in spite of a badly swollen knee Denis Compton supported him gallantly. But their bowling strength was terrific and the selectors could call on Statham, Tyson, Bedser, Trueman, Lock, Laker, Appleyard, Wardle, Loader, Titmus and Bailey. What a choice!

The one sad thing about the series was that it marked the end of Frank Chester's career as an umpire after officiating in forty-eight Tests. He had been in considerable pain for the last two or three summers and towards the end had lost some of his great judgment and authority. But up to then at least he had undoubtedly been the best umpire in the world and Don Bradman always had the highest opinion of him. The overall standard of umpiring has always been better in England than anywhere else, partly because so much cricket is played but also because our umpires in first-class cricket are mostly old professionals who have played top-class cricket themselves. This helps them to understand the problems and difficulties of players out in the middle, and accounts for the fact that the relationship between players and umpires is so friendly.

Overseas, even in Australia, very few umpires have ever played first-class cricket themselves. This led to an amusing conversation between Don Bradman and Tom Crawford the old Kent player who was watching the Test series on Peter May's tour. Australia had an umpire who wore glasses but who had been highly thought of by Len Hutton's team on the previous tour. However, four years later he was making some quite embarrassing mistakes and Tom was saying that he thought it a pity that none of the umpires in Australia had played first-class cricket, and how much better they would be if they had. Sir Don would have none of it. 'What about X?' he said, referring to our bespectacled friend. 'He played quite a lot of top grade cricket *until his eyesight went* and he took up umpiring.' He then realised what he had said!

Basically umpires are friendly people and luckily have none of the officious gear of a soccer referee such as a shrill whistle and a little black book. Numerous stories are told about them and most of them are sympathetic. I always enjoy hearing a new one and here are one or two of my favourites.

In a village match a visiting batsman was hit high on the chest by the local fast bowler, the village blacksmith. He promptly appealed. To the batsman's amazement the local umpire gave him out lbw. As he passed the umpire on his way back to the pavilion the batsman said: 'I wasn't out. It hit me in the chest.' 'Well,' said the umpire, 'you look in tomorrow's *Gazette* and you will see that you were out right enough.' 'You look,' snorted the batsman, 'I am the Editor!'

Bill Reeves probably had more stories told about him than anyone except perhaps Alec Skelding. One of the best was when Walter Robins was captain of Middlesex. One day at Lord's Walter's bowling had been carted all over the place, so he decided to take himself off. Bill Reeves walked up to Robins who was feeling hot and annoyed with himself. 'Do you want your sweater Sir?' asked Reeves. 'No,' said Robins grumpily, 'keep the bloody thing and you know what you can do with it.' 'What sir? Swords and all?' said Reeves, referring to the three seacs or swords on the Middlesex sweater.

My favourite story occurred at the Duke of Norfolk's lovely ground at Arundel. His team were playing the Sussex Martlets but just before the start they found they had only one umpire. The Duke said he would go and get his butler Meadows who was cleaning the silver down at the Castle. He did not know much about cricket but would be better than nothing. So Meadows was fetched, put into a white coat and the game began with the Duke's side batting. They did not do too well and with seven wickets down the Duke himself came into bat. He was at the non-strikers' end and Meadows was standing at square leg. The batsman thought he had better give the Duke the strike, so pushed the ball to cover and called 'Come on, your Grace'.

Unfortunately the Duke slipped and cover point threw the ball over the top of the stumps to the wicket-keeper who whipped off the bails with the Duke yards short of the crease. 'How's that?' everyone roared, and looked at Meadows at square leg. There was a pregnant silence. What would he do? Would he give his master out? After a second or two's pause Meadows drew himself up to his full height and with his two hands in front of his chest in a way butlers have, he gave his verdict: 'His Grace is not in!'

22

How far can you go?

On the radio, Light Programme asked us to do a short series of a somewhat longer *Let's go somewhere* – fifteen minutes instead of the old three to four minute routine. This gave us more scope, so we decided to make the new show a test of the public's reactions to various things – rather like *Candid camera* which came later on ITV.

This time I had a producer and other people to help me but as before each programme with one exception was to be 'live', not recorded. Our first experiment was at Victoria Station, where we staged various incidents and I reported on the reactions of people to them. I wandered around disguised with a false beard under which was hidden my microphone with a small transmitter in my pocket. We started off with our producer Doug Fleming pretending to be a newspaper seller. He bought up some evening papers and stood there in an old macintosh and peak cap shouting out: 'Paper, paper, get your evening paper.' All this was quite normal except that on his stop press were scrawled the headlines: 'Mafeking Relieved'.

I stood watching as people went up to him and bought their papers. Most of them glanced at the placard as they did so. But no one seemed surprised or even remonstrated with Doug for announcing something which had taken place over fifty years ago.

Next, I took a parcel up to the left luggage office. Inside was a human skull which I had borrowed from some students. I had purposely split the parcel open in front so that when I presented it to the man behind the counter he could see the empty eye sockets staring out at him. I had expected him to show some surprise or curiosity. Instead he just had a good look and said: 'How long do you want to leave it sir?'

We had then arranged for the female announcer to say over the public address: 'Will the passengers who took the 6 o'clock train to Brighton from platform 14 please return it as it's needed first thing in the morning!' She repeated this several times and yet I could not spot anyone in the station concourse who seemed to find anything strange or funny in the announcement.

Finally, I went behind a pillar and put on a wolf's mask which my children had been given for Christmas. I put my hat on top with the wolf's ears sticking up at the sides, turned up my coat collar and walked about among the rush-hour crowds. One or two looked at me and did a double take. But no one challenged me, nor stared for any length of time. Nor did any inspector or porter ask me what I thought I was doing. They all seemed to accept the fact that there was a man with a wolf's face among them. At the end of this broadcast we really did feel that the reputation which Britishers have for being phlegmatic was fully justified.

Even more so after another broadcast which we did with me disguised as a waiter in a restaurant, with a ginger wig, a phoney French accent and the name of Alphonse. We asked a friendly restaurateur to book us three tables close to each other one evening, and to allow us to plant a microphone hidden in a bowl of flowers on each table. We then got Henry Riddell, Doug Fleming and Cliff Michelmore to ask two people each to dinner at the time of our broadcast, warning them to be punctual. I took my cue in the kitchens and explained to listeners what we were going to do. First we switched on the microphone on Henry's table to see what he and his two guests were talking about. We quickly wished we hadn't as he had asked a Canadian and his wife and the man was busy saying how much he loathed his job and what a terrible man his boss was.

So I hurriedly went out with the soup which Henry had ordered beforehand. I placed two plates in front of the guests and when a 'commie' handed me the third one, I pretended to drop it and upset it straight into Henry's lap. He had been warned and was wearing an old suit but as arranged played up magnificently and started to tear the most terrible strips off me at the top of his voice.

I had warned listeners that this would happen and that we wanted to see how the two guests would react. They did so by pretending not to notice what was going on and started a conversation with each other about a film which they would like to see. They just left Henry to it, as if nothing was happening.

I then went to Doug's table, where I served some sole which he had ordered, to him and his two guests, another husband and wife. I gave the lady and Doug a most beautiful sole each but on the husband's plate there was just the bare backbone of a sole with only the head and tail complete. Doug pretended not to see and asked them both if their fish was to their liking. The wife said yes hers was perfect but the husband instead of being candid said something like: 'Well there's not too much of it, but it looks jolly good all the same, thanks very much.' What manners!

Lastly I went to the final table where Cliff and his wife Jean had asked a wine connoisseur to be their guest. During the afternoon we had drawn the cork of a bottle of the very best claret, poured a little away and then topped up with some Angostura bitters, tomato ketchup and a pinch or two of pepper. We had then given the bottle a good shake and left it to settle down. (I have never dared to tell John Arlott about this!)

Anyway, I presented the bottle to Cliff, saying it was the wine he had ordered and would he like to taste it. He said no but that his friend the expert would do so. This was the big moment. What would he say? I poured out a little of the wine into a glass and the expert sniffed it. 'A most unusual bouquet,' he said, then took a sip. We were watching him closely and he somehow managed to hide his true feelings.

'This is one I haven't met before', he said without wincing, 'but I am sure it will make a pleasant drink with our dinner.' Like the other two he was not prepared to embarrass his host by any criticism, but goodness knows what he was feeling.

We finished the broadcast by me dropping a pile of plates and getting the sack from the restaurateur in front of everyone. As soon as it was over he and I then rushed round to the other tables to explain what had been happening, while our three hosts made peace with their guests. They all took it very well and we made sure that they then had a super dinner, washed down with some genuine claret.

With the help of Kenneth Horne and Raymond Glendenning I next decided to test the generosity of Londoners. All of us were heavily disguised, Raymond doing something funny with his handle-bar moustache which made him look like a Chinaman. He took up a position in Leicester Square with a barrel organ, and I pushed an old upright piano to a street just off Piccadilly Circus. Kenneth was near Charing Cross Station and when the broadcast started he began to sing *Comrades* and continued to do so for the next fourteen minutes.

I played *Underneath the arches* as usual, but Raymond was luckier as he could change the tunes on his barrel organ. I am afraid the Londoners did not appreciate us much. I cannot remember the details but I know that Kenneth did best with about five bob, I was second, and poor Raymond a bad third.

It was after this broadcast that Berkeley Smith told me it would have been fun to *see* us all performing and could we not do a similar sort of thing on TV? We went into it very carefully but eventually turned down the idea, as we thought it would never be possible to keep it secret and so make it genuine. On radio it was easy with our small hidden mikes transmitting back to a near-by control van. With TV it would have meant hiding the cameras, the cables and the hordes of technicians that normally go with an OB. People would be bound to know about it beforehand and bang would go the authenticity so essential to make such a series viable. Jonathan Routh did it with great success in *Candid camera* but how he managed to keep it all secret I have never discovered.

Kenneth Horne again helped me when we proved how difficult it is to give real money away in the streets of London. We made the Victoria Palace our base and sallied forth in turn to try to give some ten-shilling notes away to the passers-by.

Kenneth had to have a large black beard to hide his well-known features, and told people that he was carrying out the wish of a dead aunt. It was the anniversary of her death and each year she wanted money to be given away in her memory. 'So will you accept ten shillings?' Kenneth asked. But believe it or not, he failed to get rid of a single note! People just stared or brushed him aside.

I was slightly more successful, getting rid of exactly one to a soldier returning off leave. He grabbed it gratefully. But everyone else seemed embarrassed or pretended not to hear me, though one rather posh elderly lady did mutter, 'disgusting'! I don't blame her really as I was dressed up as a filthy old tramp and in a wheedling, whining voice said that I had just won the pools and wanted people to share my luck with me. I suppose it was rather incongruous for a tramp to be offering brand new ten-shilling notes but I still find it strange that only one person took one.

For another of these broadcasts I was kitted out in a smart commissionaire's uniform and stood as still as I could for about ten minutes on the staircase at Madame Tussauds. I was made up with side whiskers and a wax moustache to look as similar as possible to the famous wax dummy commissionaire halfway up the stairs.

Generations of children have gone up to him and asked the way or the time, only to find that he was not real. I stood at the top of the stairs ramrod stiff, staring straight in front of me, doing my best not to move. People came right up to me, prodded me in the stomach and asked me questions. When I didn't answer one woman even tweaked my moustache! By then I think she was convinced that I was a dummy so I slowly lowered the lid of my right eye and gave her a wink. She let out an hysterical scream which gave the game away.

The one broadcast we had to record was a trip I made in a balloon from Cardington. We did it in March when the weather was really quite unsuitable, and we had to choose the moment when the wind was below the maximum allowed – 20 mph I believe it was. Anyhow we were hastily called early in the morning and told that conditions were just all right, although there was a forecast of snow. I had an engineer with me, Ted Castle, and he, myself and the RAF officer who was to be our pilot, all got into the basket.

Inside there was not much room as our basket contained some sandbags, though not as many as there should have been due to the weight of our recording gear. We were released and soared gently up into the sky, emptying some of the bags over the side as we went, to make us lighter.

We reached about 1,000 feet and cruised gently along. It was all very peaceful and so quiet that we could hear people talking on the ground below. It was freezing cold and beginning to snow so I recorded a few impressions of what it was like in the balloon. I then noticed our pilot looking rather anxiously at some high ground ahead of us and he began hurriedly to empty out the remaining sandbags. But I suppose our gear was too heavy as we did not get any higher. We got nearer and nearer to what was a range of hills and the pilot was now seriously worried that we might not clear them. So he pulled the quick-release valve and the balloon began to deflate and we sank down rapidly towards the ground.

Frankly, I was scared stiff, as we were going faster and faster but I managed to record my rather hysterical commentary on our descent. We hit a ploughed field with a tremendous bump and shot about twenty feet up into the air. Our gear was thrown all over the basket and we hung on grimly as we hit the ground a second time. The wind then caught the deflated balloon and we were dragged across the field, finally ending up against a hedge.

I have never been so relieved as when I stepped out of that basket. We had to stand about in the snow until a search party found us. Looking back I am convinced that we should never have taken off in the first place. How dangerous it really was I don't know. I was too scared to learn the truth so never did ask the pilot. Remarkably, we managed to get a programme out of my recordings though my final commentary as we were coming down was largely incoherent, and all the listener heard of the actual landing was a loud crash and then silence as our recording gear disintegrated.

Towards the end of the year I had an accident at the annual Lord's Taverners Ball at Grosvenor House. Each year there is a sporting event in which the Taverners take on the experts of a particular sport or game. Needless to say by hook but largely by crook the Taverners always manage to win.

The sport this particular year was athletics and I took part in a three-legged race with Macdonald Hobley and Peter Haigh as my partners. I was the middle man with my arms round their necks, and we were going quite well when we slipped on the polished floor. I had no arms to break my fall and landed heavily on my left shoulder. It was agony but luckily Bill Tucker the orthopaedic surgeon was there and gave me some pain-killing pills.

I went to Bill the next day hardly able to move my arm and he diagnosed a dislocated shoulder. This meant going for heat treatment, massage and manipulation for a month or two which made life a bit difficult. But in OBs we kept to the old theatrical tradition that the show must go on, and I never actually missed a broadcast as a result of it. In fact my contribution to the Christmas Day programme was to be thrown into the sea by the Shiverers Club at Brighton – the only way they could get me to join them in their daily bathe. It was of course freezing cold but my shouts were more because of the pain from my shoulder as they picked me up and swung me in.

23
The show must go on

Mention the wet summer of 1956 to any cricketer and he will almost certainly think of Jim Laker, who not only took forty-six wickets in the series against Australia but performed the incredible feat of taking 19 for 90 in the 4th Test at Old Trafford. Laker thus became the first and only bowler to take ten wickets in one innings of a Test, and I cannot believe that any of these three records will ever be equalled, let alone broken. Peter May's side won the series 2–1 and so kept the Ashes.

The Australians under Ian Johnson just could not cope with Laker's off-spin but they will also tell you that the perfidious Albion prepared pitches to suit Laker and Lock, especially at Old Trafford. As you can imagine, this match provided thrilling television as Jim took all his wickets from the Stretford end where our cameras are always situated. This meant that viewers got a perfect view of the turning ball unimpeded by the batsman and wicket-keeper. I remember going across to the pavilion afterwards to collect Jim to do an interview for TV and he was by far the calmest man on the ground. From his cool, casual air you might have thought he had taken a couple of wickets in a parents' match.

In addition to the cricket I did a mixed assortment of jobs for TV, three of them connected with water. I was surprisingly selected to introduce the Boat Race broadcast and had to talk knowledgeably about the course and the crews. They must have been pushed that year!

I also took part in a number of the *Saturday night out* programmes. One of them was from a Turkish bath in Harrogate and the cameras showed me lying on the Begoni cabinet, a kind of massage table which gives the victim a series of electric shocks in the bottom. What for, I never discovered, but it certainly made me jump up and down like a yo-yo.

The cameras also paid a visit to the Serpentine to demonstrate the life-saving abilities of boys' clubs. For some reason I was put in a boat dressed as a city gent in bowler-hat, pin-stripe suit and reading an evening paper. The boys tipped me out of the boat and then proceeded to 'rescue' me and haul me back to the bank. As I reached the water's edge one of them handed me back my bowler-hat and dripping wet I put it on my head and walked off into the crowd as if nothing had happened.

For the radio I went on one of several trips abroad with General Sir Brian Horrocks. He and I became a sort of double act for the unveiling ceremonies of the Cross of Remembrance at the War Graves Commission war cemeteries. Over the years we went to Dunkirk, Nijmegen, Caen, Athens and in this year to Mount Cassino in Italy.

Sir Brian was a wonderfully amusing companion and a great broadcaster. I used to cover the actual service and ceremony, while he did an introduction dealing with the events in that particular theatre of war. It was always a comfort to visit these cemeteries and to see how beautifully they were all kept up and maintained. What was so nice was that in Holland especially the local children used to put flowers regularly on the graves.

Pauline came to Mount Cassino with me on this trip and we spent a glorious week at Positano before going up to Cassino. We had an unusual bath in the hotel at Positano. The end of the bath, where the taps were, was a fish tank so that as you lay relaxing in the bath fish were pressing their noses against the glass of their tank watching you. Highly embarrasing!

On arrival at Cassino we decided to go up the winding road to the Monastery silhouetted at the top. Pauline and the General went ahead in one car and at the entrance there was a notice in Italian. I saw them both look at it and Pauline then say something to the General which seemed to amuse him.

It turned out that the notice said that no pregnant woman was allowed to enter. Pauline had just discovered that week that she was pregnant again, but she had not yet had the courage to tell me as we had planned to call a halt to the additions to our family. She felt she had to ask the General's advice what she ought to do, and he naturally told her to say nothing about it. He reasoned that if her husband did not even know the monks were unlikely to find out!

In November I went into King Edward VII's Hospital for Officers for another hernia operation – on the other side. There was a strange coincidence about this. I had gone to see our family doctor, Dr R. Cove-Smith, the old rugger international who won twenty-eight caps for England. He is a large, burly, genial man now but I would not have liked to have met him in the middle of a scrum. A remarkable thing about him is that for all his size and outward toughness no one could be gentler with children. Anyway he sent me to see a surgeon in Harley Street to fix up an operation.

The surgeon examined me, noted my other hernia scar and asked me when and by whom it had been done. 'By some army surgeon who came from London Hospital and who operated on me in the Military Hospital at Salisbury. I reckon he did a rather good job.' 'Yes, I agree', said the surgeon. 'I must have been in good form that day and I'll do my best to match it on the other side.' It was the same surgeon!

I don't think he remembered me but recognised his own handiwork and of course knew he had been at Salisbury at that time. Anyway he did another splendid job and I had a fortnight in hospital and then a short convalescence at Eastbourne. This was nice for me as my mother was suffering from rheumatoid arthritis and was in a private nursing home there.

I returned to work in the middle of December in time for all the Christmas activities.

As usual, Raymond Baxter and I broadcast for radio on Boxing Day from the Bertram Mills Circus at Olympia. He used to do the commentary at the ringside and I did interviews with the artists outside the ring, and this year I learnt the value of being able to keep talking. I had finished my interviews and handed back to Raymond to describe the next act, and said to Bernard Mills: 'They're not due to come back to me again, but just in case they do, be a good chap and have an animal available which we can talk about.'

Bernard went off and in my headphones I heard Raymond describing what was going on inside the ring. There was a man on a motor-bike circling round and round inside a big cage twenty feet or so above the ring. There was a hole at the bottom of the cage but as Raymond was explaining, so long as the rider kept up his pace his machine would clear the gap each time. But if by chance his speed did slacken or his engine were to stall, he would fall right through on to the sawdust ring below. As Raymond was saying all this the rider was riding the bike with one hand and trying to take off his jacket with the other. As he did so, possibly because his loose jacket caught in his rear wheel, his engine cut out and just as Raymond had said he would, he plunged through the hole on to the ground below.

Raymond had to think quickly. This was Boxing Day with an audience made up of children. It was radio, not TV, so they would not know that an accident had taken place. He made up his mind quickly and said . . . 'and as the act finishes let's go straight back to Brian Johnston behind the scenes for some more interviews.' I heard this cue as I looked through the entrance to the ring and saw the poor rider lying prostrate in the sawdust. I turned round hopefully and there to my relief was Bernard leading a nice-looking white horse towards me.

'Yes, welcome back,' I said, 'we have an interesting animal here to talk about, a horse! What's its name, Bernard?' We then proceeded to talk about this very ordinary animal for three minutes or so, while they cleared up the mess in the ring. We looked at the beast's teeth, felt his fetlocks, patted his rump and talked non-stop about him until Raymond was ready for us with the next act – some performing dogs. The next day hardly anyone knew that anything untoward had happened, though they thought the act had ended rather abruptly, and that the horse was not perhaps worthy of such a long interview. But the point was that the children at home did not have to hear details of the accident. The gift of the gab at least proved itself useful on this occasion.

1957 was a sad year for me, as my mother died after a long illness. She was seventy-seven and had been a wonderful mother to all of our family. I had been going down to Eastbourne as often as I could to see her and was due to go down again on Sunday, 14 April.

I was at home to lunch on the Saturday as I was to do some interviews in the afternoon at our local garage. It was for a record request programme and the idea was to ask drivers filling up with petrol for their choice of records. During lunch the telephone rang and it was the matron from the nursing home telling me that my mother had died. It was too late to get someone else to do the broadcast, so I had to go straight off and try to be bright and cheerful as I chatted up the motorists.

I was also due to do a commentary on some Old-Thyme dancing that night but Sydney Thompson kindly did it for me, and I was able to rush down to Eastbourne. It happened at a very busy time as the West Indies touring team arrived on the Sunday evening and I had to get back to interview their captain John Goddard. Worse still I was Chairman of the Cricket Writers' Club that year. This meant that I had to preside at our dinner for the West Indians at the Skinners Hall on the Thursday night before catching the sleeper to Cornwall where my mother was buried next to my father at the little village church of Stratton, near Bude. This was my first real personal experience of those old theatrical clichés – 'the show must go on' or 'laugh, clown, laugh', and I found it a pretty trying experience.

But a fortnight later I had something to cheer me up. Our fourth child Ian was born on 2 May. We were once again 'caught short'. This time it was in the middle of the night and at 3 o'clock in the morning I had to rush Pauline off to the nursing home. Her mother was staying with us and came along too. It was a delightful warm morning and as dawn broke I was doing the traditional pacing up and down in my dressing-gown in the middle of Avenue Road. Luckily there was no traffic but anyway I didn't have long to wait as Ian arrived only fifty minutes after we had left home.

Ian's arrival meant that 1A Cavendish Avenue was now full to overflowing, even though Barry had gone off to boarding-school. Barry was really far too young as he was not quite eight years old, but he had been attending a small kindergarden school in St John's Wood and they said they could do no more for him. He went to Sunningdale School where the Headmaster was an old school friend of mine – Charles Sheepshanks, formerly Adjutant of the 2nd Battalion Grenadier Guards for some of the time when I was the Technical Adjutant.

Sheepshanks, James Bowes-Lyon who was gunnery officer, and myself had once all been called 'a f . . . ing lot of nitwits' by one of our Commanding Officers, 'Naps' Brinkman. Naps evidently thought that we had made a mess of a gunnery inspection of the tanks. He was a somewhat explosive character who used to shake his shoulders when he laughed, just like Mr Heath. We gave him the nickname of 'spanner' because he was always trying to get a grip on things and tighten them up. Anyway I knew Charles Sheepshanks well and did not consider him a nitwit, so I knew that Barry would be in good hands, especially as Charles had a sweet sympathetic wife, who was marvellous with small boys.

But I must admit that when Pauline and I left Barry at the school after a scrumptious tea with the other new boys, we burst into tears as we drove away down the drive.

Foreigners are always amazed and, I fancy, shocked at the way some of our children are sent away to boarding-school at such an early age. I see their point of view and though I have probably gone soft in my old age, I don't think I would ever again send a son of mine away until he was at least twelve years old. All three of my sons went to Sunningdale, and although Barry and Ian never seemed to mind going back, poor Andrew used to make a terrible fuss. There are many points for and against. A boarding-school undoubtedly toughens a boy and teaches him to live and get on with other boys, and at the same time usually gives him confidence and independence. But a lot of boys and their mothers do undoubtedly go through much misery and on balance I am now slightly against boarding.

There is one thing, however, that supporters of the system quite rightly point out. A boy living at home often sees the worst side of his parents, early in the morning when no one is at their best, and later in the evening when he comes back from school and finds everyone at home tired after a day's work. They are generally telling him to do things – 'get up', 'hurry up or you will miss the bus', 'do your home-work', 'don't look at the telly', 'go to bed', etc. The advantage of a boarding-school is that all this dirty work is done by the masters, not the parents!

Our life in St John's Wood over those past ten years had been a very happy one. No. 1A was bright and cheerful, with large rooms with high ceilings and was usually full of our friends or those of our children. It had a small garden, with a lawn, a green-house and a hut for the children, and we had the normal array of pets, a lovely sealyham bitch called Smokey, guinea pigs, hamsters, and tortoises.

St John's Wood itself, though only ten minutes by tube from Piccadilly Circus, has always retained its village atmosphere with plenty of trees and gardens, and in the High Street are some small family shops putting up a bold fight against the supermarkets. St John's Church by the roundabout at the south-east corner of Lord's has always been a flourishing community ruled over for a quarter of a century with benevolence by the Reverend Noël Perry-Gore who christened all our children.

For holidays each summer we went to Cornwall, the Isle of Wight and later to Dorset for the usual family seaside holiday. I have always loved the sea to look at or bathe in but not to sail on. I enjoy nothing more than playing around on a beach. I also have a passion for those vulgar postcards, especially those by that great artist Donald McGill which I have collected for years. I had them pinned up on the wall of my office at the BBC and still send them to my friends.

My favourites tend to be rather lavatorial in humour, such as the Bishop in his gaiters dozing in an armchair at his club. The picture shows a waiter squirting some soda water into the Bishop's glass, who wakes up and says: 'Is that you out of bed again Milly?' Or the small boy outside the gents public lavatory shouting to his mother waiting with a pram full of screaming kids – 'It's all right Ma. Don't worry. Dad says he'll be out in a couple of shakes!'

During this period we did a number of radio OBs for a Saturday afternoon programme which was a mixture of sport, music and other outdoor activities. I found myself gliding, canoeing, sand yachting and riding a tandem bicycle. The gliding was an exhilarating experience, first the towed take-off, then floating serenely through the air, and suddenly finding a thermal and shooting rapidly upwards. The canoeing was fun, trying to avoid capsizing under some rapids by Teddington weir, while the sand yachting gave an exaggerated feeling of speed, racing across the huge expanse of sands at Southport.

The tandem I rode with the announcer Patricia Hughes on a trip to

Le Touquet, but we found it very difficult. It's essential for both partners to do the same thing at the same time, especially starting and stopping, and we seldom did!

Peter May captained England to a 3–0 victory in the series against the West Indies, and so became the first captain to win a series for his country, and the championship for his county, in the same season. The Test series was really decided by a remarkable record-breaking stand of 411 for the fourth wicket by Peter May and Colin Cowdrey in the 1st Test at Edgbaston. England batting first were 288 runs behind on the first innings and then by Saturday night were 102 for 2. The wily Ramadhin had taken 7 for 49 in the first innings, and in the second had already got Richardson and Insole.

On the Monday morning, we all packed up and paid our hotel bills, expecting it to be all over that day. But May and Cowdrey were still there at close of play and stayed together till ten to three on Tuesday afternoon. Cowdrey made 154 and May 285 not out before declaring with 140 minutes left in which time West Indies lost seven wickets for seventy-two runs. It was a truly remarkable recovery by England.

Ramadhin bowled ninety-eight overs in the second innings and was never the same force again. In fact, in the next four Tests he only took five wickets for 319 runs and the mainspring of the West Indies attack had been broken. England with their great bowling talents won three Tests easily inspite of the West Indies having the three 'W's, Sobers, Kanhai and that dynamic player Collie Smith, so tragically killed in a car accident two years later. Having beaten South Africa, Australia and now West Indies, England cricket was on top of the world.

For the most part, 1958 was an uneventful year. Where the big three had failed it was too much to expect New Zealand under John Reid to do any better, and although a very nice side, they lost their first series of five five-day Tests 0–4.

Their batting collapsed time after time against the strong England attack and in five of their completed Test innings they were all out for under a hundred. It was the old Laker/Lock partnership which did most of the damage and Lock had a wonderful series, taking thirty-four wickets. It was disappointing cricket for us to try and cover on TV, and due to the easy wins and the weather we lost at least ten days of viewing time.

Otherwise on TV I continued to do *Ask your dad*, regular jobs for

Sportsview and even encroached on the world of racing by doing interviews at the Greyhound Derby at the White City.

On radio I sat several times on the panel of *Twenty questions* and also spent a week covering the Brussels Exhibition. I cannot remember much about it except that one day our producer Geoffrey Topping and myself decided to tour the exhibition in a cycle-cab. As we were representing the BBC abroad we dressed smartly and Toppers even wore a Homberg hat at a jointy angle. We sat side by side facing the front like two twins in a pushchair, with the driver pedalling like mad behind us. He must have thought that we were in a hurry as he cut a corner too fine, hit the pavement and tipped us both out head first into the crowds walking along. It was highly embarrassing, especially as we did not know how to apologise in Belgian, but as we brushed ourselves down we made good use of our English in cursing the driver. Perhaps it is the memory of this incident which has always made me against the Common Market.

I was also beginning to do more and more interviews for various programmes and one of these was *Spot the headliner,* which went out on Saturday night on the Light Programme. It was a sort of quiz show based on someone who had 'Hit the Headlines' during their lifetime. I asked questions about the event or incident, when and how it happened and by so doing provided clues for the listener.

I then asked them to guess who the headliner was. We came back about ten minutes later, revealed the identity of the person and I then talked to them about what had happened. Among our headliners were included: Monty's double, M. E. Clifton James – Arthur Bell a survivor of the R101 – Lieutenant Commander Kerans of HMS *Amethyst* fame – Miss Mathieson who had helped take the Stone of Scone from Westminster Abbey – and so on. It was fun meeting all these interesting people and hearing their stories and the series ran quite a long time.

24

It's digger time

By the end of 1958 I realised that I had been with the BBC for nearly twelve years. In that time although I had done all the television cricket commentary I felt my cricket education was incomplete. I had never been on a tour abroad with MCC and I decided that it was time that I did. Peter May's side had already left for Australia and I applied for something called 'Grace' leave – nothing to do with the cricketer – to join them for the last four Tests.

The BBC were very kind and gave me eight weeks absence on full pay but I would of course have to pay my own expenses. I fixed up some articles with a weekly boys' paper, the Australian Broadcasting Commission said I could join their commentary team and finally the BBC said that once I was there they would of course use me for commentary, reports and interviews. That being so they felt they should pay some of my expenses, which they did! So all was set and I even managed to have Christmas at home with my family.

I flew off to Melbourne in a Britannia on 27 December. It was a forty-eight-hour journey in those days, [today I believe the flight lasts around thirty hours.] This trip to Australia was to change the pattern of my broadcasting life for the next twelve years, until I retired as a member of the BBC staff. I reached Melbourne on 30 December and was commentating on my first Test Match overseas on the morning of 31 December – not bad going.

I hadn't expected to work quite so soon, and despite having slept the clock round I was still a bit shaky after the journey. I had also, for the first and only time, flown first-class and actually enjoyed some free champagne for breakfast. What is more, Alan McGilvray's plane from Sydney had been delayed so I was thrown in at the deep end and was the second commentator on twenty minutes after the start.

And what a start! In the third over of England's innings Alan Davidson had dismissed Peter Richardson, Willie Watson and Tom

Graveney with his first, fifth and sixth deliveries, and England, having already lost the 1st Test at Brisbane, were 7 for 3 when I took over the commentary.

To make matters worse, no sooner had I begun to introduce myself to Australian listeners than a pigeon from a rafter overhead dropped a message of welcome on to my wrist. Luckily no more wickets fell while I was commentating but England lost this Test and the 4th and 5th as well to lose the series 0–4. This result was a complete surprise as May's team had been hailed as world champions and the best side ever to leave England.

There were several reasons for their defeat. First they suffered an unprecedented number of injuries. Watson had to have an operation on his knee, Subba Row broke a wrist, and Milton and Evans each broke a finger. With three of their opening batsmen injured and Richardson out of touch England never got off to a good start and except for May and Cowdrey were simply not good enough against the class of Davidson and Benaud.

There was, by the way, a good story told about all these injuries which were reported back here with unwelcome regularity. It had been announced that MCC were sending out two replacements, Ted Dexter and John Mortimore. Two deaf old gentlemen were discussing the state of affairs in their club in St James' Street.

'Terrible, all these injuries. They must be running out of players. I see MCC are sending out replacements,' shouted the first member. 'Who are they?' bellowed the other. 'Dexter and Mortimore', replied number one. 'Dexter and how many? Forty more?!' roared the second member in disbelief.

England also had to compete against the blatant chucking of Meckiff, Rorke and Slater, blatant that is to all English and most Australian writers and broadcasters, but not to the umpires. In addition Rorke with his tremendous drag used to deliver the ball from about eighteen yards. But to be fair, Australia under the dynamic captaincy of Benaud did look the better side regardless of all these handicaps.

It was on this tour that Bailey, Tyson and Evans founded the Bowers Club which involved wearing a natty bow-tie every Friday with a motif of wine glasses, and a bat resting against some stumps. We used to meet every Friday, drink wine and go through certain rituals. This must not be confused with the Saturday night club which was for the team only.

It was quite an experience being a commentator in Australia for the first time as I had to learn to say 'sundries' instead of 'extras' and give the number of wickets down before the number of runs scored. In other words our 108 for 7 becomes 7 for 108. This method is all right so long as the score is not 10 or less when it becomes hopelessly muddling. 4 for 7 or 7 for 4 could mean different things to different listeners.

I got back to England towards the end of February after two months of wonderful hospitality and with my appetite whetted for more such tours in the future. It was great fun travelling round with a team and sharing in their triumphs and disappointments – usually the latter on this tour. I also felt it was adding to my cricket education and therefore helping to improve my commentary. Luckily my boss Charles Max-Muller thought the same. He was a white-haired old Etonian who had taken over from Lobby in 1952. They could not have been more different in character.

While Lobby was somewhat puritan and quiet living, Charlie was a cheerful extrovert who enjoyed going out and meeting people. He was highly strung and always jingled the coins in his pocket when he got enthusiastic or excited about something. He fought hard for the department and did a marvellous job of public relations with all the heads of various sporting bodies. Luckily for me, he himself adored travelling and used to go all over the world at the slightest excuse – planning for the Olympic or Commonwealth Games or for some Royal Tour in the far distant future. It was a great race between him and Peter Dimmock as to which clocked up the biggest world mileage in any one year!

Anyway, Charlie realised the value of having someone from his department travelling with a touring team abroad. I had been able to arrange broadcasts and interviews which would never have been possible without personal contacts or a good relationship with the captains and members of both teams. Charlie therefore proceeded to fight to get me appointed as the first BBC cricket correspondent, so that in future I would automatically accompany an MCC team abroad. He won, as he usually did, but it took a long time and it was not until 1963 that I became the first cricket correspondent of the BBC.

Back home in England I seemed to be doing more and more tele-vision and had a hat-trick of new commentaries. First I was one of the commentators at the Miss World Contest; great fun reading out all the statistics but very frustrating. Then there was the Lord Mayor's

Banquet, full of tradition and pageantry but rather starchy, and finally the Lord Mayor's Show which I always enjoy. Rather more I imagine than the Lord Mayor himself, whose coach has no springs but sways in a sickening way.

I also began to introduce two programmes, both angled towards children. I suppose they thought that as a father of four I ought to know how to deal with the kiddies! Little did they know!

One was an animal programme called *Dog's chance* in which we used to have various obedience tests, discuss a different breed of dog each week and invite celebrities to bring their own dogs along.

The other was *All your own* which I gradually took over from Huw Weldon who was going on to higher and better things. This was a programme in which children demonstrated their hobbies and it was my job to chat to them and find out all about them. It meant travelling round to the BBC TV studios in Glasgow, Manchester and Bristol but it was rewarding, and I never ceased to be amazed at the keenness, ingenuity and originality which the children displayed. I suppose I must add to this *Ask your dad* which still continued, so the poor children of that generation had a large overdose of Johnston.

On radio, the *Today* programme in the early morning had now been running for about eighteen months, and Jack de Manio was breaking all previous records in getting the time wrong. I started to do for it a weekly birthday spot called *Many happy returns*, in which I picked out the most outstanding birthday of the week and interviewed the person concerned. It ran for about four minutes and I kept it to a regular pattern: How were they going to spend the birthday, what sort of presents, a short bit about themselves and ending with a birthday wish.

My records are fairly hazy, but it seems that I did about eighty of these over the following year or so, speaking to some fairly prominent people – usually on a tape-recorder in their own home as near as possible to their birthday. What does surprise me now on looking at my guest-list, which figures personalities and public figures like Lord Longford, Sir Compton Mackenzie, Gracie Fields, Stirling Moss and Alfred Hitchcock, is that very few people ever refused to take part which in a way I suppose was rather flattering.

Running currently with this during the nest three years was *Meet a sportsman*, in which I interviewed a famous sportsman or sportswoman and if possible played a recording or commentary on their most out-standing achievements. I did over sixty of these and covered every conceivable sport – even tobogganing. It's really rather frightening as I write this about the year 1959 – and with all the later years still to come – to think just how many questions I have asked people in the course of my career.

One of the best answers I ever had was from that lovable character Uffa Fox, the yachtsman. When I interviewed him he had just married a French lady and it was rumoured that she could not speak a word of English and that Uffa could not speak a word of French. I asked him to confirm this and he admitted it was roughly true. 'How then,' I asked, 'does your marriage work?' 'Oh,' he said, 'it's easy. There are only three things worth doing in life – eating, drinking and making love. And if you speak during any of them, you are wasting your time!'

So far as cricket was concerned, the weather was glorious but the Test series against India a terrible disappointment, England winning all five Tests easily, three of them by an innings. India, under D. K. Gaekwad, were simply outclassed. Trueman took twenty-four wickets in the series and as a comment on the Indian bowling eight England batsmen averaged fifty or over, including Statham of all people, who was top with an average of seventy.

Our TV commentary box was enlivened by the arrival the previous year of Denis Compton as the expert between overs. He brought a cheerful but professional analysis of the play with his emphasis always on attacking cricket. Unlike some expert summarisers, he could claim to have practiced what he was now preaching.

Over the next ten years or so we were to have a lot of laughter mixed with our cricket and although some of our jokes may have offended the more serious pundits, I genuinely believe that that is what cricket is all about. It is a game to be *enjoyed* by player, spectator, viewer and listener alike.

Before the year was over I had become an 'angel' for the first and last time. At William Douglas-Home's suggestion I invested £100 in his new play, *Aunt Edwina*, and I am sorry to say that I lost the lot. If it were presented today the play would probably be a roaring success, but it was ten years before its time.

Aunt Edwina was all about a Master of Foxhounds who during a holiday abroad with his wife and two grown-up children, suddenly changes sex and comes home a woman. I thought it extremely funny but the critics slated the play and it never recovered, though William kept it going for six weeks. Possibly Henry Kendall who played the

MFH. was too 'camp', and the play might well have got by if it had been played straighter. During its short run, as an angel I received a weekly breakdown of the takings and the outgoings, and though none of the latter came my way I found it all very intriguing.

William had previously had his two big successes *The Chiltern hundreds* and *The reluctant debutante* but at about this time was going through rather a thin patch. It's perhaps fairer to say that it was the kitchen sink era and his witty country house drawing-room comedy was out of fashion. But in recent years he has come right back into form with three big hits *The secretary bird*, *The Jockey Club stakes* and *Lloyd George knew my father*. Alas he has never asked me to be an angel for any of these but he does very kindly give me seats for all his first nights. So perhaps we are quits.

25

A sporting chance

1960 was another disappointing series, with England winning the first three Tests and beating South Africa 3–0. For some reason Jackie McGlew's team never quite clicked and their batting and fielding were below their usual standard. A wet summer did not help them nor the fact that Cowdrey won the toss five times for England.

In addition, there was the unhappy Griffin affair. This likeable young fast bowler was no-balled for throwing twenty-eight times by seven different umpires in first-class matches. He never bowled again on the tour after the 2nd Test at Lord's where, in spite of being no-balled eleven times by Frank Lee, he also managed to do the hat-trick – another unique record unlikely ever to be equalled.

Naturally there was no real tension in the 5th Test at the Oval and on the last morning things became particularly dull, with light rain falling and England batting drearily. As usual we were televising and thought we would try to liven things up. We got an envelope from one of the many telegrams which we had received and inside it put a rather rude photograph. We re-addressed the envelope and persuaded Griffin who was twelfth man for South Africa to take it out to Neil Adcock at the end of the next over. He did so and Adcock stuffed it into his trouser pocket until he had bowled another over. He then opened the envelope, saw the photograph and began to roar with laughter. He signalled to the rest of his team to come and have a look and even the two umpires Charlie Elliott and Eddie Phillipson could not resist taking a peep. Soon everyone on the field was laughing and all we could say on TV was that Adcock had obviously had some very good news from home.

We heard our radio colleagues speculating: 'Could it be that his wife had had twins', or 'had he won some raffle or pools?' At the lunch interval a representative from the Press came up to see Adcock to ask him for a statement. But though by now he had guessed who had sent the 'telegram' he did not give us away and said something about a practical joke. But he did keep the photograph, and incidentally still has it!

On radio we started a new quiz called *Sporting chance* in which the New Towns competed against each other every week for a cup presented by the BBC. The teams were asked to identify bits of commentary on matches, races or fights, answer questions on laws, records and statistics, and also identify a mystery sporting personality. I was the Chairman and before the broadcast used to test the teams with some trial questions to get them confident and relaxed. They were not always serious and included the following:

Q. Who played at Twickenham one Saturday and at Wembley the following Saturday – both international matches?

The teams used to try to think of a double international who had played both rugger and soccer for England but of course never succeeded. The answer was:

A. The Band of Her Majesty's Grenadier Guards.

Another one was:

Q. Who was the last person to box Jack Johnson?

A. The undertaker.

The next two really have to be spoken and are given away if written properly. So I will cheat slightly.

Q. When did fog last stop the Cup Final at Wembley?

A. In 1935. Fogg was the name of the referee.

Or:

Q. A football team won a match 3–0 yet never scored a goal. (Their opponents did *not* score through their own goal.) How do you explain this apparent contradiction?

A. Never was the name of the winning team's centre-forward.

The quiz was devised and produced by Michael Tuke-Hastings who since then has established himself as the roving quiz king of the BBC with *Sporting chance* and *Treble chance*, touring the British Isles, Europe and the Middle and Far East regularly over the following twelve years.

Sporting chance was such a success that we were immediately asked by Paul Fox to do a special version for TV to go out every Saturday afternoon at the beginning of *Grandstand*. To make it more visual we included clips from films of sporting events, photographs for the team to identify and the silhouette of the mystery personality hiding behind a screen.

After one or two shows Paul Fox began to change his mind, as he felt *Sporting chance* was too static indoors and lacked sufficient action for a programme like *Grandstand*. He finally decided to scrap it and was in the BBC club having a drink when Kenneth Adam, then Head of BBC TV, came up to him and said: 'That's a jolly good quiz show you've got on *Grandstand*. I can't get my two boys away from our set while it's on.'

So we were saved and *Sporting chance* lasted for some time, with dear old Roy Webber as scorer, adjudicator and question-setter. He was a large, friendly person with a fantastic photographic memory, and after a few casual scorers including John Woodcock, now cricket correspondent of *The Times*, Roy became the regular TV scorer and statistician. He also did a lot for radio other than the Tests and he and I spent many happy hours together 'at the cricket' as he used to say. He collapsed and died suddenly in 1962 and our commentary box was never the same again without him, though there was much more room!

Arthur Wrigley – a Lancastrian who bowled a useful leg-break and had a dry sense of humour – was the radio scorer and used to carry a mobile reference library round with him. He always came up with the right answer as of course did Roy but usually out of his head. These two were the first of the invaluable TV and radio statisticians and were ably assisted by Jack Price and Arnold Whipp. By a sad coincidence they all four died within a few years of each other. Since then Ross Salmon and Irving Rosenwater on TV and Bill Frindall (the bearded wonder) on radio have continued to provide the high-class and near infallible service of information and statistics which is so indispensable to all of us commentators. Some people may feel that too much emphasis is put on records and the like but from the large number of letters which we receive it is obviously also much appreciated by most viewers and listeners.

One unusual job I found myself doing on TV was interviews at breakfast time at the Savoy Hotel. It followed the night of the results of the American Presidential Election and was one of the few breakfast-time programmes ever to go out on TV, except of course for our own elections. It was also my one and only foray into the political arena. Just as well perhaps as I am sure I would never be able to hide which side I was on.

I also entered the TV world of sequins and white ties and tails, and for the next eight years or so I was the commentator at the International Ballroom Championships from the Royal Albert Hall. My expert co-commentator was Elsa Wells who had an attractive drawl and was always exquisitely dressed. I named one of her outfits her religious dress – lo(w) and behold!

Elsa did a fabulous job as she not only organised and put on the whole event but was also one of the judges in the two grand finals which we televised. She used to commentate and judge at the same time which was quite unique as it meant that the viewer knew what at least one of the judges was thinking before the results were announced.

But I suppose the most important occasion on TV that year was Princess Margaret's wedding in May. It was especially crucial for the BBC as for the first time ITV were to challenge the BBC's right to a big occasion and were to match the BBC's coverage with their own cameras and commentators.

We were all very carefully briefed and exhorted to make special efforts to do a good job. I was in a comparatively unimportant position on the Horse Guards Parade, and all I had to cover was the procession crossing the Parade on its way to and from Westminster Abbey.

It was a field day for the TV critics who had two sets in front of them and next day compared the performances of the two channels. Naturally Richard Dimbleby won hands down in the Abbey and later at Tower Bridge. But along the route things were more even and opinion was divided as to who had done best – the BBC or ITV commentators. Of one thing though Peter Black of the *Daily Mail* had no doubt whatsoever: 'By far the silliest remark of the whole day,' he wrote, 'was made by Brian Johnston of the BBC, who when Princess Margaret passed a statue in Whitehall commented: "Princess Margaret is now passing the statue of the 2nd Duke of Cambridge. I am sure he would have waved at her if he could."' On reading it again I am inclined to agree with him but at the time I was very upset!

Peter and I are in fact old friends as we have two things in common, cricket and convertible cars. He has had one of the latter for a long time and I had Zephyr convertibles for at least fifteen years, though I am now content with a sliding roof. It lets in nearly as much air, is quicker to open and does not leak. Peter has also always been sympathetic with my attempts to portray the funny side of cricket. He agrees with me that even Test matches can be fun and should not be taken *too* seriously.

This was a great year for all of us at 1A Cavendish Avenue as it heralded the arrival of Mrs Callander alias Cally. She and her son Jack and daughter Ann came to live in our downstairs flat, and except for a few weeks she has been with us ever since. She has looked after all the children, cooked, cleaned, mended, washed and answered the telephone. Remarkably, she has remained cheerful throughout and been a real friend of the family. How she has put up with us all I don't know. Just possibly she enjoys being with us as much as we enjoy having her with us. I hope so anyway.

1961 was a much better year for cricket and Richie Benaud's popular Australian side won the series 2–1 and so kept the Ashes which he had won from Peter May's team in 1959. I flew out in April with a TV camera crew to meet their liner SS. *Canberra* at Port Said. I then travelled with them to Malta doing interviews and taking shots of their life on board, which we flew back to England in advance of their arrival.

For a couple of nights we stayed in Cairo and saw the Pyramids and rode a camel before we went down to Port Said to wait for the ship. It was pouring with rain, so to get some shelter I went into a shoe shop where I spotted a pair of brown and white correspondent shoes. They fitted me perfectly so to pull his leg I told the Arab shopkeeper that I would take the left one, and would he wrap it up for me. He got terribly excited and waved his arms about in protest, so I relented and said I would take both. These are the same shoes which I have worn ever since, and they are famous among cricketers all over the world. They are supposed to bring England luck and it is true that England have won more Tests than they have lost since I started to wear the shoes. Now everyone expects me to wear them, even though they look a bit shabby.

Australia were severely handicapped by Benaud's bad shoulder which prevented him bowling his leg breaks and googlies properly throughout the tour. But in spite of a lot of pain he bowled Australia to victory in the 4th Test at Old Trafford.

Australia under Neil Harvey had won at Lord's where the famous ridge reared its ugly head. England then won on a suspect pitch at Headingley where Trueman took eleven wickets. At Old Trafford England looked all set for victory thanks to a brilliant seventy-six by Ted Dexter. But Benaud then bowled round the wicket into the rough outside the leg stump and England lost their last eight wickets for forty-three runs, Benaud taking 6 for 70. He was one of the greatest Test captains and an inspiring leader. He always did his best to see that his sides played attractive and attacking cricket but on the few occasions when they did not, his public relations were so good that it never seemed to be his fault! He broke all tradition by giving a Press Conference at the end of each day's play, and never refused to answer a question. It often appeared that he was writing the correspondents' articles for them.

Richie was indirectly responsible for my giving up wicket-keeping some years later. I had been terribly lucky since joining the BBC to play in Sunday charity matches with all the famous Test cricketers of the time. I have let byes or missed countless catches and stumpings when keeping wicket to bowlers like Lindwall, Miller, Trueman, Bedser, Statham, Laker, Worrell, F. R. Brown, Gover, R. W. V. Robins, Compton and Titmus.

One Sunday in the late sixties Richie and I were playing for John Woodcock against the Rugby School Boys' Club at the Dragon School in Oxford. I was crouching behind the timbers reading Richie's googlies, flippers and top spinners. I read them all right but many of them still went for byes. However, when the last man came in Richie bowled him a leg break. He went down the pitch, missed it and with all my old speed – so I thought – I whipped off the bails and appealed. The umpire put up his finger and there it was: St. Johnston b. Benaud. I felt very proud and pleased with myself as I walked off.

Then the school bursar came up to me and said: 'Very well stumped.'

I looked suitably modest and thanked him. 'Yes', he went on, 'I should also like to congratulate you on the sporting way you tried to give him time to get back!' I was speechless and much shaken. If that's what people thought of my lightning stumping it was time I hung up my gloves. So I did.

It was during the Headingley Test that I made my most famous gaffe of all. Australia were fielding and Neil Harvey was at leg-slip. Suddenly without warning the camera panned in on him so that he filled the screen. I had to think of something quickly to say. 'There's Neil Harvey', I said, 'standing at leg-slip with his legs wide apart waiting for a tickle.' I realised immediately what I had said and wished the earth would open and swallow me up. Jack Fingleton made matters worse by drawing attention to it saying: 'I beg your pardon. I presume you mean waiting for a catch.' I did not answer. For once I did not dare to speak.

Jack and I were to have an interesting adventure after a dinner which the BBC gave to the commentators during the 5th Test at the Oval, I was giving Jack a lift back to his hotel near Lord's, and we were passing through Portman Square to Gloucester Place. Suddenly from a car park on the corner a man shot across the road followed some distance behind by a large fat policeman minus his helmet and desperately trying to blow his whistle. But his breathing wasn't too good and the man was gaining on him rapidly.

At Jack's suggestion I accelerated and drew level with the policeman, and shouted to him to jump into my car. He did so with evident relief and sunk back on the seat as we chased the man down a mews. As soon as we had passed him, I stopped, and the policeman leaped out. After a short struggle he got a grip on the man and asked us to drive them back to the car park. When we arrived there the policeman bundled the man out but they immediately began to fight and were soon wrestling on the ground.

Jack and I got out, and while I rushed off to dial 999 Jack carefully rolled the two contestants over until the policeman was on top. He then sat on the man's head so that he could not move. I must say the 999 worked very well and inside two minutes an ordinary-looking van rushed up and deposited about six policemen. It was one of their QZ cars. They quickly went to the aid of their colleague on the ground and when Jack had got off the chap's head, they clapped a pair of handcuffs on him and bundled him into their van.

Jack and I stood watching all this and heard the police talking to their colleague: 'Are you all right Ted? Sure you're not hurt Ted', and so on. But not a word to us. No thanks, no appreciation of what we had done. Nothing. Off they went in their van leaving us there fuming. Blast their colleague. What about us, we thought, and both swore it was the last time either of us would ever 'have a go'.

After this Pauline and I had a very pleasant holiday in Marbella which had not yet become as fashionable as it is today. I returned home a couple of days early to do my first big commercial job – introducing a close-circuit sales conference for a big firm from an ITV studio. It was in the morning before their transmissions began so that we were able to use all their facilities and links to large cities like Glasgow, Birmingham and Bristol where all the sales representatives were gathered.

My job was to act as linkman and interviewer in a sales boost pro-gramme which included a brains trust in which the directors answered questions asked by the reps from the various other studios in the big cities. It was well organised and worked quite well.

I had met the organisers before I went off on holiday at a sumptuous lunch at the Mayfair Hotel. When we got to the coffee they asked me what sort of fee I would like. I told them I would leave it to them, thinking to myself I would say yes to anything over £50.

'What about £300 then?' they said and must have noticed the look of utter astonishment on my face. 'You see,' they went on, 'we are on rather a tight budget.' So trying not to look too pleased with life, I accepted. It was beyond my wildest dreams and a remarkably good fee for those days, especially as they decided to throw in a brand new washing-machine as well!

It was during this year that Rex Alston on reaching the age of sixty retired from the BBC staff and became a freelance commentator. I missed him a lot as he was a kind and charming person, but in fact his departure did make me the number one cricket man on radio so far as the staff were concerned. It also opened up the way for me to be the BBC representative on future MCC tours.

Rex continued to commentate for the next decade, specialising as he always had on cricket, tennis, rugger and athletics. He had a very clear precise delivery with a touch of the schoolmaster about it, and looked, and still does wiry, fit and amazingly young for his age. I have always thought that he was at his best when doing athletics, which is not surprising as when up at Cambridge he had been second string to Harold Abrahams in the 100 yards.

Throughout his broadcasting career Rex was plagued, possibly more than most of us, by a small word which is the bugbear of all commentators. He is recorded as saying: 'It's a colourful scene here during the tea interval. The ground is full of small boys all playing with their balls.'

Or again at Wimbledon when there was a pause while the ball boys were getting the new balls and Louise Brough was waiting impatiently to serve. 'There's a slight hold-up here. Miss Brough hasn't got any balls.'

After he left the BBC, Rex did a 'voice-over' commercial on ITV, advertising a well-known brand of soft lavatory paper. Someone commented: 'If he *is* going to do commercials he is quite right to start at the bottom.'

26

Busy 'B'

1962 was a busy year. On radio in addition to *Sporting chance*, the birthday spot in *Today* and some more *Twenty questions*, I was asked to do another series called *Married to fame*. In this I talked to the wives of well-known people to find out what sort of life they led, and how they helped their husbands in their careers.

Among the wives I visited and recorded were those of Sir Compton Mackenzie, Herbert Morrison, Ted Dexter, Douglas Bader, Jimmy Greaves, Lord Robens, Graham Hill, Jack Warner, Scobie Breasley, Humphrey Lyttleton, H. E. Bates, Harry Secombe and Sir Francis Chichester.

The ladies were an interesting and varied selection who proved to me how important it is for a man to have a wife who can provide sympathy, encouragement and a happy and peaceful home life. Admittedly I picked successful marriages but some of us have indeed been lucky. The series was brought to an end with a 'cod' interview with Dick

Emery using one of his sexy female voices, which somewhat spoilt the saintly image of my previous wives!

Sporting chance was replaced by *Treble chance*, a quiz with more varied ingredients, general knowledge, current affairs, show-business, guess the year or the voice, etc. I was Chairman and a BBC panel toured the sea-side towns each week to take on the local team. The town which got the most points against the BBC eventually won the cup.

There were three people on the panel – Nan Winton (the first lady ever to read the news on BBC TV) who was an expert on music, films and the theatre, Charles Gardner the old BBC air correspondent, who covered all the sporting, technical and scientific side and Wynford Vaughan-Thomas, who covered almost everything else. Wynford is a man with a vast knowledge of history, geography, literature, serious music, food, wine, travel and world events.

Our panel was strong, but even so the occasional town used to beat us, and gained bonus points for so doing. This quiz has been tremendously popular and is still running, and it has always amazed me not only that so many people are keen to air their knowledge but that they have so much knowledge to air. Wherever it goes large audiences turn up to watch the show and support their teams, which is highly encouraging in this TV age.

Talking of television, I had a fleeting appearance as one of those people for whom I always feel so sorry – the compère in *Come dancing*. He must sit at a table surrounded by a bevy of beauties (?) and act as a sort of local cheerleader.

The venue was a vast ballroom in Purley and my team represented South-East London. I did my best but I am afraid we lost and in spite of a polite note of thanks from the producer I think the BBC rightly thought that in future the beauties deserved a younger and more 'with it' cheerleader. I wasn't sorry.

But I was pleased to join Peter West, Polly Elwes and David Dimbleby in an information-type programme on TV called *What's new?* It was produced by Brian Robins and as its name suggests was a forerunner of *Tomorrow's world*. We weren't quite as technical and scientific as Raymond Baxter is today, but did try to explain new inventions and ideas. *What's new* became a regular feature for the next year or two and was great fun to do, though we were all terrible gigglers and always trying to make each other dry up.

Brian was the ideal producer to work for, and always took great care of the human needs of his team. He was small, wiry and full of infectious energy and enthusiasm and the word 'no' did not exist in his vocabulary. He was also a man of instantaneous decisions, and once when I reported to Lime Grove in my best suit to do a studio interview, I was suddenly whisked off to catch a plane to Switzerland. I just had time to collect my passport and next day found myself on the top of a ski-slope, interviewing some skiers – still in my pin-stripe suit. They must have thought I was mad. All I know is that I was jolly cold.

Life was full of surprises like that. I had had a lovely family holiday in a cottage at Swanage which Pauline had bought with some money left to her by her mother. It was on the top of a hill two miles above the town in a small quarry village called Acton. It had the most perfect view of the sea and of the Isle of Wight too on a clear day. To my mind Swanage was, and still is the most unspoilt and delightful place for a seaside holiday.

The bathing is safe, it is usually near the top of the sunshine league, and there are sandy beaches for the children, good sailing for the sailors and perfect walks for miles round the cliff paths. In recent years we have spent most of our holidays there, and now have a holiday home on the cliff-tops.

On my return from a family holiday in Swanage my telephone rang and it was TV Light Entertainments from the White City. Was I free that evening and if so could I come down to the TV Theatre at Shepherd's Bush and introduce *This is your life*? My heart sank. Me do an Eammon Andrews for half an hour? My first thought was that I would break down and blub when some aged sister whom the victim had not seen for thirty years hobbled in, just flown by the BBC from Sydney.

But I need not have worried. They just wanted me to open up the programme and explain that Eammon was busy trying to trap the victim and would appear, they hoped, at any moment. It was in the days when the programme was done live and it often really was touch and go whether the victim would turn up, and having done so, agree to appear. In case he or she failed to do so, there was always one pre-recorded show in the can, but so far as I know the only person who turned up and then refused was Danny Blanchflower.

Somewhat reassured I went down to Shepherd's Bush and after the dramatic opening music walked out on to the stage, much to the surprise, and I'm sure the disappointment, of the audience. But I soon explained what was happening, and luckily Eammon and his victim appeared more or less immediately. It was Rupert Davies, whom Eammon had trapped in another studio.

Pakistan under Javed Burki were the cricket tourists and after the excitements of 1961 it proved to be another disappointing series. England won 4-0 and would have won all five but for the weather at Trent Bridge. Parfitt, Graveney, Dexter and Cowdrey were the main run-getters for England and Trueman with twenty-two wickets the best bowler. But all these runs and wickets were cheap as Pakistan were completely outclassed and none of their bowlers took more than six wickets in the series.

The Pakistanis were a friendly side and strictly managed by a military consortium of Brigadier R. G. Hyder the manager and his assistant Major S. A. Rahmann. The Brigadier was a genial and charming soldier who did not profess to know anything about cricket. He was determined that his team should behave well, be popular and be good losers and he succeeded in all three.

At times the Brigadier's methods were more suitable to a military campaign than a cricket tour. In the 3rd Test at Headingley Pakistan were beset by injuries and player after player left the field which became full of substitutes. This was too much for the Brigadier who decided to put a stop to it when he saw another of his bowlers hobbling from the field. It turned out afterwards that this bowler had a very serious groin injury and did not in fact bowl again on the tour. But as he stumbled up the steps to the dressing-rooms he was met by an irate Brigadier who waved him away: 'Go back on to the field at once and fight for Pakistan,' he cried, and back limped the unfortunate bowler.

In this same match Pakistan had collapsed in the first innings and were 123-9. The Brigadier walked into the dressing-room and saw the opening bat, who had actually made fifty, lying asleep on the massage table. The Brigadier shook him awake: 'Get up, and get your pads on at once.' 'But I have already been in', protested the batsman. 'No matter', said the Brigadier, 'get your pads on again. We are fighting for Pakistan!'

On the other hand the Major was quite a useful cricketer and played for me one Sunday in an annual match which I used to run against the village of Widford in Hertfordshire. The local side was captained by

John Pawle the old Cambridge blue and Racquets players. It was a perfect setting surrounded by trees and gardens with a little thatched pavilion. I usually got some well-known players to join me and my broadcasting friends and over the years people like Jack Fingleton, Arthur Morris, Richie Benaud, Gerry Gomez, Jeff Stollmeyer and Russell Endean all played for me.

My regulars were Jim Swanton, John Woodcock, Michael Melford, Anthony Craxton, Charles Gardner, Peter West, Rex Alston, Arthur Wrigley, Trevor Howard, Gordon Ross and John Warner. The latter was 'Sir Pelham's Boy' and could have been mistaken for nobody else. He was as bald as his distinguished father.

We had numerous 'incidents' such as when Jim Swanton was brilliantly caught and bowled low down by a young bowler from the village. Rex Alston the non-striker applauded and shouted 'well caught'. But Jim stood his ground and said: 'I'm not going for that one', and didn't!

Another year we thought that Jim had made enough runs, so we told Gerry Gomez to run him out. Alas Jim saw what was up, sent Gerry back and ran *him* out! John (Pom-pom) Fellows-Smith had also once been in too long, but no matter how hard we tried we could not run him out. In spite of each in-coming batsman telling him to get out he soldiered on regardless. We were so annoyed that we thought we would rob him of his hundred so when he had reached ninety-six we all applauded and a small boy even put 100 up on the tiny scoreboard.

But 'Pom-pom' paid no attention and did not even touch his cap. He proceeded to make four more runs, *then* touched his cap, and got out deliberately next ball. He always counted his runs!

When he was up at Oxford, Pom-pom used to have his leg pulled unmercifully by Jumbo Jowitt. One day Pom-pom was sitting writing letters in the dressing-room in the Parks. This is at the back of the pavilion and is underground so that it is impossible to watch the game from it. Jumbo rushed in and said: 'You are in, Pom-pom.' Pom-pom picked up his batting gloves and bat and walked out, and as was usual with him, kept his eyes fixed on the ground with his bat trailing behind him. When he had got about halfway to the wicket he heard roars of laughter from the crowd. Looking up he saw that the game was going on in the middle and that no one was out.

In the next match *v*. Middlesex he was again writing letters in the dressing-room when a young chap being tried for the University went in to bat. Pom-pom was the next man in. After about two minutes Jumbo Jowitt again rushed in and said: 'Lawrence is out, you are in, Pom-pom', but this time Pom-pom refused to believe him and went on writing letters. He wasn't going to be caught twice! However, a few moments later Lawrence came into the dressing-room and began taking off his pads, so Pom-pom realised that this time his leg had *not* been pulled.

He picked up his batting gloves and again rushed out to the wicket. But still determined not to be caught out a second time he looked up as he walked, and to his surprise he saw that there was no one on the field except the two Umpires. J. J. Warr, who was captaining the Middlesex team had been let into the joke and had taken all his team and hidden them behind the sightscreen!

In 1962 when Major Rahmann was playing we were twelve-a-side and created what must be a record. When the village batted I made the usual bowling changes to start with and found that the first four wickets had fallen to four different bowlers. So from then on whenever a bowler took a wicket I took him off and put on someone else. Believe it or not, at the end of the innings eleven bowlers had each taken one wicket apiece. It must be unique and we did not cheat in any way. No catches were deliberately dropped, nor did any bowler stop trying once he had taken a wicket.

We were all highly delighted with the record and celebrated in the village pub – all except Major Rahmann who was exceedingly puzzled as to why he had been taken off immediately after taking a wicket. They did not play cricket that way in Pakistan! Incidentally, Roy Webber used to be our regular umpire and on one occasion called off play for bad light, before he discovered he still had on his dark glasses!

During the summer I started to do a column for the *Cricketer* magazine in which I used to relate my experiences round the grounds, and tell the occasional story. I see that I reported on the match between Lord's Taverners and Old England which was played at Lord's one Saturday before a large crowd.

Denis Compton could not be with Peter West and me in the TV box as he was playing for Old England, so we thought we would try an experiment. We gave him a small pocket transmitter and a micro-phone the size of a button pinned to his shirt. We also fitted up Richie Benaud, who was playing for the Taverners in the same way.

When Denis was batting and Richie bowling we had a combined commentary. Richie would tell us what type of ball he was going to bowl, googly, leg-break or top spinner. But Denis could not hear this and as the ball was delivered he told us what he thought it was and how he was going to deal with it. The viewer sitting at home could then judge who was right. It was a fascinating experiment, and it is a pity that it has not been repeated more often as with two such good players who could also broadcast it made a marvellous way of coaching young boys.

During the same match Norman Wisdom was playing for the Taverners and when he was batting kept the crowd in roars of laughter with his clowning and antics at the crease. He finally did a succession of his mock falls in the middle of the pitch and collided with and knocked down his partner. The crowd's laughter shook Lord's.

In the pavilion there was an elderly MCC member in a Panama hat with I.Z. ribbon who hadn't really cottoned on to what match he was watching. However, Norman made him chuckle and he nudged his neighbour: 'I don't know who this player is but he'd earn his fortune as a comedian.'

I see that I also reported that at one match we televised at Lord's we had spotted John Warr and his fiancée Valerie sitting hand in hand in the grandstand. When the cameras picked them up I'm afraid I perpetuated the ghastly pun: 'Ah, Warr and Piece.'

1962 had been a happy year with a touch of nostalgia for me as Barry left his private school at Sunningdale and went to Eton. In spite of dour reports from Mr Sheepshanks, he had passed the Common Entrance quite easily and in fact 'took' two forms higher than I had done when I entered Eton.

It was amusing to go back as a parent and notice the changes after thirty years. The fees were at least double what they had been and the boys though still in their tails and white ties, no longer had to wear top-hats – they were too expensive. There was no longer such an emphasis on games and in the summer, for instance, the boys were now allowed to play tennis, golf or do athletics, rather than being forced to play either cricket or row. This I think is a good idea as it means that those playing cricket, though fewer, are keen and want to play. Towards the end of his time at Eton I fear that the only thing Barry played was his guitar and he spent most of his leisure hours composing and writing songs. This has turned out wonderfully for Barry and was due entirely to Pauline.

During one summer holiday we made friends with a young comedian in the local concert party. He was called Johnny Pearn and Pauline asked him up to our cottage to teach Barry the basic essentials of how to play the banjo on which he used to perform in the show. Barry soon picked it up, Pauline bought him a secondhand guitar and since then his life has been involved in nothing else – playing, singing, composing and recording.

One other thing I noticed about Eton was that the masters no longer live in the comparative luxury to which they had been accustomed in my day. Then all housemasters and masters in digs had butlers and cooks. Now Barry's housemaster spent hours chasing round Windsor looking for Spanish maids while the poor young masters had now to cook their own breakfasts after early school. *Tempus fugit* seemed to me the appropriate cliché.

I ended the year by flying off to Australia to join Ted Dexter and his MCC team. It was rather sad in one way as it was the first time I had ever missed Christmas at home with Pauline and the children. But the BBC, urged on by Charles Max-Muller, this time were keen that I should go and represent them, though they had not yet officially appointed me their cricket correspondent.

This was the tour on which the Duke of Norfolk was the surprise manager. There had been much speculation as to who it was going to be and late in July the Press and the BBC were all asked to assemble in the Press Box at Lord's, to hear the announcement, and meet the mystery manager. It had been an amazingly well-kept secret and not even the keenest ferrets in the Press had the faintest idea who it was going to be.

When the Secretary of the MCC Ronnie Aird came into the box followed by his assistant Billy Griffith we all thought: 'Ah. They are going to release Billy from his winter duties, to send him as manager.' But then we noticed a few yards behind the figure of the Duke of Norfolk, though even then until Ronnie made the announcement some of us did not suspect the truth.

It was a cricket sensation and the box rapidly emptied as corres-pondents rushed to their phones to warn their sports editors. They were even more surprised when they returned and heard a statement from the Duke telling how and why he had got the job. He had evidently woken up in the middle of the night and thought that he would rather like to go to Australia. So he woke up the Duchess and asked her if she thought it would be a good idea if he told Lord's that he was available, if required, for the job. She said yes, so he did and he got it.

But more surprises were to come. The Duke explained that due to private business he would only be joining the Team in Australia and that he would also have to return home for three weeks over Christmas and so miss the 2nd and 3rd Tests. He later modified this slightly and did in fact fly out and join the team's ship at Colombo. But this unorthodox choice proved a great success and the Duke was extremely popular and a wonderful ambassador for MCC wherever he went. He owed a tremendous lot to his assistant Alec Bedser who worked like a beaver and carried out most of the day-to-day chores of the Tour with admirable efficiency.

During the Tour the Duke used to visit as many race-meetings as possible and even had an interest in a horse, and the following story was told about him. He went to a small country meeting to see the horse run and strolled into the paddock to see it saddled. It was in a far corner and as he approached the Duke noticed the trainer put his hand in his pocket and slip the horse something to eat. Remembering his position at home as a member of the Jockey Club and the Queen's Representative at Ascot, coupled with all the dope scares of recent years, the Duke went up to the trainer and said: 'What's that you've just given the horse to eat?'

'Oh, your Grace', said the trainer looking a bit guilty, 'Not to worry. It was just a lump of sugar. Here, have one yourself. I am going to.'

So saying, the trainer gave the Duke a lump and popped one into his own mouth. The Duke somewhat relieved thought he better follow suit and eat his too. He walked off to talk to someone and the jockey joined the trainer who began to give him his riding instructions, 'Take the horse steadily for the first five furlongs, just keep him on the bit and tuck him in behind the leaders. But when you have only two furlongs to go, let him go and give him all you've got. If anyone passes you after that, it will either be myself or the Duke of Norfolk.'

I joined the team at Adelaide just before Christmas and we stayed at a beach hotel about ten miles along the coast. I was greeted by *When shepherds watched their flocks by night* over the inter-com of my plane from Sydney and it was strange to be celebrating Christmas with temperatures in the eighties and nineties.

On Christmas Day itself the Press and BBC played MCC in a riotous game of beach football and then gave them a champagne party before lunch. During this Ted Dexter conducted a masterly auction for players in a golf tournament which had been organised by Sir Donald Bradman. I was rather cunning and bought Ken Barrington, not by any means the best golfer but someone on whom I knew I could rely to go to the first tee fighting fit. As soon as he knew, he restricted himself to one glass of champagne and decided to forego his turkey and plum pudding, which actually was not much of a sacrifice in that heat. This forebearance must have been worth at least a stroke a hole to him and he walked away with the tournament and we split the winnings.

With the Rev. David Sheppard in the team we were kept on our religious toes and not only attended early service but went to hear him preach in the Cathedral. He did this in every city and people used to come in from miles away in the outback to hear him and he always had a full house.

On this occasion I went with Colin Cowdrey and John Woodcock and we decided to have a sweep on the length of his sermon. I had taken my stopwatch with me and there was great excitement as he approached the various targets. He had a habit of pausing so that it seemed as if he had finished and once I was about to pay out to John Woodcock when David suddenly went off on another tack and did another four minutes. His final time was twenty-eight minutes which may seem long but he spoke superbly and appreciated that people had come especially to hear him. Cowdrey assessed his form better than us and won the sweep.

David had a good tour with the bat and made a fine hundred in the 2nd Test at Melbourne which we won. Unfortunately his absence from regular first-class cricket had made his fielding a bit rusty and he dropped a lot of catches. As so often happens in cases like this, the ball seemed to follow him wherever he fielded and down it would go. This surprised Fred Trueman who commented: 'After all, when the Rev. puts his two hands together he must stand a better chance than any of us.'

There was also the young English couple who had recently settled in Australia. They had just had their first baby and the wife suggested that they should get David to christen it. 'Not likely,' said the husband, 'in his present form he'd be bound to drop it.'

The series was drawn, each side winning one Test. This meant that Australia kept the Ashes and it was the first time that a Five-Test series in Australia had ever been left undecided. The teams were evenly matched but in the last two Tests both seemed scared of losing and the final Test at Sydney played on a very slow pitch was the dullest I have ever watched.

Barrington had a marvellous tour averaging seventy-two in the Tests, and was well supported by Dexter and Cowdrey. Trueman and Titmus were the best bowlers and each took twenty wickets or more, but somehow the team lacked spark. This was surprising considering what a dynamic batsman Dexter could be. At that time his head often seemed to be in the clouds and his thoughts anywhere but on the cricket ground. He had a funny habit of completely ignoring people one moment and then being his own charming self the next time that they met. He was always most helpful to me and was patience itself answering my numerous questions.

Ted has always had a splendid sense of humour and one night I thought he would never stop laughing. He, Ron Roberts, John Woodcock and I were dining in a restaurant in Launceston. I have told you earlier how our groom had taught me to tuck my ears in, so I thought I would challenge my dining companions to do the same. Ted and Ron both failed but John promptly tucked both in as if he had been doing it for years. We all began to laugh and the noise attracted the attention of all the other diners. Soon everyone in the room, including the waiters were trying to tuck their ears in, and John and I went from table to table to give them aid and advice. We found ourselves trying to twist complete strangers' ears into the right shape in order to tuck them in. The whole place was in an uproar and everyone including Ted became quite hysterical. I must add that we found no one's ears pliable enough to 'take the tuck'.

After Christmas, Pauline flew out to join me travelling with the Duke's three daughters. As Sue Dexter and Grace Sheppard were also accompanying their husbands we didn't lack female support and company, which all helped to enliven the social scene. When there is no cricket many of the team and Press nowadays play a lot of golf but I have always gone off to the nearest beach to swim and sun-bathe. I must confess though that I have never mastered surfing and gave Jack Fingleton some good laughs once when he took me to Bondi beach. I know all the technical terms to shout – 'one out the back' which means a big wave is coming or 'there's too much water in that one' which still means nothing to me. But however small the wave I am usually well and truly 'dumped'.

At the end of the tour I had to fly back to England but Pauline went on to New Zealand where she had an amusing experience.

On her last day, Ted Dexter gave her lunch and she then said that she would like to have a short sleep before flying off that night. Ted suggested that she should use one of the beds in the Duke's suite, the sitting-room of which was used as a team meeting-place. Ted explained that the Duke was away for the day and that she would not be disturbed. So she took off her dress and lay down on one of the beds and was soon fast asleep. She awoke some time later to hear a gruff voice saying: 'Who's that sleeping on my bed?' It was the Duke who had returned unexpectedly. But unlike the three Bears he did not chase Pauline away. After hearing her embarrassed explanation he did the British thing and gave her a cup of tea.

27
Cricket correspondent, BBC

On my return to England at the end of February 1963 I found an additional assignment lined up for me in April. Jack de Manio was going to take three weeks' leave and they asked me to take his place and introduce the *Today* programme while he was away.

This was quite a challenge, as it's never easy taking over someone's regular spot and there was also the contrast in our styles. Jack has the most casual and natural approach of any broadcaster I have heard, and speaks with a slow rather upper-class drawl. I would not dare to analyse my delivery but I do know that I talk fast – too fast probably – and that compared to him my presentation must have sounded like machine-gun fire.

In those days there was only one presenter and I used to get a call from the BBC and set my alarm at 5.50 am. The BBC sent a car for me and I was in the studio by 6.30 am. The overnight staff and producer had prepared most of the items and a secretary was usually typing out a rough script when I arrived.

I quickly scanned through all the daily papers to bring myself up to date with any news item with which we might be dealing. I also looked for any 'funnies' to use as fill-ins between items or in an emergency. There was sometimes an interview to be recorded before the programme with someone in their home or abroad or perhaps one or two people were actually in the studio to be interviewed 'live' in the programme.

This meant chatting them up beforehand to find out what the interview was all about. Once the script was typed with the timings allowed for each spot, I went through it and made adjustments to suit the way I would normally say it. It was therefore quite a hectic forty-five minutes before the programme went on the air at 7.15 am.

An hour later we had a second edition with one or two of the items changed and in between we were given a rather poor breakfast of coffee, fruit juice and soggy toast and marmalade. The toast was always soggy because the BBC claimed that if they provided a toast rack it was always pinched. We were usually short of a bottle-opener too for the same reason.

One thing I was determined to get right was the time. The main danger was getting the hour wrong so for each edition I always wrote a large 7 or 8 on a pad in front of me, and though even then I sometimes got it wrong, I never touched Jack's form. It was all a good experience but at the end of three weeks I felt pretty tired, as I was doing my normal work as well. It also made any social life extremely difficult, as I tried to have a 10 o'clock curfew, and it was especially tough on Pauline who had to put up with an alarm and the telephone at 5.50 am every morning. I just don't know how Jack stood it all those years.

Except for odd shows for TV like the Ballroom Championships and the Miss World Contest, *Treble chance* and the Royal Variety Performance for radio, I shall always remember 1963 for its cricket. It saw the start of the Knock-out Competition now known as the Gillette Cup and when Sussex beat Worcestershire in an exciting final, Lord's for the first time experienced the real cup-tie atmosphere which has existed every year since then.

The West Indies under Frank Worrell beat England 3–1 in an

exciting series which produced some brilliant batting, some fine fast bowling and attracted huge crowds. For England Dexter, Close, Sharpe and Barrington made the runs and Trueman with thirty-four wickets had his best-ever series.

Led by the genius of Kanhai, all the top West Indies batsmen came off and Sobers proved himself a great all-rounder. Wes Hall and Charlie Griffith made a devastating and frightening pair of opening bowlers, though they both bowled too many bumpers and there was considerable doubt about the legality of some of Griffith's deliveries.

The match of the series was undoubtedly the 2nd Test at Lord's – almost certainly both the best and the most dramatic that I have seen. For four days the fortunes of the two teams fluctuated, and then on the fifth day came that famous last over at the start of which any of four results could have occurred.

As Wes Hall started his long run eight runs were needed by England to win with two wickets in hand, one of them being Cowdrey with his left wrist in plaster. David Allen and Derek Shackleton were together and they each scored a single. Then off the fourth ball Shackleton was run out and out of the pavilion emerged Cowdrey to cheers and counter cheers from the excited crowd. Six runs were needed and two balls left and Allen resisted the temptation to try for a six for victory and played the two balls out. So Cowdrey did not have to bat, but had he done so he had intended to stand as a left-hander but using only his right hand.

Once again I had my usual luck and was the TV commentator for the finish. Earlier as the excitement grew, the TV programme planners decided that we should not return to Alexandra Palace for the usual 5.50 pm news. But in the middle of the second last over someone apparently changed their mind, as I was told to wrap up quickly and hand over to Alexandra Palace for the news, which so far as I can remember started with a rather boring item about President Kennedy.

Luckily for cricket viewers Kenneth Adam, Head of BBC TV and himself a cricket fanatic was viewing and got straight on to the news people and ordered them to return to Lord's at once. So we had the unique event of the national news fading out for cricket. They just got back in time for the start of the last over. So all was well in the end and it was certainly the most dramatic of all our television broadcasts of cricket.

It was in 1963 that I was at last appointed the first-ever BBC Cricket Correspondent and from then on my broadcasting life gradually centred more and more on cricket and less on other types of programmes. It was also the year in which we brought off a leg-pull double on Jim Swanton.

The first was too good an opportunity to miss and happened on the Friday of the Lord's Test. The Sacred College of Cardinals were in conclave at the Vatican to elect a new pope to succeed the late Pope John XXIII and the whole world was waiting in expectation for the traditional signal that they had reached a decision – smoke coming from a chimney in the Vatican. We were televising from Lord's that morning when I spotted black smoke pouring from the chimney of the Old Tavern. I quickly directed the cameras to it and could not resist saying: 'Ah – I see that Jim Swanton has just been elected Pope.'

The other leg-pull was prearranged by Peter West, myself and our producer Antony Craxton, when we were televising the August Bank Holiday match at Canterbury between Kent and Hampshire. Also in our commentary team were Jim Swanton and Colin Cowdrey who had been recruited by the BBC as a commentator the day after he had broken his wrist at Lord's. Before play started we had a conference with Peter Richardson and Bill Copson the umpire. Peter was captain of Kent and was also due to be batting. We laid our plans which were to start as soon as a handkerchief was waved from our TV scaffolding as a signal that Jim Swanton was actually commentating.

As soon as he saw the signal Peter had an earnest mid-wicket conference with his partner, ostentatiously gesticulating in our direction. He then went over to Copson and spoke gravely to him, still pointing at us. Anthony Craxton zoomed in and said over the talkback to Jim: 'I wonder what's going on? What's the conference all about? Comment on it please.' At this point Copson turned and made his way towards our commentary position.

'Ah,' said Jim, 'obviously some small boys are playing about below us here and putting off the batsmen – or perhaps it's the sun shining on the windscreen of a car . . .'. Copson stopped when twenty yards away, cupped his hands and shouted so that the millions of viewers could hear: 'There's a booming noise coming from up there. It's putting off the batsmen. Please stop it.'

Colin, just to rub it in, shouted down to Copson: 'Sorry. We can't quite hear you. Can you repeat it?' Copson did so, twice as loud and there was much laughter from the crowd at that end of the ground.

By now, Jim had realised what was up and told the viewers that Peter Richardson was up to one of his usual silly tricks and perhaps we could get on with the game. He soon saw from our laughter who was really to blame and the next morning in his column concentrated more on the stupidity of the leg-pull, than on the cricket. The idea for it came from a similar incident that had taken place at Dover when Kent were playing Yorkshire in 1961. Then Jim was commentating for radio, looking down from a height on to the large bowl which forms the cricket ground. Here his voice genuinely could be heard echoing round the ground and Brian Close in all seriousness had asked for him to speak more quietly.

Possibly the best remark of 1963 was made by the great Sydney Barnes in a programme which the BBC recorded in honour of his ninetieth birthday on 19 April. Asked by John Arlott what was the peak of his career, he replied without hesitation: 'From 1905 to when I retired from first-class cricket.' Since he played his last first-class match in 1930, twenty-five years later – this great player still showed tremendous confidence in his own ability, and this was perhaps the secret of his greatness.

In 1964 *Treble chance* gave me the opportunity of seeing more of the world, and we set off on a six-week trip to Aden, Bahrein, Nairobi, the Island of Gan in the Indian Ocean, Singapore and Hong Kong.

Led by our producer Michael Tuke-Hastings, our team consisted of the panel Wynford Vaughan-Thomas, Nan Winton and Charles Gardner, a secretary, an engineer and myself as chairman. We travelled everywhere by RAF Transport Command and played teams from the three services wherever we went. We had a fantastic time and were royally entertained.

This was my first experience of the mysteries and customs of the East and of course the smells and the heat. I couldn't believe it when we went on to one beach and were told that the —— of —— had a close-circuit television set on which he watched the beach, and invited 'up to tea' anyone he particularly fancied. None of us were asked!

In the main square of Aden I watched an interesting game of cricket played on a dry mud service, and saw what could so easily be the answer to the current slow over-rate. All the bowling was done from the same end with the next bowler fielding at mid-off or mid-on. At

Ian's christening at St John's Wood Church in 1957. Barry, Clare, Andrew, and Ian.

(*Top*) Riding bareback at the Harringay Circus – just before standing up and losing my trousers! (pages 132–3).
(*Bottom*) The BBC Production Team for *Treble Chance*. Left to right, Anne (secretary), B.J. (question master), Michael Tuke-Hastings (producer) and Roy Webber (scorer).

(*Top*) A *Radio Times* picture when *Sporting Chance* went on the telly. B.J. (question master), Roy Webber (scorer and adjudicator), and Michael Tuke-Hastings (producer). (*Bottom*) Discussing technicalities with South African cricket captain Jack Cheetham before a *Sportsview* programme from Alexandra Palace in 1955. (Now you know who Robin Day copied!)

(*Top*) I interview MCC Captain Mike Smith after the 1st Test at the Kingsmead Ground, Durban in 1964, after England had beaten South Africa by an innings and 104 runs. (*Bottom*) Relaxing between Tests – 1968. Some of the MCC party on the Sandy Lane Beach in Barbados. Colin Cowdrey, B.J., Freddie Titmus, John Snow, Penny Cowdrey, John Edrich, John Woodcock.

(*Top*) The BBC Cricket Correspondent about to broadcast his views on the latest Test Team.
(*Bottom*) As P.R.O. I qualify for a seat with the Derrick Robins Team at Newlands, Capetown, January 1973.

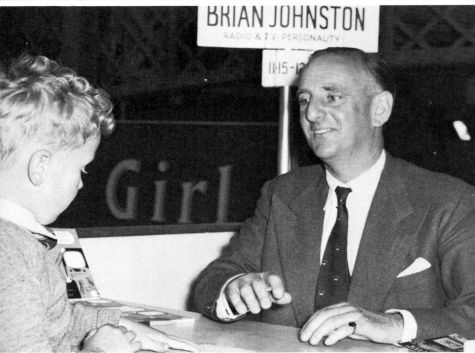

(*Top*) Little Offley in its winter coat (pages 1–2).
(*Bottom*) I look delighted to be asked for my autograph at the Schoolboys Own Exhibition.

(*Top*) All dressed up ... Pauline shakes hands with the Lord Mayor of London at a reception given at the Guildhall to celebrate the BBC's 40th anniversary.

(*Bottom*) The MCC Team recording The Ashes Song at Decca Studios. April 1971.

Say 'Cheese'! Barry, Ian, P.J., B.J., Clare, Andrew.
Mini   Joanna

the end of an over the batsmen had to hurriedly change ends which they did at the run and there were one or two minor field changes. But the whole thing only took about ten seconds instead of the forty seconds or so which is usually taken between overs in first-class cricket, while they wait for the next bowler to trudge slowly up from third man or long leg. A saving of even twenty seconds between the overs would add over half an hour's extra playing time each day. On our pitches of course, there would be the question of wear and tear if one end only were used. But a compromise could surely be worked out so that ten or even twenty overs in succession came from one end and then a change made over to the other.

In Nairobi we visited the big game reserve just outside the city early one morning and enjoyed an unique experience – or so we were told. We saw a pride of lions and witnessed the lion and the lioness 'performing' twice within a quarter of an hour. Just to put the record straight I must add that it was definitely the lioness who wanted and instigated the repeat performance.

The Island of Gan is an RAF staging post in the Maldives Islands in the Indian Ocean – it has a large air-strip, some huts, some powder-white beaches and coral strands, and clear blue water containing multi-coloured fish of all shapes and sizes. It was an idyllic place to stay for three or four days and we spent hours with our snorkels watching the fish.

The RAF do a two-year stint and when we visited them, there was only one lady on the island – a senior WRAF welfare officer. So you can imagine the sort of reception which Nan Winton and our secretary received!

There were several small islands dotted around from which the natives used to row across to work on the air-strip. We visited one of these called Hitadu – as near to a Robinson Crusoe setting as you could find. No domestic pets nor wheeled vehicles were allowed except bicycles and we pedalled our way along steamy jungle paths to visit the Chief of the Island in his hut. He bade us welcome and gave us a delicious cup of tea.

We attracted the attention of the children who followed us around with large staring eyes. We demonstrated cricket to them with a piece of wood and a stone and they soon began to copy us and join in. When we got back to England we sent the Chief some cricket gear for the boys but whether they ever played or not I never heard. It was all so beautiful and peaceful with the tropical trees and plants and no one seemed to have a care in the world. Yet sadly we were told that the maximum age most of them reached was about forty-five.

Singapore and Hong Kong were every way as good as I had expected though Singapore was perhaps too sticky. The view from the heights looking down on Hong Kong harbour at night is one of the most breathtaking sights I have ever seen. The city itself is overcrowded and teeming with people, but there is a wonderful atmosphere of bustle and activity and as so often in the East a painful contrast between the living standards and conditions of the very rich and the very poor.

As one arrived on the steamer from across the harbour there were queues of rickshaws lined up like taxis. But I could never bring myself to ride in one. I felt it was the final degradation for the poor rickshaw 'boys' – many of them tired, thin, old men, doing the job of an animal.

My one complaint was the Chinese food which I just could not stomach. While the others picked away at a communal dish and ate birds' nest soup and the like, I used to settle for a fried egg and bacon. I visited the famous Hong Kong Cricket Club with its ground right in the middle of the city, surrounded by skyscrapers and giant office blocks. The site is worth millions and there was always tremendous pressure to get them to move. They rent it from the civic authorities and now at last they are being ejected and given another ground outside the city. It was here that Keith Miller hit a six through a window of the Red Bank of China and nearly lost us Hong Kong – fifty years before we *have* to hand it back to the Chinese.

At one time, a big property developer tried to make the best of both worlds. He offered to buy the site and build a massive block of flats and offices, on the roof of which he proposed to recreate the cricket ground – like a giant roof garden. Whether they thought that the grass would not grow up there, or that they would lose too many balls over the edge I don't know. But his scheme came to nothing.

We returned at the beginning of March in time for me to fly up to the Hirsel for the wedding of my god-child Meriel Douglas-Home. Sir Alec was then Prime Minister so the telly, radio and Press made a lot of fuss about it. I was able to help the happy couple escape from their clutches as I travelled down in the same plane and smuggled them out of London Airport in the back of my Ford Zephyr. We thus avoided hordes of newshawks waiting in cars to follow them to their honeymoon destination.

My first big job after I had welcomed Bobbie Simpson's Australians at London Airport was to commentate on a firework display from Southend on the opening night of BBC-2. It was due to take place on Sunday, 19 April 1964 but due to an electricians' strike there was a black-out, so the opening was postponed for twenty-four hours.

A commentary on fireworks is almost an impossibility. What is there to say? I remember in 1951 at one big firework display on the embankment Stewart Macpherson had a list of adjectives written down in front of him – brilliant, fantastic, magnificent, dazzling, sparkling, etc. and he crossed out each one as he used it. Anyway, I asked the man in charge to give me a list of all his fireworks, the order in which he was going to let them off, and their correct names. We also asked him to pause between each lot so that they could register on TV and I should have time to describe what they were.

Alas all my well-laid plans went for a Burton. When he got the signal, the man panicked and rushed from rocket to display, from display to banger, from banger to catherine wheels – in any order and at a terrific pace. All my notes were useless, and not only did I not know what to say but would not have had time to say it anyway. But muddle or not at least the opening of BBC-2 went with a bang!

It was in general a fine summer but, typically rain spoilt three of the Tests, otherwise England might at least have drawn the series. As it was Australia won the 3rd Test at Headingley and then made certain of not losing the series by winning the toss at Old Trafford. They batted into the third day and made 656 for eight before declaring, Bobbie Simpson making his first-ever Test hundred – a small matter of 311! England replied with 611 with Barrington and Dexter, England's chief run-getters of the series making 256 and 174. So with rain at the Oval Australia won 1-0 and still kept the Ashes.

The series against Australia had been made brighter for us by yet another leg-pull on Jim Swanton during the 1st Test at Trent Bridge. For some reason at the start of the season Jim decided to have a chauffeur to drive him around. The only other cricket writer I ever remember having one was C. B. Fry when he wrote for the *Evening Standard* in 1934 and coined the lovely phrase about Bradman: 'The Don was at his donniest today.'

Jim as usual was doing television with us and Trent Bridge was packed on the first morning. At about 12 noon Denis Compton went down to see the man on the public address and asked him to read out a message. We had composed this up in the TV box when Jim wasn't looking, and during a silence between the overs the loudspeakers gave out: 'If Mr E. W. Swanton has arrived on the ground yet will he please go to the back of the pavilion where his chauffeur has left the engine of his car running!'

I have rarely heard such a roar of laughter on a cricket ground and I'm afraid Jim soon knew where to put the blame! You must think that we devote a lot of time to Jim and it is certainly true that wherever cricketers meet his name is bound to crop up sooner or later. He looks big and thinks big and is fearless in giving his opinion no matter how unpopular he knows it is. People who don't know him sometimes think that he is pompous. So I suppose do his many friends – and he has legions – which is why we enjoy pulling his leg.

Jim also has a habit of staying with Governor-Generals or dining with Prime Ministers when on MCC tours, and this produced the now famous but rather unkind remark by someone about him: 'Jim is such a snob that he won't travel in the same car as his chauffeur!'

He is one of the really great cricket writers and has had the necessary strength of character to ensure that he is given adequate space to reflect his opinions. He is still the senior cricket broadcaster having started way back in 1938 and goodness knows how many Tests he has covered on TV or radio. Jim's summaries are still infinitely superior to those by anyone else in the business though they are now restricted to radio only.

There were some classical moments when he did the summaries on TV. He had the guts – and it needed them – to stop in the middle of one, snap his fingers and tell some small boys to stop moving about behind the camera. When they did so, he continued quite unabashed. But he *was* slightly taken aback once at Trent Bridge when he finished his summary and removed his field glasses from around his neck and placed them on the table in front of him, as he always did. 'Well it's been a day we shall never forget. A fine day's cricket. Let me just give you the final score once again.' So saying, he looked up at the giant electric scoreboard and to his horror saw that it had been switched off! As happens on occasions like that his mind went blank and he could not remember what the score was! But a snap of the fingers and a hurriedly written note was slipped in front of him on the table and all was well.

When I told Jim I was going to write about him in this book he said that he hoped there would be an index so that he could find it easily!

Just in case he does find it I am going to make him blush by saying that although I know he often disapproves of some of my antics he is a very kind and long-standing friend and would be one of the first people to whom I would turn if I were ever in any serious trouble.

28

Johnston's choice

Dexter had now lost three series as captain – against India, West Indies and Australia; with the general election in October he turned his attention to politics and stood as a Conservative for Cardiff S.E.

This meant that Mike Smith was given the captaincy for MCC's winter tour of South Africa. The BBC had decided that we should give it full coverage, so towards the end of October '64 Pauline and I sailed for Capetown in the *City of Exeter* – a pleasant ship of the Ellerman Line.

An aunt kindly moved into 1A to help Cally run the house and look after the children. But I must admit that I did not enjoy the voyage as much as I had hoped. The sea does something to people: within a few minutes of meeting a complete stranger you are hearing intimate details of his or her private life, often accompanied by a show of photographs. Ugh! Pauline is far better than I am at this sort of thing and thoroughly enjoyed herself. But I got plenty of sunshine, scrabble and swimming so I don't really know why I am complaining!

This tour was one of the happiest on which I have ever been. It was without incidents, the country was beautiful, the people friendly and the hospitality superb. But most important of all was the MCC's team spirit. As on all his three tours as captain Mike Smith proved himself to be the ideal leader of a touring side. As a batsman he was utterly unselfish and on the field he never asked anyone to do anything which he would not do himself. As a result he was usually to be found in the most dangerous close-catching positions.

Mike never flapped or got excited and had the ability to deflate gently anyone who tended to get temperamental or swollen-headed. His teams would do anything for him and he was rightly known as 'the players' captain'.

By winning the 1st Test at Durban on a spinner's wicket, England won the series 1–0 and although the next four Tests were drawn they were usually good to watch. But the pitches were too placid and the batting of both sides stronger than their bowling. For MCC that great tourist Ken Barrington averaged 101 in the Tests and all the other batsmen averaged over forty-two. For South Africa the batting and fielding of Colin Bland and the batting of Eddie Barlow and Graeme Pollock were outstanding.

From a personal point of view, there was the added enjoyment of seeing my sister Anne for the first time for nearly thirty years. She came down to Durban to meet me on our first visit for the Natal match and when we returned for the Test, Pauline and I went up to visit her in the little fishing village of St Lucia Estuary, about 150 miles up the coast from Durban. As Anne had been there since 1937, she became a mother-figure to the RAF during the war, for they spent their leaves up there.

If you like the quiet life, that part of the globe is a paradise. It has a lovely climate, monkeys swinging from tree to tree in the garden or hippos wandering around at night. It only has sandy roads and is now a popular week-end fishing resort and a good centre for two game reserves. Anne loves the simple life, has her grandchildren around her and goes to bed at about 8 pm and gets up at 4 am. Definitely not the life for me!

My popularity with the team sunk somewhat when we were at Port Elizabeth the first time round. We were playing football on the beach and I was racing through the centre with the ball at my feet when I was tackled by Bob Barber. Our feet met and he came off worse with a suspected broken toe. He missed a match and at one time it looked as if he would not be able to play in the 1st Test. But luckily for me he recovered in time.

I renewed my friendship with Charles Fortune (nicknamed 'Outrageous') and he and I were the regular commentators throughout the series. With his slow, articulate delivery and good command of English Charles is a fine broadcaster and has a big following in South Africa, where for years he commentated on cricket, rugger, tennis and soccer.

There are, however, critics of Charles' cricket commentary who maintain that he neglects the score and the play and talks instead about the seagulls, scenery or what have you. They quote the story of him commentating at Adelaide one day when Lindwall was bowling. At the beginning of the over he gave Lindwall's analysis as o for 32 and then proceeded to describe the beauties of the ground, the backdrop of the blue hills and Mount Lofty, the spire of St Peter's Cathedral, the gum trees, the seagulls settling by the sightscreen and the gay frocks and hats of the ladies. After about three minutes of this he is reported to have said: '. . . and that brings us to the end of Lindwall's over, his analysis is now 3 for 32 . . .' A likely tale! But Charles loves to hear it told. He has made his name with that particular style of commentary and why should he change it? He was kindness itself to me and we had a most friendly atmosphere in the box. I was a bit shaken though on one hot and sticky day in Johannesburg. I handed over to Charles who had just slipped into the seat alongside me, and after so doing noticed that he was sitting there in his underpants, his trousers hanging on a peg.

Pauline had left us before Christmas to spend it at home with the children but before leaving she bought a small present for each member of the team which I duly presented to them on Christmas Day. We had turkey and plum pudding up at the magnificent Wanderer's Club and I spent the rest of the day with Bob Barber, David Brown and one or two others round a swimming pool.

At the end of the tour I flew to Cyprus via Athens to join the *Treble chance* team for another tour of the forces. This time it was a short one in the Middle East, taking in Cyprus, El Adam, Tobruk, Malta and home via Gibraltar. It was a tour of contrasts, with snow in Athens, sunshine in Cyprus and a dust storm in Tobruk. It was a case of 'Join the BBC and see the world'.

On returning home I was selected to introduce *Housewives choice*, quite an accolade in those days. The producer picked out twenty or so requests for each day from the many thousands of postcards received, and the compère then wrote his own links based on what was written on the postcards. As you can imagine, it gave me ample scope for corny gags and I think my worst one was about a request by a Mr and Mrs Morley for the Seekers to sing *I'll never find another you*. I couldn't resist adding: 'Sounds the sort of song that a blind ram might sing.' I remember writing the scripts one week-end at our cottage at Swanage, where during the course of a walk on the cliffs Pauline revealed that Johnston No. 5 was due in November.

For this year's Boat Race, radio decided to have a second commentator in addition to John Snagge on the launch: the previous year, the launch had failed to keep up with the race and listeners had had to listen to the TV commentator. In case this should happen again, I was stationed on Chiswick Bridge just beyond the finish – so that at least listeners would know who had won, in the event of the launch breaking down altogether.

After Barnes Bridge, John Snagge also loses sight of the two boats for about a minute as they go round a big right-hand bend. At this point he hands over to me for about a minute, though I am always extremely careful to hand back to him in time to describe the finish.

What a marvellous career John has had with that deep, distinctive voice. Until he became famous as a newsreader with his *This is London*, he was in OBs and not only started *Let's go somewhere* but even commentated on a cricket match! John was also the voice in the background at rugger matches which came in with 'square one' to denote where play was on the field, the listeners' crib being a numbered chart in the *Radio Times*. This is not to decry Teddy Wakelam as a commentator, but nowadays it's considered the job of the commentator to indicate in his commentary exactly in what part of the field the ball is.

John has always had his leg pulled about his famous remark during that thrilling boat race in 1952. The boats were racing canvas to canvas and John shouted: 'It's a desperately close race – I can't quite tell from here who is ahead – it's either Oxford or Cambridge!' Yet his worst gaffes are minor compared with some of mine. Once when reading the cricket score he said: 'Hutton ill – I'm sorry, 111!'

1965 was the first year of the experimental double tour. Following the tremendous success of the West Indies in 1963 it was generally agreed that they ought to have another tour as soon as possible, so a series of shared tours were arranged.

New Zealand and South Africa were the guinea-pigs and New Zealand were unlucky to come first and to experience cold wet weather for most of their tour. They were a young, inexperienced side and the wet wickets and damp atmosphere proved too much for them – they lost all the Tests.

South Africa were luckier with the weather, and by winning the

2nd Test at Trent Bridge won the series 1-0. They owed a lot to the two Pollock brothers – Peter and Graeme – and to the thrilling fielding of Colin Bland. His policing of the offside and his swift accurate throwing alone were worth the price of admission. For the first time I heard people saying that they must go to a match especially to watch a fielder. His two run-outs of Parks and Barrington at Lord's when he hit the stumps each time from an 'impossible' angle were fantastic.

At Canterbury, Colin Bland gave a special demonstration for us on TV of picking up and throwing at a single stump. Watched by hundreds of small boys, he hit it more often than not. This was putting fielding where it belongs – at the top of priorities for all classes of cricketers. To attain this perfection, Bland used to practice for hours on end throwing at a single stump with a hockey net at the back to stop the ball. I can't help feeling that his example on this tour did much to encourage some of the many fine fielders whom we have in county cricket today.

At about this time BBC-2 entered the cricket arena and broadcast on Sunday afternoons the limited over matches between the International Cavaliers and the counties.

These were usually run for a charity and the county beneficiary and attracted large and enthusiastic crowds. They came to see the great Test cricketers from all the countries playing together in one team and these Sundays became a family occasion. The matches not only brought money into the game but also a fresh approach with the gay dynamic cricket which was played. The counties certainly owe a debt to Rothmans, the sponsors, who, in my opinion, were rather shabbily treated a few years later when their matches were superseded by the John Player' League.

I shared the commentaries with John Arlott, Peter West and Richie Benaud with Sir Learie Constantine as the regular summariser – and how he used to enjoy it. This type of cricket was just up his street and he would have played it superbly. I once heard him give his philosophy on cricket . . .' 'I never wanted to make a hundred. Who wants to make a hundred anyway? When I first went in my immediate objective was to hit the ball to each of the four corners of the field. After that I tried not to be repetitive! . . .'

Sunday, 28 November was to be a very important day in our lives. In the early evening Pauline went into the nursing home to have her baby and I sat waiting in the hall downstairs. It seemed an awful long time, but at last a nurse came down the stairs to tell me that I had a daughter and that Pauline was fine. But she looked embarrassed and didn't look me straight in the face, and went off before I could ask any more questions.

Dr Cove-Smith then came down and said that our little daughter was in an incubator and that he wasn't quite happy about her and would consult a specialist the next day. I went up to see Pauline who was still in the delivery room and had not yet really seen the baby, but seemed blissfully happy at having a daughter. I didn't say anything about it to her but already I suspected that something was wrong.

After leaving her, I was allowed to peep at the tiny baby lying naked in the incubator and then went home to tell Cally the news that we had a daughter. She was thrilled as she loved children and had we not had another might even have left us in search of one to look after! At this stage I told her nothing but I realised that everything was not quite right.

I spent as much of the next day as I could with Pauline but it was a busy one for me and she was left much on her own, without yet seeing the baby. I felt desperately sorry for her as she had so looked forward to another child. Meanwhile Cove and a paediatric specialist from St Mary's hospital had examined the baby again and as a result Cove came in during the evening to say that the specialist would like to see Pauline and myself alone together the next day, with the baby.

You can imagine how we felt and neither of us slept much. I told Cally what was going on and she was wonderful and said she didn't mind what the baby was like, she would look after her. The next morning, the specialist came to Pauline's room. He was a charming man, gentle and kind but did not beat about the bush. The baby, he said, had Downe's Syndrome as a result of having too many chromosomes: this meant she was a border-line mongol but without all the usual features. He and Cove had made sure that she was physically perfect but she would undoubtedly be backward and not quite like other children. He said she was a mosaic and that she would be pretty, loving and a source of great happiness. (He was right on all three counts.)

The specialist also pointed out that some parents in our position might have to put the baby into a hospital due to their circumstances at home, but that a happy home life was the best medicine a child

like this could have. Of course we didn't hesitate. Talking it over after
he had left, we both realised how lucky we had been with our lives
and that most of its worst features had passed us by. Now we felt it
was our turn, and that this whole thing would be a challenge to us
which we would accept. We promised there and then that we would
do everything in our power to make Joanna – as we named her – as
near as possible the same as any other child.

One thing was certain. With Cally, three brothers and a sister she
was not going to lack love and care. Because she was such a rare type
Guys Hospital took a special interest in her and for the next five years
she went regularly to them and Great Ormond Street for blood and
development tests and an EEG on her brain. The reports got progres-
sively better but the doctors never led us to believe that she would ever
be completely normal.

Although Joanna was a happy and loving child she was naturally
not always easy to bring up and train, and Pauline and Cally had to
exercise a great deal of patience. They also noted down every detail of
her progress in walking, talking and so on, and compared this with the
rest of the family at her age. The three boys and Clare were wonderful
with her from the moment we told them the facts a few weeks after
she was born. They helped look after her, bathing her and playing with
her. Except for her big saucer eyes she didn't look so different to them.
I am sure that this happy home life has helped her enormously and she
has certainly added to the happiness and enjoyment of our own lives.

Meanwhile my life and career in the BBC had to continue, and on
Boxing Day I once more flew off to Australia to cover the MCC tour
for the BBC. I arrived just before the 2nd Test at Melbourne, and as
usual went straight to bed and slept round the clock in the comfortable
Windsor Hotel – one of my favourites anywhere in the world. They
have the gift of making their guests feel welcome and all the porters
and reception greet one like a long-lost friend.

I have always found that after twelve hours sleep I am as good as new
and quite unaffected by a long flight, whereas some people take several
days to recover. One quite good tip is to keep your watch on English
time instead of advancing it as you go further east. You can then eat
something at normal English mealtimes, even if it means refusing the
regular airline meals, and making do with snacks. By so doing, your
usual eating habits remain unaltered and your stomach will be duly
grateful.

This was another enjoyable tour under Mike Smith's captaincy and Billy Griffith's friendly and helpful management. England won the 3rd Test in Sydney and Australia the 4th in Adelaide, and so the Ashes remained in Australia. England's victory at Sydney was due to some fine fast bowling by David Brown and the spin of Freddie Titmus and David Allen but more especially to a magnificent innings by Bob (Ali) Barber. Going in first he made 185 off only 255 balls and thrilled the Sydney crowd with his stroke play. It remains one of the most exciting Test innings which I have ever seen.

Among the large crowd on the famous Sydney Hill was someone who cheered every stroke Bob made. It was his father Jack, who arrived out from England on the morning of the match. He spurned the posh VIP seat reserved for him in the Noble Stand, preferring to stand out in the hot sun and share his son's triumph with the beer drinkers on the grassy slopes of the Hill. What a day he had and the nice thing is that his fellow-onlookers were as pleased as he was. They are still the best barrackers in the world and the stories about them are legion, many of them attributed to the loudest shouter of them all, called 'Yabba'.

On one occasion, the umpire George Borwick was signalling to an attendant who was moving the sightscreen. George had his right arm raised above his head to indicate from where the bowler would bowl. Yabba spotted this and shouted: 'It's no use, umpire – you'll have to wait till the lunch interval, like the rest of us.'

Nowadays, they all have their transistors and several times I have deliberately pulled their legs by saying something critical about the Australians and then waiting for their roar of disapproval. Once I asked them to wave their handkerchiefs if they were hearing me, and when they did I apologised for what I had said.

There was one surprising innings on the tour which I shall always remember. It was played by Ken Barrington who as usual had a marvellous tour averaging sixty-six in the Tests with two hundreds. His first – 102 at Adelaide – was a typical effort and took him five and a half hours. But in the final Test at Melbourne he scored one of the fastest Test hundreds since the war. It only took him just under two and a half hours, and more important still he only faced 122 balls. He reached his hundred with a six over long-on and I have seen him do this in two of his other Test hundreds.

Ken started life with Surrey as a stroke-player but after playing for England twice in 1955 was dropped by the selectors for four years.

He decided then that what they wanted was runs and he turned himself into a grafter to get them. Ken was a wonderful tourer and a great mimic and comedian and was idolised by the crowds in India and Pakistan. His Indian Colonel batting is a classic, so is his W.G. complete with beard and I.Z. cap. He was underrated and under-used as a leg bowler, since he could really spin the ball and overseas got a lot of bounce. I ought to know, as once in a Sunday game in South Africa I missed an easy stumping chance off him which hit me on the right tit. He seldom fails to remind me of it whenever we meet.

As on all my five tours of Australia my regular partners in the commentary box were Alan McGilvray and Lindsay Hassett, with the local State commentator making up the quorum.

Alan is a high-class cricket commentator who reports and assesses each ball and stroke with accuracy and expertise, as you might expect from an ex-captain of New South Wales. He sees it as his job to stick to cricket only without any of the 'colour' we tend to use on BBC, and like all Australian commentators would rather give the score too often than too little. He is meticulously fair and unbiased in his criticisms and I would describe him as the cricketers' ideal commentator.

Lindsay is a wise and lovable clown and his comments and summaries are also strictly fair, backed up by all his experience as an old Australian captain. Before joining the radio commentators I had heard of temperamental clashes in the box. But I have been lucky all over the world and have always enjoyed a friendly light-hearted atmosphere, which over a seven-hour day is an absolute essential.

29
The compleat commentator

By now, I had come to look on Australia as a second home with cricket, sunshine and friendly hospitality. I particularly like the contrast in its cities. Melbourne is sedate and dignified, with its large city offices, vast department stores, wide tree-lined streets with trams still running, and the fashionable and social suburbs. The Melbourne Club is a wonderful institution and I have been lucky to be elected an honorary member on all my visits. Its peaceful olde worlde atmosphere rivals that of the Athenaeum in London – without the bishops.

This reminds me of the two bishops who were having tea together at the Athenaeum during one of the Synods which are periodically held at Church House. They were discussing the agenda for the next day which included a debate on pre-marital sex. Both were married and they were trying to decide what line they would take. '. . . For instance,' said one of them, 'I never slept with my wife before I married her, did you?' The second bishop paused for a few seconds as he nibbled a crumpet. 'I can't remember,' he finally said. 'What was her maiden name?'

Anyway, to get back to Melbourne. The cricket ground is an enormous arena about 190 yards across, surrounded by towering stands. It looks a desolate sight when only a few thousand spectators are present, but when full it is unique so far as cricket goes. It has held 90,800 *on one day* of the 5th Test against West Indies in 1961 and I have seen over 80,000 there. The noise and excitement has to be seen to be believed, with the players looking like small white puppets at the bottom of a large bowl.

Sydney is one of the most exciting cities in the world. In the centre near its famous bridge is the crowded business and shopping centre. At Kings Cross – a combination of Montmartre and Soho – there is every kind of entertainment, restaurant and hotel. Then only fifteen minutes away are the magnificent beaches. The standard of living is high and because of the influx of Europeans, the quality of food and drink in the restaurants is now extremely good. It's a friendly place and if I were a millionaire I would buy a flat overlooking Rose Bay and fly out there in the winter. The cricket ground ranks high with all cricketers and many consider it the best in the world on which to play.

Adelaide is the most beautiful city with its broad streets, gardens and lakes and its quiet cathedral-like atmosphere. The tempo of life is slower, there is some lovely countryside and its oblong cricket ground is top of the pops for beauty.

Brisbane, where the 1st Test is usually played is more down to earth and has no attraction for me. But Perth on the River Swan is delightful and undoubtedly the city of the future, though it is so far to the west that one gets the impression of being on another continent.

From this latest MCC tour, I flew back via San Francisco and New York, spending two of my six days in America aboard the train the *California Flyer*. Fitted with an excellent observation car, the *Flyer* wended its way across America, round mountain gorges, through deep valleys or over miles and miles of flat dull plains. It was a good way to see America – but I had never realised before that the country had so much space and so few people. Sometimes we would travel for miles without seeing a living soul!

I could have stayed longer in hilly San Francisco with its trams, Chinatown and Golden Bridge. But two days in a freezing New York was enough, for me. I saw two musicals – *Funny girl* and *On a clear day* – went up the Empire State Building and watched skaters on an open-air ice rink in the heart of the city. I don't suppose I would dare to do so now with all this mugging, but then I wandered for miles looking at famous landmarks like Broadway, Times Square, Central Park, Fifth Avenue, Wall Street and Greenwich Village.

Yet the pace of everything in America was too fast. Everyone seemed to be in a mad rush. It was nice to get back home to the family for a rest at the end of February. But I was soon off again with *Treble chance* to Germany, this time including West Berlin. It was unpleasant standing by the wall thinking of what went on behind it, and equally eerie peeping out from our sealed train as we travelled through the Eastern Zone on our way to the Rhine Army. It was a relief to go on to Gibraltar where Pauline joined me to try to get a sun tan while we played quiz games with the Forces.

In the summer the West Indies beat England 3–1, the tour being a personal triumph for their captain Gary Sobers who averaged 103 in the Tests with three hundreds, and also took twenty wickets. His performances at this time certainly justified the claims made that he was the greatest all-rounder cricket had ever seen – though it is something impossible to prove. It was not just his batting but the fact that he was three bowlers in one and a brilliant fielder close to the wicket – and incidentally a charming and most modest person.

England were a disappointing side under three captains M. J. K. Smith, Colin Cowdrey and Brian Close. But I have some happy memories of the series.

First of all, after an absence of three years, the return to Test cricket of the graceful Tom Graveney on his thirty-ninth birthday. It was a fairy-story return, as in his first innings at Lord's he just missed his hundred by four runs, but then made up for it by making one in the 3rd Test and another in the 5th. I have always been a Graveney fan and consider that he was grossly under-played for England. But selectors, and some of his fellow players too, always maintained that he had no stomach for a fight when the chips were down. Be that as it may, to me he always *looked* a class above most of his contemporaries. Just before he retired he was sweeping the leaves away from the door of his house in Winchcombe. Two boys passed him on their bikes and he heard the following conversation: 'I say, I think Tom Graveney lives somewhere here' – 'Yes, he does, in that house where the old man is sweeping the leaves.'

Next came the emergence of Colin Milburn as a Test player. He was run out for 0 in his first innings at Old Trafford but followed with ninety-four in the second and 126 not out at Lord's. He was a magnificent hitter of a cricket ball and with his Billy Bunter figure was the type of crowd-puller that cricket so badly needs. But he too failed to be one of the selectors' favourites over the next three years.

Finally, there was the splendid last wicket partnership of 128 between John Snow and Ken Higgs at the Oval which helped England to win their only Test of the series under their new captain Brian Close. Alas, he was to have a short reign.

It was during this summer that the BBC decided that I should divide my commentary time between TV and radio. They felt that as the BBC Cricket Correspondent it was only natural that I should do both, especially as I was now doing so much broadcasting overseas during the winter months. So long as I stayed on TV for home consumption only, my voice would not be familiar to the audiences of the various cricketing countries, and with the West Indies tour coming up it was important that the Caribbean should learn what to expect!

The two techniques are, of course, totally different and I am often asked which I have found the more difficult. The answer, perhaps surprisingly to many people, is television. On radio, with a gift of the gab and a knowledge of cricket, you are halfway there. Personality and broadcasting technique learned by experience, make up most of the other half. It is important to remember that you are the eyes and ears of the listener at home in his armchair, in his car, on the beach or listening surreptitiously to a small transistor in the draw of his office desk.

Lobby always told us to imagine that we were describing what was going on to one particular person, and so try to make the commentary as intimate and conversational as possible. You have in effect to paint the scene with words and that is why John Arlott has been such a great commentator. He is a poet at heart with an immense knowledge of cricketers and their history, and his vivid word pictures of a cricket match have won large radio audiences for cricket. To many people his gravel voice and Hampshire burr *are* cricket, and to me certainly they conjure up the smell of bat oil and newly-mown grass.

Cricket owes John Arlott a great deal and his witty, picturesque phrases are something unique to him. Who could better his 'Mann's inhumanity to Mann' when Tufty Mann bowled George Mann in South Africa in 1948. Or of a bowler with a crab-like run with bent knees: 'He looks like Groucho Marx chasing a pretty waitress.' So given a knowledge of cricket, a good vocabulary, the ability to talk and a personality to put it across, radio cricket commentary is certainly an art but not an impossible one.

Perfect television commentary is on the other hand virtually impossible. There are certain golden rules such as: 'Never speak unless you can add to the picture' – 'Do not try to describe what the viewer can see on his screen' – 'Let the camera tell the story.' But that is really putting it all far too simply. I have always maintained that a TV commentator can never hope to please *everybody any* of the time. He will also be extremely lucky if he can please *anybody all* the time.

Cricket has a mixed audience made up of possibly 25 per cent experts who know and understand what cricket is all about. The remainder are what are called fringe or marginal viewers, ready to be entertained and even educated but not essentially keen on cricket. All the experts want to hear from a commentator is who has won the toss, the state of the weather and the pitch and of course the score. They know the players by sight, they know the fielding positions and the laws and regulations of the game.

In contrast, the marginal viewer will almost certainly not know the names of all the players. He or she will not have detailed knowledge of the very difficult laws, such as what constitutes a no-ball, or how is someone out lbw. Furthermore, they will want an explanation of such place-names as gully, silly mid-off or 3rd man. What is a googly or a chinaman? So what is the poor commentator to do? Satisfy the expert, keep comparatively quiet and infuriate the marginal viewer craving for more information? Or try to explain everything to the uninitiated and get people ringing up telling him to put a sock in it?

The commentator is on a hiding to nothing, and if he compromises which perhaps seems the obvious thing to do, he may end up by pleasing *nobody* any of the time! You may think I am exaggerating about the viewers' lack of knowledge. But over the years we have received some extraordinary letters. Only recently I said that Ray Illingworth had two short legs, one of them square, and a man wrote in to say that there was no need to draw attention to people's physical disabilities. Or again Ken Barrington had once just completed a hundred and I said: 'He is batting well now. But he had a bit of luck early on. He was dropped when two.' A woman wrote in deploring the carelessness of the modern mother!

Even better, was an occasion when I was commentating at the annual Whitsun match at Lord's between Middlesex and Sussex. John Warr was captain of Middlesex who by tea-time had made a large score. We returned to the studio during the tea interval and soon afterwards the announcer in Broadcasting House returned to me: 'The latest news here,' I said, 'is that Warr's declared.' An old lady who had just switched on at that moment actually rang up the duty officer to see who it was against!

By the way, people often ask me whether I ever feel nervous before or during a broadcast. I know the right answer should be 'yes', because it's always said that a performer can never be at his or her best without butterflies in the stomach. But to be truthful, except at the start of my broadcasting life, I never worried, and have no nervous tension or pains in the tum. Perhaps it would have been better if I had!

One final word about giving the score. It is laid down by the BBC that it should be given every time a run is scored, and at the end of every over, be it a maiden or not. Remember that a maiden over by a fast bowler with one of these long runs can take up to four minutes. So if no runs are being scored even every four minutes can be too seldom. There is nothing more infuriating than switching on and not getting the score almost immediately, plus a certain amount of information about what has already happened.

Too much giving of the score is better than too little, even though it may be annoying to those who are lucky enough to be able to view or listen right through a session. They occasionally send telegrams saying: 'Why give the score every run. We can add up.' So they can, but I know that when I am at a cricket match I always look up at the score board *every* time a run is scored – just to check. Talking of letters and telegrams, there is an interesting contrast between those received by TV and radio. Those to radio commentators are in general, even when critical, polite and appreciative, those to TV commentators can be vitriolic in their criticism or declared preference for one commentator over another. These are admittedly a fairly small percentage of the post but it does help to prove my point how difficult it is for a TV commentator ever to satisfy everybody.

Once the cricket season was over, the Johnston ménage prepared to make its first and so far, only move. Our lease of 1A Cavendish Avenue was due to end in 1968 and our road was losing a lot of its peaceful charm since the arrival of Paul McCartney in a house opposite to us. At all hours of the day and night there were crowds of fans outside his gate. There were occasional screams and cheers as he rushed out of the electronically-locked gates in his black-windowed Mini, but usually the house looked unoccupied with drawn blinds and no sign of anyone.

The explanation of this I got from Paul's butler whom I used to meet when taking their large black dog for a walk. He said that because of the crowds the pattern of life at the house was topsy-turvy with breakfast at 11 pm, and night becoming day for the Beatle and his friends. Anyhow with the arrival of Joanna, and the other four growing up and needing rooms of their own, we felt that it was time to move. But not far! Once again my brief to Pauline was St John's Wood and almost immediately she found just what we wanted, about a quarter of a mile away in Hamilton Terrace, a broad tree-lined road between Lord's and Maida Vale.

Our new house was large and bright with plenty of room for all of us, and Cally and her two grown-up children Jack and Anne. Furthermore, it has a wonderful garden, unusual for London, with a large lawn, a big copper-beech, pear trees and plenty of flower beds. We moved in during November and for the first time were able to enjoy central heating, something we had never had at 1A. We were naturally sorry to leave after eighteen years, but we soon liked our new house even better and I was still only ten minutes' walk from Lord's.

Unusually for me I spent the winter at home as the only tour abroad was by MCC's under-25 team to Pakistan. This gave me the opportunity to go round the country in my spare time and give lectures or make speeches at Dinner Clubs or Ladies' Luncheon Clubs. These were fun to do and quite lucrative, though I have never taken money for speaking at any cricket function – a small way of paying back all I owe to cricket.

The Luncheon Clubs are great institutions and especially strong up in the North. I have often been the only male present among two hundred women, most of them wearing exotic hats of all shapes and sizes. I normally talk for around fifty minutes about my life and experiences at the BBC, and then answer questions afterwards.

Until he died, there was always one question which I could guarantee would always crop up: 'What is Gilbert Harding really like?' It was a jolly difficult one to answer as he was such a complex character. As an ex-schoolmaster, he was extremely well-read and knowledgeable about most subjects, and especially meticulous about the use of the English language. He was usually a sick man with bad asthma, heart trouble, and even dropsy in his later days. This, plus a distinct liking for drink, accounted for his intolerance and irritability and for his frequent loss of temper, especially in public.

Gilbert could not tolerate fools, or inefficiency and bad service and was never afraid to say so. But he was always most contrite afterwards, and if he had insulted a lady she would be inundated with flowers the next day. If one of his friends had been the victim, then a lengthy and sincere apology on the telephone would follow. He was a sad and lonely character and I used to visit him towards the end of his life. In fact Pauline and I lunched with him in his house at Hove just a few weeks before he died. He had by then been forbidden all drink, but I noticed that when his housekeeper was not looking, he slipped himself a large brandy as we were talking after lunch. He was mourned by many friends and his memorial service in Westminster Cathedral was packed out.

I have never been taught the art of public speaking. I just stand up and with a few notes in my hand rattle off a succession of anecdotes and stories, linking them with my life at the BBC. From experience I have learned the importance of getting a good start and for years have used the following . . .

'I was extremely flattered to receive Mrs X's kind invitation to speak here today, especially as she added: "You are such an expert at this sort of thing I am sure it will be no trouble to you." I told my wife: "There's someone here who thinks that I am an expert. Isn't that marvellous?" But you know what wives are: "Better look it up and make sure," she said. So we got out an Oxford Dictionary and of course she was right. There it was. *Ex* means you've had it and *Spurt* is a drip under pressure – which is exactly what I feel standing up in front of all you ladies.' It usually gets a laugh.

30
Some sticky wickets

Besides standing in again for Jack De Manio in *Today* for a few weeks, I was also called in to chair a TV quiz called *Top firm* when the late Kenneth Horne suddenly fell ill. On reflection, except for my cricket, *Let's go somewhere* and *Treble* and *Sporting chance* I have been one of the biggest 'stand-ins' in the business. For Richard Dimbleby on *Twenty questions*, for Leslie Mitchell in *How do you view*, for Huw Weldon in *All your own*, for Jack De Manio in *Today*, for Peter Dimmock in *Sportsview* and as I write this for the late and much-missed Franklin Engelmann in *Down your way*.

I suppose that in some ways it is a compliment to be a stand-in, though in fairness I must point out that there was an added incentive for the BBC to use me. Against my name in the final accounts for the programme were the letters *SNF* in brackets. They stood for 'staff no fee', so that in place of the fee that some of the others got I cost the BBC nothing!

There was another double cricket tour with India and Pakistan as the two visitors. It was a terrible May, the worst for nearly two hundred years and India lost all three of their Tests, and Pakistan two of theirs, drawing the first one at Lord's. Neither of these countries, normally so difficult to beat on their home pitches, had yet learnt to master English conditions. Their chief weakness was a lack of fast bowlers and their batsmen's inability to play the moving ball.

Boycott and Barrington were England's chief run-getters though Boycott was dropped after scoring 246 not out in the 1st Test against

India at Headingley. He batted all the first day for only 106 not out and to show their disapproval of his methods the selectors dropped him from the next Test, just as they had Barrington for similar reasons in 1965.

Illingworth got forty-three victims in the two series but they lacked any glamour or excitement, and sadly the main cricket news of the summer was the dropping of Brian Close from the captaincy of the MCC side to tour West Indies in the winter.

It all happened just before the 3rd Test *v*. Pakistan at the Oval. Yorkshire were playing Warwickshire at Edgbaston and were accused of unfair delaying tactics when Warwickshire were chasing a target in the 4th innings. Yorkshire in fact bowled twenty-four overs in the last ninety minutes – a rate of sixteen overs to the hour (pretty good by modern Test standards!). But in the last fifteen minutes they went off for rain, leaving the umpires and the batsmen out on the pitch, and only sent down two overs in that time, leaving Warwickshire nine runs short of victory.

Whatever the rights or wrongs of the case, it was significant at the time that such respected Yorkshiremen as Bill Bowes, Jim Kilburn and A. A. Thompson all condemned the Yorkshire tactics. In addition, Close was alleged to have had words with a spectator as he left the field. He was immediately summoned to Lord's to appear before the disciplinary committee to put his case. MCC were apprehensive of what would happen if such tactics were adopted by their captain in front of the volatile West Indian crowds.

Close was asked to apologise and to give an assurance that he would never do that sort of thing again. Had he done so – and he was urged to do so by all his friends and advisers – he would undoubtedly have been forgiven and would have led the MCC side to the West Indies. But Close comes from Yorkshire where they have a reputation for stubbornness, honesty and straight-speaking, and he brought all three into play on this occasion.

He said that he was not sorry for what he had done and that in similar circumstances he would do the same again. How then could he publicly apologise even if by so doing he would achieve his life's ambition of leading an MCC team abroad? How can you argue with honesty like that? And so Colin Cowdrey was given the captaincy and the popular press had a fine old time bemoaning the victory of the establishment and public schools against the rest of England.

It was all very sad, as Brian is a thoroughly likeable person and certainly one of the bravest ever to play cricket, whether facing bumpers or fielding within a few feet of the batsman. Once against Gloucestershire he was fielding suicidally close at forward short leg. Freddie Trueman was bowling and the batsman Martin Young hit a bouncer on to the right of Close's forehead. From there it ricocheted to Phil Sharpe at 1st slip who caught it, and Young was out. Close received attention but at first refused to leave the field. Finally, however, he had to go off to stop the bleeding and someone in the dressing-room pointed out to him the dangers of fielding so close.

'What would have happened if the batsman had hit you slap in the middle of the forehead?' 'Oh', replied Close, 'he would have been caught at cover'! A typical reply and one which sums up his whole personality. His career has been one of ups and downs, and after being dropped by England and sacked by Yorkshire, how nice it has been to see him batting better than ever for Somerset, and ironically being asked to captain England in the one-day Internationals against Australia in 1972.

After spending a happy family Christmas at No. 98 I flew off on 31 December to Barbados where I joined the MCC party in the middle of their New Year celebrations, and quickly sampled my first rum punch.

This was Colin Cowdrey's first MCC tour as captain, though he had been vice-captain five times before. He started off at a disadvantage as the selectors had somewhat irresponsibly let it be known that they would still have preferred Brian Close in spite of the Edgbaston incident, and that Colin was only their second choice. However, with his fellow Kent Hopper Les Ames as his manager, Colin did a great job, and England won the series 1–0, so gaining the Wisden Trophy for the first time. Even more important than the result was the fact that Colin's side was a very happy one, with the most wonderful team spirit. They hardly put a foot wrong the whole tour, in spite of several incidents not of their making.

Colin is by nature a modest, gentle character, a practising Christian who sets himself a very high standard, and expects the same from others. As a result he has often been severely buffeted by this evil world of ours. But by his own example and understanding he has always inspired great loyalty from his players, both on this tour and during his fifteen years as captain of Kent. His Achilles' heel has been a lack of confidence in his own ability – remarkable in a man who has played in 113 Tests – and a certain difficulty in making up his mind, due largely to his efforts to see and listen to everyone else's point of view. But on this tour he grew from strength to strength both on and off the field, and England were unlucky not to win the 1st and 2nd Tests as well as the 4th.

The batting of Wes Hall of all people saved West Indies in the 1st and England were undoubtedly robbed of the 3rd at Kingston by the now famous bottle-throwing riot. This occurred when the West Indies followed on and was sparked off when Butcher was caught by Parks down the leg-side, with West Indies still twenty-nine runs behind and only five wickets standing. Bottles poured on to the field, mostly from an open stand to the right of our broadcasting box. The combination of heat and rum had obviously affected the crowd, who shouted and jeered at the police as they tried to restore order.

At considerable danger to himself, Cowdrey went and pleaded with them to no effect, so the police decided to use tear gas to empty the stand. Unfortunately, they forgot all about the direction of the wind. It blew the gas away from the stand, past the Press and broadcasting boxes, and right across the ground to the Pavilion, where VIPs and their ladies, players and officials were caught in its flow. There was a mad dash by both sexes to take shelter in the ladies loo at the back, but everyone was weeping and holding handkerchiefs to their eyes as if they had just heard Al Jolson sing *Sonny boy*.

We tried hard to continue broadcasting but were spluttering and choking so much that we had to hand back to the studio, while in the Press box next door the clattering of the typewriters gradually ceased altogether. Pauline, who had joined me in Jamaica, took some splendid photographs of the cloud of gas drifting over the ground with Colin reluctantly leading his players off the field.

Play was resumed about eighty minutes later in front of a half-empty ground. But England were naturally affected by what had happened and lost the tight hold they had had on the game, and in fact nearly lost it when extra time was played the next day. If ever there was justification for the expression 'we was robbed' this was it.

The victory by seven wickets in the 4th Test was a splendid performance by England, though poor Gary Sobers was crucified by his home Press for setting England to get 215 in two and three-quarter hours – about seventy-eight runs per hour. As it was, England only won with three minutes to spare, and I believe it needed a tea-time conference in the MCC dressing-room to persuade Colin that he was a great enough player to do the job. He did it with a magnificent seventy-one at a run a minute, with Boycott in control at the other end with a masterly eighty not out. There were plenty of celebrations in an English-style pub that night.

Even more exciting was the draw in the 5th Test when on the sixth day England just held out with the last man Jeff Jones playing a maiden off the last over bowled by Lance Gibbs. He was surrounded by the entire West Indies side and I doubt if his bat touched the ball once! The whole success of the series depended on him staying there, and I have always nominated this as one of the most thrilling Tests which I have ever watched.

Off the field we had a fabulous time on the glorious beaches and especially enjoyed the scenery of the smaller islands like St Lucia and Antigua. But though it was paradise on the surface underneath it all one felt a current of nationalist and political feelings. Barbados was, and still is, the least spoilt and is the most friendly to visitors. It was here that we had the near tragedy of Freddie Titmus's toes.

We were all bathing at Sandy Lane Beach, and some of the boys were playing around with a small motor boat, which had a propeller underneath the middle of the boat instead of at the stern as in most boats. Freddie went to give it a push and in the buoyant salt water his legs were sucked under the boat and his four toes on his left foot were cut off, luckily just above where the nerves go into the foot. He was rushed to hospital where an efficient team of doctors were waiting to operate on him. The remarkable thing is that he felt no pain at all at the time and has never done so since. What's more, he played for Middlesex in the summer and nearly did the double, taking 111 wickets and making 924 runs, which only goes to show how small a part our toes play in our movements. It's the big toe which is the vital balancing factor and had he lost that, Freddie might never have played again.

A happier occasion was the night when some of us were dining in a restaurant full of American tourists. Our waiter – as they all do out there – soon got talking about cricket and told Colin Cowdrey that he was a useful fast bowler and would like to bowl at MCC in the nets. We decided to try him out and cleared a few tables from near the dance floor. We then put down an ice bucket as the stumps and Colin with a large serving spoon took up his position at the wicket.

Then, to the amazement of the Americans this tall, athletic looking waiter took a long run, wending his way through the tables and delivered a fast yorker with a round breadroll. It hit the base of the ice bucket without Colin getting a touch and he there and then invited the waiter to bowl at the nets next day, which he duly did. Where else in the world could such a thing happen?

I have spared you most of my puns which I fear have been the bane of my friends' lives for countless years, but I can't resist telling one I made in Port of Spain. One of my press colleagues had made friends with a pretty American girl who was staying out there and he used to see quite a lot of her! One evening we were going to have a drink and a swim at the Hilton and as we arrived my friend and the girl emerged from the hotel. He couldn't avoid us, so rather sheepishly introduced her to us as Annette: 'Oh', I couldn't stop myself saying, 'that's what you've been doing. I thought you were going to practice cricket every time you said you were about to have a net (Annette!)', I am glad to say that she laughed but I'm not so sure about him!

It was also in Port of Spain that I played a dirty trick on Tony Cozier who was one of the commentators. Rain had stopped play and he had gone across to the Press box on the other side of the ground while I stayed in the box in case the broadcasting people wanted any up-to-date report on the weather. I saw him returning after a short time, so as he entered the box I pretended that we had been called up and that I was broadcasting.

'Well', I began, 'there are the up-to-date statistics of the MCC team, their exact batting and bowling figures, and their ages and dates of their birthdays. Ah, I see that Tony Cozier has just returned so I will ask him to give exactly the same details about the West Indian side. Tony . . .'

I have rarely seen a greater look of horror on anyone's face. He sat down at the mike and began to stammer, making frantic signals to our scorer to hand him *Wisden* or any other book which would give him the necessary information. 'Well, Brian, I'll try to tell the listeners in a moment but I've just seen the pitch and perhaps you'd like to hear something about that first.' 'No, sorry Tony', I said, 'we've just talked about it while you've been away. All they want – and straight away please – is the information about the West Indies statistics.'

At this point I just couldn't go on, he looked so miserable and desperate so I said: 'Well, if Tony won't give us the details I suppose we had better return to the studio, so goodbye from us all.' There was a deathly hush for about five seconds and then I broke the news to him that we had not been on the air. It took him quite a few minutes to recover from the shock and I still feel guilty at playing such a trick and am always on the look out that it doesn't happen to me.

One interesting side to the tour was that BBC TV sent out a producer, two cameramen and a sound recordist to film the Test matches. Denis Compton and I did the commentaries and the films were flown back to London each night. We filmed every ball and did not miss a single wicket. What made the operation unusual was to have commentary recorded at the same time as the film was being taken. Normally the commentary is dubbed on in a studio after the film has been cut and edited. But the 'live' commentary gave a sense of urgency to the whole thing, though it was obviously not as neat and tidy as an edited version.

We used to sit alongside the cameraman as it was not technically possible for us to have a monitor in which to see what the camera was showing. We had to develop a close understanding, and assumed that he would always take the head and shoulders of the bowler delivering the ball and then pan up to see the batsman's stroke. If the ball then went to the slips, short legs, wicket-keeper or just in front of the batsman on either side of the pitch, we also knew that the camera could follow it. But if it was a hard hit or a snick away from the square then we had to lead the camera gently towards where the ball had gone.

It was tricky and had never been done before at cricket but it seemed to work well, and we actually received a congratulatory note from the TV chiefs on returning to England – a rare enough event to be recorded! It meant a lot of hard work for me, as no sooner had I finished my ball-by-ball commentary session on radio, than I had to climb a ladder to join our TV team and do a stint for them.

I got back to England in early April after what had been a lovely tour, and I am glad that I did it then, as from what I hear the Caribbean is not now such a happy and carefree place as it was.

As soon as I returned, I completed the editing of *The wit of cricket*, which I had been commissioned to do. It was a collection of the best stories, both true and fictional, articles and cartoons and was in fact my third cricket book. I had edited *Armchair cricket* for the BBC, which was all about the broadcasting of cricket on TV and radio, and also another collection of funny cricket stories called *Stumped for a tale*.

Roy Webber helped me with this before he died, and we had the cheek to write to a lot of famous people and ask them to send us their favourite story. We then collected and published them and one or two of my friends rightly pointed out that this was rather an easy way of making money!

Bill Lawry captained the Australians and the series was drawn with Australia winning the 1st Test at Old Trafford and England under Colin Cowdrey the 5th at the Oval, though it's probable that bad weather robbed England of victory at Lord's as well. Except for a swash-buckling eighty-three by Colin Milburn at Lord's, my main memory of the series is of the dramatic finish to the 5th Test and the repercussions which followed Basil D'Oliveira's 158 in the same match.

To take the result first. At lunch on the last day Australia, set 352 to win, were eighty-six for five with three and a half hours left. It looked odds on for an English victory until during lunch there was a cloudburst and the Oval became a lake.

Although the sun came out, further play looked impossible to everyone except Ted Warne the groundsman and Colin Cowdrey. Ted recruited volunteer labour from the crowd who with a collection of blankets, mops and squee-gees helped the ground staff to dry out the ground. It drained rapidly until only miniature lakes were left. Soon even these disappeared, and miraculously the umpires decided that play could start at 4.45 pm, giving seventy-five minutes of possible play.

Thanks to Derek Underwood who took seven for fifty on a pitch made to measure for him, England won with six minutes to spare. I still think that the photograph of all eleven Englishmen appealing for the final lbw against Inverarity is one of the most remarkable cricket pictures I have ever seen – every man in the team within a few yards of the bat.

But much as England owed to Underwood and the volunteer band of drier-ups, they owed as much to Basil D'Oliveira, who, although missed when thirty-one, and three more times after his hundred, went on to make a magnificent 158, and so started one of the most unfortunate chapters in the history of modern cricket.

31
Simply not cricket!

Basil had had an unsatisfactory tour of the West Indies where he not only missed a lot of catches but was out of form with both bat and ball. After his performance on that tour, I think it is fair to say that of those who went to the West Indies, either to report, broadcast or just watch, very few would ever have picked him for any future MCC tour.

D'Oliveira was, however, selected for the 1st Test at Old Trafford where he made a fighting eighty-seven not out. But he then damaged a finger, lost his form for Worcestershire and did not play in the next three Tests. He was not therefore many people's choice for the MCC team to South Africa which was to be picked after the Oval Test.

It was then that fate played a hand. Roger Prideaux who had played well at Headingley had been selected for the Oval but had tonsilitis. He was playing for Northants v. Hampshire and on the Tuesday reported to Doug Insole, the Chairman of Selectors, that he was not yet match fit, and would have to cry off the Test.

The selectors had allowed for such an emergency and Phil Sharpe was on the stand-by list for batsmen. Doug was about to ring him when he thought that he had better just consult the captain, Colin Cowdrey. Had he not done so, cricket history would have been different. Colin's opinion was that Dolly's bowling might be useful and that he'd like him to play. So he did, and if Jarman had caught him when thirty-one nothing more would have come of it. But after his 158, made when England were up against it, everyone agreed that the selectors could not leave him out of the MCC party.

They met at Lord's on the Wednesday and Thursday after the Oval Test and there was a conference called for 6 pm to announce the team. It was my job to give the team first to the world as I had a microphone just outside the committee room and the 6 pm news were prepared to take me 'live' as soon as the team was chosen. With the smell of drama in the air, the meeting was packed, as it was realised that if Dolly were chosen the tour could be in jeopardy as no guarantee had been given (or asked for) that he would be acceptable to the South African Government. They had announced in April that teams of mixed race would be able to tour South Africa if they were teams from countries with which South Africa had traditional sporting ties, and 'if no political capital was made out of the situation.' This last sentence was vital and seemed to put a question-mark against Dolly. As a native of South Africa his presence might be political dynamite to the South African Government.

There was a deathly hush as Billy Griffith read out the names of the team selected in alphabetical order. By halfway down it was obvious that Dolly had NOT been chosen and there was a buzz of excitement round the room. I could not wait to hear the explanations and I rushed out to announce the team over the air, within seconds of it being given. I read it out in my usual way when giving teams, batsmen first, then bowlers, wicket-keepers and all-rounders. As Dolly would have been in the last category listeners did not know whether he was in or not until I had finished.

From that moment on, all hell was let loose. The ordinary man in the street could not understand how he could have been left out after his 158. The Press as a whole took a cynical view of Doug Insole's statement that the selectors had looked on Dolly as a batsman and not as an all-rounder for overseas purposes. The selectors were accused of bowing to political pressure, a group of indignant MCC members called for a special meeting to censure their committee and the *News of the World* finally put the cat among the pigeons when they engaged Dolly to report the tour for them.

Few of those who criticised the selectors of almost everything ranging from racialism to sheer incompetence, stopped to assess the characters of those concerned. Doug Insole, Alec Bedser, Peter May, Don Kenyon, Arthur Gilligan, Gubby Allen and the captain elect Colin Cowdrey. Nor did many people remember the bad tour which Dolly had had in the West Indies, nor the fact that Colin Milburn, who some thought had better claims than Dolly, had also been left out. There was no outcry about that.

Things were not helped when ironically Tom Cartwright the *all-rounder* who had been selected, declared himself unfit and cried off the tour. The selectors then promptly chose in his place D'Oliveira whom they had previously said they did not rate as an all-rounder for overseas.

This was the last straw so far as the South African Government was concerned. Mr Vorster announced that he could not receive a team forced on South Africa by 'political influences', and MCC accordingly cancelled the tour.

It was all terribly sad for cricket and everyone felt great sympathy for Dolly, the unwilling cause of all the trouble, who behaved impeccably and with dignity throughout. I still think the selectors were right in their original selection, but some of their statements made their final choice of Dolly appear to be contradictory and to justify the accusation that they had yielded to pressure.

And so robbed of a winter in South African sunshine, the rest of the year slipped quietly by with the usual number of quizzes and interviews, and a month introducing *Today*. But MCC managed to arrange a short tour of Pakistan and Ceylon and I persuaded the BBC to let me cover the three Tests in Pakistan, arriving in time for the first one at Lahore in the middle of February.

Except for the occasional stop-off at an airport, I had never been to either India or Pakistan and it was quite an experience. The pungent smells of the East, the heat and dust, the beggars, the noisy markets and the apparent lack of care for either human beings or animals, were all quite new to me. So were the disorderly crowds at the matches. It was a time of political unrest and the left-wing students seemed to be in control almost everywhere, in spite of the efforts of the police in Lahore and Karachi.

During one of the noisiest demonstrations in the 1st Test seats were being hurled about in all directions and it was a wonder that no one was seriously hurt. Aftab Gul the local student leader was batting for Pakistan at the time and when he was out, instead of returning to the pavilion, he went straight across to the students and appealed to them to be quiet, and this had some affect.

MCC were due to play the 2nd Test at Dacca in East Pakistan but the trip was on and off because of serious street fighting there which had resulted in many deaths. Colin Cowdrey and Les Ames who managed the tour with great patience and tact, had conferences with the British High Commissioner who finally persuaded them to go, on the assurance that they would have full police protection at the match and that the army would meet them and escort them from the airport. If MCC had refused to go and play a Test in Dacca the local students threatened more riots and burnings, and the lives of the Europeans would obviously have been in danger. So a cricket tour had become wholly political and MCC were being used as a lever to achieve the students' ends.

We flew off to Dacca full of foreboding but encouraged by the promise of police and army support. Imagine everyone's surprise when the local representative of the British High Commission welcomed Colin and Les with the news that there was no army about, though he hinted they were in reserve if needed, and that there would be no police whatsoever at the Test match. The students had insisted on organising the whole thing and Colin had several conferences with their leaders in his hotel bedroom before agreeing to go on with the match. Remarkable to relate, the crowds were the best-behaved of the whole tour, though admittedly they were behind wire-netting so could not invade the field of play. But whenever there was a disturbance in a stand the students' committee sorted it out straightaway, and we never saw a single policeman during the whole match.

But the police were back in force at Karachi where political tension was just as high and there was strong feeling against the Pakistan selectors for failing to make the local hero Hanif captain in place of Saeed. On the first two days there were the usual interruptions of play and scuffles with the police. The third day had been declared a general strike in Karachi and the students made it known that they thought that there should be no cricket either on that day. There was clearly going to be trouble.

Colin after making fourteen had flown home on the death of his father and Tom Graveney was captaining England who went on batting into the third day. I was doing TV commentary for the local Pakistan station when Alan Knott reached ninety-six. David Brown was his partner and together they had put on seventy-five runs for the eighth wicket. All seemed set for Knotty's first Test hundred when a section of the crowd suddenly erupted and jumped over the fence, reinforced by a crowd of students who had somehow gained entry to the ground. They raced across the ground towards the pitch shouting and screaming as they went. It was bedlam. Both Knotty and David had seen them coming and though hampered by pads and bats set off for the pavilion followed by the fielders and umpires.

They must have been near to breaking the Olympic 100 metres record as they dived into the safety of the dressing-rooms. I tried to commentate on the TV but someone pulled the plug out and picture and sound disappeared. The rioters did what damage they could to the pitch and then swept towards the VIP stand where there were comfortable armchairs and thick carpets under a giant awning. The VIPs were no fools and had already sensed danger some time before and were sheltering in the pavilion. Just as well.

Their stand was completely wrecked, chairs broken, carpets ripped up, tables overturned. It was a horrifying sight to watch a mob at work and I admit to feeling scared even though I was up in the TV tower. But there was no guarantee that they would not wreck that too. However, they decided to set fire to some of the other stands and the English Press and myself managed to dash for the safety of the English dressing-room.

Police reinforcements arrived and we were smuggled into cars and whisked back to our hotel. I think there were at least twelve of us in our car, piled on each others laps – and the driver's! I had to go out again to the local radio station to send my report back to England but this was not easy, as there were no taxis and the streets were not too safe. Anyway I managed somehow after first doing a quick recording with Les Ames, who was busy arranging an immediate flight home, the match obviously having been abandoned.

We hurriedly packed and flew back that night, arriving at London Airport on Sunday morning highly relieved but not highly amused. The team had all behaved extremely well under all the stresses of the tour but politics had come first and cricket had suffered.

Both the first two Tests were drawn on deadly slow pitches, but in the final one England had scored 502-7 when play was stopped. Top scorer was Colin Milburn with a brilliant 139. He had been summoned from Australia to join the team and arrived in Dacca the day before the second day.

Colin didn't play there but his arrival boosted the morale of the team. They went to meet him at the airport and as he came down the steps of the aircraft they garlanded him with flowers.

He then solemnly shook hands with the lined-up team to the amazement of the airport staff, who were even more amazed when Olly and the team burst into a chorus of his theme song *The green, green grass of home.*

Here was a cricketer who by his exciting batting and his cheerful Billy Bunter personality exuded an aura of fun whether on or off the cricket field. The crowds loved him. So did his fellow players. He and I used to sing *Underneath the arches* and *Me and my shadow*, using the question and answer technique.

B.J.   Where were you last night, Ollie?
C.M.   Underneath the Arches.
B.J.   Did you have a bed?
C.M.   On cobblestones I lay.
B.J.   Where did you say?
C.M.   Underneath the Arches.
B.J.   What do you do there?
C.M.   I dream my dreams away . . . *and so on.*

Luckily, his singing drowned most of my wrong notes on the piano. You can imagine therefore how I felt when our newsroom rang me at Lord's on Saturday, 24 May and asked me to do a piece about Colin Milburn in the 1 pm news. He had had a car accident and had lost his left eye.

I was really shattered. What a loss to cricket. Just when he had shown that he must be a regular choice for England. Only a week before, Colin had made what was possibly his most brilliant hundred – 158 in seventy-seven overs with five sixes and sixteen fours. I did my best to do him justice but for the first time on radio I nearly broke down. I took him a bottle of champagne the following week when I went to visit him in hospital at Northampton. There he was, as big and smiling as ever, and we even slipped into *the Arches* for a few bars. But cricket had been his life, not just playing but the whole social side of it, and in the winter he had become just as big a favourite in Western Australia. He was to find the next few years hard going, in spite of a bumper benefit of over £20,000.

Later in the season it was laughter instead of sadness for me, albeit quite unintentionally. It was during the 1st Test against New Zealand, at Lord's when Glenn Turner carried his bat for a brave forty-three not out in their second innings. I was commentating for TV (I did three Tests for TV, three for radio) and Alan Ward playing in his first Test was bowling particularly fast from the pavilion end.

Off the fifth ball of one of his overs he struck Turner a sickening blow in the box, and Turner collapsed at the crease. After a minute or so he staggered to his feet looking very pale but he collected himself and amidst much applause took up his stance at the crease. 'Well' I said, 'he's bravely going to carry on – but he doesn't look too good. One ball left'!

This was one of the double tour years with West Indies in the first half, and they lost two Tests and drew one. Colin Cowdrey had damaged his Achilles tendon in a Sunday match at the end of May so Ray Illingworth, after only a month as captain of Leicestershire found himself captain of England for all six Tests – the start of a long sequence.

As England also won two Tests against New Zealand Illy got off to a good start. But the Tests were undistinguished and there were few outstanding performances. The most important feature of the season was the start of the John Player League in which each county plays the other once on Sundays in a single innings match of forty overs each. It was an immediate success and drew large family crowds who had learnt the fun and excitement of instant cricket from the International Cavaliers.

As I said earlier, the Cavaliers were badly treated by the counties who dropped them as soon as a sponsor came up with some money, seemingly forgetful of how the Cavaliers had helped their bene-ficiaries, besides providing their members and crowds with some capital entertainment.

With no MCC tour scheduled I was delighted to receive a novel invitation from Charles Fortune in South Africa. He invited me to be the 'neutral' commentator in the Four-Test series between South Africa and Australia due to start in January. So far as I know this was the first time that any cricketing country had asked an outsider to join their commentary team except when his own country was taking part in the series.

The BBC very kindly allowed me to accept, and after spending Christmas in bed with 'flu I looked forward to two months of sunshine and sharing the commentaries with my old colleagues Charles Fortune and Alan MacGilvray.

We were to see the annihilation of the Australians, tired after a strenuous tour of India. They were completely outplayed by the superb South African team who captained by Ali Bacher won all four Tests by large margins.

For pure perfection, I doubt if I have ever seen a partnership to rival that of Barry Richards and Graeme Pollock in the 2nd Test at Durban. They added 103 in one hour for the third wicket, matching each other's strokes boundary by boundary. It was technically perfect cricket, Richards scoring 140 and Pollock 274. I shall never forget it.

There was obviously much talk of the coming tour of England in the summer. Would it take place? Would Peter Hain and his friends carry out their threats to stop the games? Was barbed-wire really being put up on the cricket grounds of England? The South African cricketers themselves were keen to make the tour, no matter what difficulties lay ahead. They were undoubtedly the best team in the world and they wanted to prove it against their old opponents England.

I am one of those people who do not think that politics should interfere with sport. I happen to believe that in spite of the inevitable minor incidents, it is still a good thing for people of all races, religions and colours, be they capitalists or communists to play and compete against each other.

I do not approve of what happens in Russia, of what India and Pakistan do to each other, of the way dictators like General Amin of Uganda rule over people or of the civil wars and massacres that have taken place in countries like the Congo and Nigeria. Nor do I approve of governments like those of East Germany, Greece, Cuba, or the Argentine. I could go on indefinitely.

I only want to make the point that there would soon be no people left to play, if we only competed against those whom we liked or of whose politics we approved. Which brings me to South Africa. I love the country and have many friends there, but I definitely do not support apartheid and the way it inflicts unnecessary indignities and restrictions on the coloureds and black people. But this does not stop me visiting the country – any more than I would refuse to go to Spain, Greece or Russia if I wanted to.

I can never understand why South Africa is picked out for special treatment, particularly where cricket is concerned. The white cricketers in South Africa are doing all they can to try to play cricket on a multi-racial basis *inside* South Africa, but at the moment are up against the laws of the country. But I am convinced that things are slowly getting better and will continue to do so if the people there are left alone to sort out their great problem. There are plenty of liberal-minded people among the South Africans who are working towards that end; if do-gooders from outside try to force changes too quickly, then I think there could be real trouble, just as there was in all the other new states of Africa. Anyway, do-gooders would be better employed working in the countries where they advocate change, instead of sitting here in comfort on their backsides urging everyone else to do something! I can never forget what happened in India. We were told that separation was the only hope for the continent and our Parliament voted for it to take place. Fine for the idealists. But it cost over two million lives and they have not been very happy or prosperous since. Still, I am getting too serious and pontificating about things on which I am no expert – which is always fatal . . . I simply wanted to explain my philosophy. The world is alas an evil place. Dreadful things occur in almost every country. But I personally do not think it helps if we all pull up the drawbridge and refuse to mix and play with someone because we don't like the way they live. Our Lord made a good statement about this once. 'First cast out the beam out of thine own eye . . .' As Lord Montgomery once said in a speech when quoting a saying of our Lord '. . . and I quite agree with Him'.

32
From ashes to Ashes

As soon as I got home in the middle of March I had a personal problem to deal with. I heard whispers that while I had been away TV had decided not to use me as a cricket commentator any more.

As I had heard nothing official, I went to seek confirmation from my boss Robert Hudson, the head of radio OBs. He confirmed it unofficially but said that he would rather I waited to be told officially by TV. But to my relief he did add how delighted he was, from radio's point of view, as this would mean he could now have me for all the Tests. His remarks were cheering, as I must admit that I was a bit shocked at the suddenness of it all, though relieved that it had happened.

For the last few years, TV had been changing. The powers that be said they wanted an increasingly professional and disciplined approach – which so far as cricket was concerned meant sticking rigorously to the play to the exclusion of all else. Jokes, stories, anecdotes or light-hearted asides were frowned on and the camera was no longer encouraged to find off-beat pictures of a blonde in a bikini on the grass or small boys playing cricket round the boundary edge.

The emphasis was to be on an analysis of technique and tactics with an efficient appraisal of what was happening on the twenty-two yards of pitch. So be it. But it was not my cup of tea. A cricket match includes so many other things besides what goes on in the middle. It is a game full of character and fun and there is always laughter not far away. But not if you have a producer shouting down your ear . . . 'Steady – no jokes – stick to the cricket!'

As a result of this policy TV has now become a highly efficient purveyor of cricket with superb camerawork and great expertise from the old Test players who now do the commentary. But it has lost its soul and humour and is angled towards the cricketer viewer, and not the majority who don't play and don't know too much about the game, either.

As I write this just after a Test match, four newspapers have praised the efficient and highly technical service given by TV. But each one has added that it lacks the humour and friendliness of the radio ball by ball. It is because of this that more and more people watch the TV picture and listen to our radio commentary.

The same thing was happening in Australia when I was last there. So although my pride was hurt – no one likes to be dropped, whatever the reason – I was secretly pleased to be leaving TV after twenty-four years. *But it would have been nice to have been told!* It is unbelievable but true that I am still waiting to hear from the Head of Sport in TV OBs. He presumably made the decision but I have never heard from anyone in TV that I was being dropped nor the reasons for it.

After about a month, when told I had heard nothing, Peter Dimmock, General Manager of TV OBs, wrote me a short note in his own hand saying he personally would miss me but that it was radio's gain! But no explanation, no thanks nor appreciation from the Head of Sport, which was not too much to expect after twenty-four years in which I had re-started the cricket after the war and helped to create and develop the commentary technique. In addition I had done countless cricket interviews and programmes and had been their consultant on all cricketing matters for a quarter of a century.

I am afraid I sound bitter, and in this very small context I am. I think it is time that TV grew up and learned to deal with people properly. I know it's the technical playground of whizz-kids but they still ought to have good manners and behave as normal human beings in their relations with the people they employ.

I am saying all this, partly to get it off my chest but also because some freelances whom I know have been treated far worse than me. I at least had the welcome refuge of radio. This is my only complaint against the BBC in my long career with them. They have always been kindness itself. But I just hope that this may catch the eye of one of the top TV men who may then ensure that in future TV matches radio in the quality of its manners and behaviour.

The spring was largely taken up with speculation about the coming South Africa tour. It would take a book in itself to go into all the details of meetings, conferences and demonstrations, and the why and wherefore of all the arguments. I stuck to my belief that it is a good thing to keep in touch by means of sport, and these feelings were reinforced when Peter Hain and Co. threatened to disrupt the matches if the tour did take place.

These seemed to me thoroughly dangerous tactics and a threat to democracy as we know it. A group of people – however sincere their cause – were going to prevent a lot of others from the perfectly legal activity of watching cricket. If it were to succeed in such a small field where would it stop? I have always felt that the final capitulation of the Labour Government to these threats, influenced the result of the general election that June.

Anyway it brought me my one and only scoop as the BBC Cricket Correspondent. At 7 pm on 19 May there was to be a Press Conference at Lord's at which the Cricket Council would announce its final decision about the tour. For days beforehand TV, radio and press were full of programmes, articles and interviews about the whole business. Feelings ran high. Colleagues and old friends found themselves on opposing sides. The general consensus of opinion was that the tour would be called off. On the day itself one of London's evenings actually headlined that it *was* off.

But I had a hunch and went on to *The world at one* on Radio 4 and calmly announced that I was sure it would go on. It was awful cheek really, as all Fleet Street was against me and throughout the afternoon news editors came down to my office before each hourly bulletin to see if I had changed my mind. But I didn't and even in the 6 pm news I kept to my opinion. You can imagine therefore how relieved I was when Billy Griffith announced to a packed Long Room that the tour was on. Our News Department too were mightily relieved and were kind enough to send me a note of thanks. But three days later I knew that all was up and this time rightly predicted the cancellation. This was when Maurice Allom as Chairman of the Cricket Council went with Billy Griffith to see Mr Callaghan at the Home Office.

As a result of this meeting, the Government 'requested' the Cricket Council to withdraw the invitation to South Africa. That was as good as a directive, and the tour was off. The cancellation saved cricket commentators from possible verbal embarrassment. In the South African side was A. M. Short of Natal. I personally was dreading having to announce that Boycott had been caught Short in front of the pavilion!

In place of the South African tour a Five-Test series was quickly arranged against a strong 'Rest of the World' side containing ironically five top South African players, the two Pollocks, Barlow, Richards and Procter. The Cricket Council designated these Tests as unofficial and the England players were to be awarded home caps. On this basis the series was sponsored in order to give an extra incentive to win and to avoid suspicion that they were in any way exhibition matches.

On the guarantee that the Tests were to be unofficial – and so count in Test match records as unofficial – BBC TV and radio both gave their usual full coverage. But ever since the International Cricket Council has queried the right of the Cricket Council to have staged even unofficial Tests without their approval.

Statisticians too have had heated arguments among themselves as to whether the figures should be included in records of Test careers. The ICC are entitled by their constitution to authorise *official* Tests, but nothing is said about *unofficial* ones. The solution to my mind would have been for the ICC to have formally approved that the records in this series should be allowed. There were extenuating circumstances, the most important being the severe financial loss that English cricket would have sustained without it. The ICC could then at the same time have laid down that in future all unofficial as well as official Tests must have their prior approval. But the argument still rages.

At the last count, *Wisden*, the bible of cricket and BBC radio were still including the Tests in their records. BBC TV after first supporting this view switched to the other side in 1972. So we have the somewhat Gilbertian situation of the BBC giving out to the world two different sets of statistics. Personally I am strongly in favour of recognising the Tests but think that an awful lot of unnecessary fuss has been made about the whole thing.

England, not unexpectedly, lost the series 1–4 against this very powerful Rest of the World side captained by Gary Sobers. In addition to the South Africans it included Lloyd, Kanhai, Murray from West Indies, Mustaq and Intikhab from Pakistan, Engineer from India and McKenzie from Australia. If a game against a side like that is not a Test match, what is?

Ray Illingworth captained England and remarkably was top scorer with 476 runs averaging 52.88. This form ensured his selection as captain of MCC for the winter tour of Australia and New Zealand, but not without a certain amount of unpleasantness and controversy. Cricket was in the wars yet again.

The trouble was that many people in authority felt that Colin Cowdrey would make a better *tour* captain than Illy. After all he had already been vice-captain on three previous Australian tours.

Accordingly David Clark, a Kent farmer who had captained Kent and was a top administrator on TCCB committees, was appointed manager, before the captain was selected. This pointed to Colin for whom David Clark seemed tailor-made, whereas he and Illy could in the nature of things have very little in common – not even in their philosophy of the way cricket should be played.

So, in spite of his form, Illy's selection *was* a surprise and a bitter disappointment to the sensitive Colin. He 'retired to his tent' to think things over, and it was some time before he could be persuaded to accept the vice-captaincy for the fourth time. You can hardly blame him. But it was not a good way to start the tour and was unfair both on Illy and Colin.

The obvious solution in the future is to select the captain first and then choose a manager to fit in with him. The whole trouble was in the new set-up in cricket whereby the Test and County Cricket Board selectors now chose the touring team without any representative or approval of MCC, although the team was still called MCC! Another example of where change is not always for the best.

For the first time there were to be six Tests in Australia so as to include Perth for the first time, and for the first time too I was to cover all the Tests for BBC. Previously I had always missed the 1st Test at Brisbane.

But before making my preparations to leave for Australia Pauline and I spent a delightful holiday in Jersey at the end of September, when most of the crowds had gone. It was a splendid place to relax after all the excitements of the last few months. Maurice Allom and his wife Pam were also there, and Don Wilson of Yorkshire and his wife Jill.

Maurice had borne the brunt of all the South African crisis as Chairman of the Cricket Council and badly needed a rest. In his Cambridge days he had played the saxophone in Fred Elizalde's Band at the Savoy and with Maurice Turnbull had written a most amusing book about an MCC tour of New Zealand called *Two Maurices*. So he had show-business in his blood – which was just as well when he, Don and I were invited to sing at a night-club. A few days earlier Pauline and I had gone to the same place and had been recognised. The compère, an eccentric extrovert called Ronald Ronalde (not the whistling one) announced that he would sing a song in our honour which he had recently sung in front of the Queen at the Royal Variety Performance. The holidaymakers lapped it up. Here is the song, sung to a catchy old music hall tune:

> *Show me your winkle tonight*
> *When the lights are low.*
> *Show me your winkle tonight*
> *And set my heart a-glow.*
> *Oh, what a surprise*
> *When it dangles in front of my eyes.*
> *My heart is thumping with fright*
> *Show me your winkle tonight*
> *That's right!*

So a few nights later Maurice, Don and myself stood up and sang this to the night-club audience. Not a bad advertisement for cricket I thought at the time. President of MCC and Chairman of the Cricket Council, a Yorkshire and England cricketer, and a BBC commentator, singing a trio in a night-club. I don't know about the singing but at least it proved the harmony which exists among cricketers.

This was to be the last tour which I covered for BBC and except for one or two incidents, I enjoyed it as much as I had all the others. Pauline joined me after Christmas and we saw more of Australia than we ever had before when we motored the 1,100 miles from Adelaide to Sydney with John Woodcock as our companion. The first part of the journey was miles and miles of nothing with the temperatures in the nineties. But then we came to the peaceful Murray Valley and the beautiful Snowy Mountains. Many of the small towns we passed through were reminiscent of the one street cowboy towns of the films and it was an education to see how the other half of Australia lived, away from the big cities.

On our way down to Sydney we stopped to pay homage at the house in Bowral where Don Bradman was brought up as a child. We saw his tiny bedroom and the small backyard where he started his cricket.

Ray Illingworth was not the usual type of MCC captain. He saw it as his sole job to win back the Ashes and if he had to devote more time to cricket than to the social side of the tour then that was too bad. He had always appreciated the tough way Australians play their cricket and he was prepared to match them. They respected him for it.

So far as the Press and broadcasters were concerned, Illy was the most honest and uninhibited of any captain with whom I have toured. If you asked a question, you got a straight answer. An Australian press man once asked him if he thought X threw his off-spinner. When Illy replied yes, he did, there were screams of protest in some quarters. But surely it was the questioner who was to blame? Why ask a question if you don't expect a truthful answer?

Illy was more Yorkshire than Yorkshire itself. Honest, blunt, fair, with not too much time for the niceties of life. But he had the backing of his team, who were intensely loyal to him, and he got the best out of them on the field, including John Snow! Illy is a good tactician and reader of a game and an accurate assessor of his opponents' weaknesses.

Off the field, it would be untrue to say that all was one hundred per cent happy at the top. Through no fault of either of them, David Clark and Illy were never on the same wavelength. It was just an unfortunate pairing. Nor did Illy make enough use of Colin Cowdrey's talents and cricket knowledge. Perhaps Colin, who as ever performed wonders off the field with his visits to schools and hospitals, was too sensitive to offer his advice, and Illy possibly interpreted this as lack of interest. It was a great pity, as had they combined their varied talents what an extra asset it would have been to the team.

But Illy achieved his object of regaining the Ashes by winning the two Tests at Sydney and the series 2–0, though the final Test at Sydney was at one time a close thing and a magnificent team effort.

Geoff Boycott was the outstanding batsman of the tour, scoring 657 runs in five Tests averaging 93.85. But he had his left wrist broken by McKenzie in a one-day game and he could not play at Sydney.

Similarly, John Snow was the outstanding bowler taking thirty-one wickets in the series. But he broke a finger when fielding in the vital second innings at Sydney and could only bowl two overs. But even without their two best players, England in the end won by sixty-two runs, and his team chaired Illy off the field.

Once again – as in 1953 when England last regained the Ashes – I was lucky to be on the air for the *coup de grâce* and Radio 2 stayed open all night to hear our ball-by-ball commentaries. Once again, too, I was able to share the triumph of a team with whom I had been touring for four months, living with them through the good times and the bad.

It would be wrong if I did not deal with two incidents which marred the total success of the tour. The first occurred at Adelaide in the 6th Test (an extra Test was played because the 3rd Test at Melbourne had been abandoned without a ball being bowled).

Boycott was batting beautifully and he and John Edrich had put on 107 for the first wicket when Boycott going for a quick single on the off-side was given run out at the bowler's end. It was certainly a very close thing, and Boycott in disbelief and disapproval of the decision threw his bat down on the ground, and stood with his hands on his hips, like an annoyed washerwoman. One of the Australians picked up his bat for him and directed him back towards the pavilion.

It was a dreadful thing to happen in front of a big crowd, coming as it did from England's number one batsman. The crowd were stunned and so too were the English supporters on the ground. But these sort of things, though not excusable, do happen and the only way to put matters right is for the person concerned to say he is sorry. It is as simple as that. But for some unknown reason Geoff would not apologise either to the umpire or to Ian Chappell the Australian captain, and Illingworth had to do it for him.

Here, surely, was a cut and dried example of where management should have shown leadership, and ordered Boycott to apologise or else . . . But they did not and it is something that Geoff will have to live with for many years to come. He is now desperately sorry that he did it but how much better if he had said so to the people concerned at the time.

Geoff is a complex character whom I like very much. But he is so dedicated to his own success, that he often forgets that there is a world outside his own. By hard work and practice he has achieved near perfection in relation to his batting. He is now working equally hard to perfect his relations with other people. I only hope that he succeeds, for the sake not only of Geoff Boycott, but of Yorkshire and England.

The other incident was the now famous walk-off in the last Test at Sydney. Ian Chappell captaining Australia for the first time put England into bat and got them out for 184. By tea time on the second day Australia were 165 for six. Shortly after, O'Keeffe was out and the second new ball was taken with Jenner joining Greg Chappell. Then followed the famous 'walk-off' incident.

I was broadcasting at the time so most of what happened is clear in my mind. For the rest I have checked and double-checked the events. I have set out the facts below so that you can judge for yourself and make up your own mind what *you* would have done had you been the captain in Illingworth's place – always remembering that you have a chance to sit back and think whereas he had to act on the spur of the moment.

The first two overs with the new ball were bowled by Snow and Lever with no suspicion of a bouncer. With the seventh ball of the third over, Snow, however, did bowl a bouncer at Jenner who ducked into it, was hit on the back of the head, collapsed, and had to be carried off. The crowd naturally enough booed and shouted, roaring their disapproval of Snow.

While the new batsman Lillee was on his way out to the wicket, Lou Rowan, the umpire at Snow's end, told Snow that he should not have bowled a bouncer at a low-order batsman like Jenner. Snow became incensed at this and asked Rowan in not too polite a way whose side he thought he was on. Umpire Rowan then seemed to lose his temper and in what appeared to be an emotional decision, promptly warned Snow under Law 46, Note 4 (IV) for persistent bowling of short-pitched balls.

Then it was Illingworth's turn to protest at what he considered a wrong interpretation of the Law. How could *one* bouncer come under the heading of persistent? Unfortunately, in the heat of the moment, Illingworth also became annoyed and was seen by thousands on the ground and tens of thousands on television to wag his finger at Lou Rowan. What in fact he was doing was trying to indicate that Snow had only bowled *one* bouncer.

Amid a storm of booing – I've seldom heard such a noise on a cricket ground – Snow completed his over by bowling one ball at Lillee. He then turned to go off to his position at long leg. When he had got halfway there some beer cans were thrown in his direction from the small Paddington Hill to the left of the Noble Stand. Snow turned back and returned to the square where Illingworth told the umpires that he would not go on playing until the field was cleared of the cans. The team sat down while this was being done by the ground staff. After a few minutes the ground was clear and Snow set off again for long leg.

I remember saying on the air at the time that I thought the whole incident was going to end happily as members in the Noble Stand and people on the hill started to applaud Snow and a man stretched out over the railings to shake hands with Snow. Snow went up and shook hands but a tough-looking spectator who had obviously 'had a few' then grabbed hold of Snow's shirt and started to shake him.

This was the signal for more cans and bottles to come hurtling on to the field, narrowly missing Snow. Willis ran up and shouted something to the crowd. Then Illingworth came up, saw the bottles flying and promptly signalled to his team to leave the field. The two batsmen and the two umpires stayed on the square. Then the two umpires made their way to the pavilion – the first time they had left the square since the trouble started.

Rowan made it plain to Illingworth that if he did not continue he would forfeit the match and an announcement was made that play would be resumed as soon as the ground had been cleared, not only of the cans and bottles but also of a number of spectators who had clambered over the fence. This, in fact, took only ten minutes and Illingworth led his men back thirteen minutes after leading them off. In the remaining forty minutes, the England side somewhat naturally seemed to have lost their zest, and Chappell and Lillee added forty-five runs so that Australia finished the day at 235 for seven – a lead of fifty-one.

That was the incident as I saw it, though it is true to say that opinions differ about what *exactly* did happen. I said at the time, and I still believe, that Illingworth was right to lead the side off. Not only was it becoming dangerous with bottles flying around, but this action so stunned the crowd that the throwing stopped immediately and play was very soon restarted. In other similar circumstances in the West Indies, the fielding side had stayed on the field and play had to be abandoned for the day.

There was, of course, no excuse for Illingworth to argue in such a demonstrative manner with the umpire. He has since publicly said he was sorry he acted as he did and also concedes that he should have gone back to the square and warned the umpires that he was taking his team off. But he had to make a quick decision and it is surprising that neither umpire left the square at any time to go to deal with the incident at the trouble spot. Illingworth and Snow have also been criticised for Snow's return to long leg after the first lot of cans had been thrown at him.

There are two views about this. As captain, you either take the peaceful way out and give way to force and threats or you stick to your right to place your fieldsmen where you like. And finally, Snow was criticised for going up to the fence and accepting the proffered hand-shake. Who can say what the reaction would have been if he hadn't? I apologise for dealing at such length with this unhappy incident and now you must judge for yourselves.

After the stress and excitements of Australia we spent a very happy and relaxed eighteen days in New Zealand. I am ashamed to say it was my first visit as the BBC had never thought it worth the expense to send me. In fact, even this time I went at my own risk being paid by the New Zealand Broadcasting Corporation for all my commentaries.

This was an unusual procedure, as in the past McGilvray, Fortune, Lawrence and myself have always been paid for by our respective bosses and so have broadcast without fee when visiting other countries. We were lucky with the weather and the team thoroughly enjoyed the chance to unwind slowly before returning home.

New Zealand is a gorgeous country with magnificent scenery and I hope one day to return there for a long holiday. During our stay we decided to try and emulate the England World Cup XI and record a victory song. I scribbled out some words and aided by John Henderson of Reuters we produced four verses designed to fit the tune of the *Winkle Song* which at least we all knew.

We rehearsed in hotel bedrooms and even on the plane home via Los Angeles, and finally gave the song full treatment as we crossed the English coast, much to the surprise of some American passengers, who kept on looking for the Ashes we said we were bringing home.

Although we got back on 12 March we did not record the song until 19 April when the team were all going to be in London for an MCC dinner in their honour. This delay was to prove fatal to the success of the song. At any rate that's our excuse!

The Arsenal pipped us with their song which, because they could advertise it on public address and put it on sale at their matches, were able to sell in sufficient quantities to get into the charts. Ours, in spite of quite a lot of publicity and airings on Radio 2 never caught the public's fancy and try as we might we failed to get on *Top of the pops* on TV.

But though we failed to make a fortune we had a great deal of fun doing it. We had to wait for the spring of 1973 before we heard that our royalties had reached the princely sum of £53.86! We decided to have a draw for four prizes rather than distribute it among all of us. I asked Illy to do the draw at the Test Trial at Hove in 1973 and guess whose name came out of the hat first. It was Illy himself who won the first prize of £25, John Henderson, John Edrich and Bob Willis being the other lucky ones. Here are the words of the song and perhaps they are the best explanation of why it never became a hit!

We've brought the Ashes back home
We've got them here in the urn
The Aussies had had them twelve years
So it was about our turn.
But oh! What a tough fight
It's been in the dazzling sunlight
In spite of the boos of the mob on the Hill
We've won by two matches to nil.

When we arrived people said
The Aussies would leave us for dead
But we knew we would prove them wrong
And that's why we're singing this song
Oh! The feeling is great
For losing is something we hate

So Sydney we thank you for both of our wins
But not for those bottles and tins.

Our openers gave us a good start
And the others then all played their part
We usually made a good score
Seven times three hundred or more
The Aussies however were apt
To collapse at the drop of a hat
If they were bowled any ball that was short
It was ten to one on they'd be caught.

In the field it was often too hot
So sometimes we felt very low
Whether rain was forecast or not
We always knew we'd have Snow
So now to go home we are free
And we're sure the Aussies agree
Though the series has been a long uphill climb
We've all had a real bumper time.

But there is one happy note with which to end the saga of our Victory song. The Prime Minister, Mr Edward Heath, gave a reception to the team, the accompanying Press, and the broadcaster at No. 10, and we presented him with a disc of our song. This was rather a cheeky and presumptuous thing to do in view of his love of good music and skill as an organist. But he was kind enough to send a letter to me and my opinion of him as a judge of good music rose even higher than it had been before.

He said of the record: 'I enjoyed listening to it – and congratulate you on your musical and literary skills'! It is my exclamation mark, not his, but I think you can now better understand why he has become the top politician in the country.

33
A bang, not a whimper

In addition to my involvement with the *Ashes song* I was also busy working on a cricket book which I had been commissioned to write. It had the somewhat optimistic title of *All about cricket*. But this was not as bad as it sounded as it was one of an *All about* series published by W. H. Allen. The book was not intended for experts but rather as a guide to young cricketers, and I found it a most enjoyable task.

I did my best to justify the title and tried to include all aspects of cricket – its history, organisation, the main competitions, a glossary including the laws and regulations, a chapter on batting, bowling and fielding techniques, all the main records, a quiz and a few of my favourite cricket stories. But the part which I enjoyed doing most was selecting my six best Tests and my twenty-seven best players over the period in which I had been commentating. It was not easy and I am afraid that I had to leave out a lot of my best friends among the cricketers.

I also managed to spend a week on a boat on the Thames with my sons Andrew and Ian, and we travelled up as far as Oxford and down just below Windsor. I appointed myself non-playing captain and let the boys do everything.

All went well except once when we forgot to pull up the anchor and dragged it for several miles before we discovered why the boat was going so slowly! Travelling like this is a holiday which I thoroughly recommend. There is a splendid *camaradarie* on the river, and it was encouraging to see as many novices as ourselves doing equally clottish things. We spent a pleasant day at Oxford seeing the colleges and I must admit it did my ego good when we went into the pavilion on the New College Cricket Ground and found my picture as captain of the 1934 side still hanging on the wall, with my sealyham Blob sitting at my feet.

The double tour by Pakistan and India gave final proof that they were both now in the top league and that England were not going to have it their own way on future tours of this country as they had had in the past. Pakistan lost their series 0–1 but rain undoubtedly robbed them of victory in the 1st Test at Edgbaston, and England only just won at Headingley by twenty-five runs.

India were more successful and at the Oval in the 3rd Test beat England for the first time in this country amidst scenes of tremendous enthusiasm. Back in India there was wild rejoicing and the team became such national heroes that their Prime Minister had their plane diverted so that she could personally congratulate them on their success.

If not so good for England, it was wonderful for cricket, especially as India's success was largely due to superb *spin* bowling by Venkat, Chandrasekhar and Bedi. What a relief from the dreary old seam, and the England batsmen short of practice against class spin, just could not cope. There was one unusual feature of the England batting. John Jameson the hard-hitting opener played in the last two Tests and was run out in three of his four innings. None were his fault and Boycott was not playing in either match. How unlucky can you be!

My co-commentators on the six Tests were John Arlott, Alan Gibson and Neil Durden-Smith, with caustic, expert and witty comments from Trevor Bailey. We also had summaries from Pakistan and India but in truth did not always find them easy to understand. But we had plenty of fun in the box and offered the listeners a variety of styles in our commentaries. I am afraid that some of the names offered tempting opportunities to make puns. When the wicket-keeper let byes off Bedi's bowling they became 'Bedi byes', or when comparing two of their batsmen it was 'Sardesai' which was the better.

After a pleasant holiday with Pauline in Cornwall I returned to the BBC for my last year as a member of the staff. Retirement age is sixty and I was to reach that frightening target on 24 June 1972. As this would be in the middle of the cricket season it was decided that I should stay on until the end of the season and retire on 30 September. I was due for a lot of compensatory leave so I arranged to take it at the beginning of the following year which would enable me to go to Australia to follow the series there against a World XI, which as with us, had taken the place of a cancelled South African tour.

I filled in the autumn by temporarily taking over the chairmanship of *Sports forum* from Peter West. This was a sporting brains trust which was recorded at some sports club on Thursday nights and transmitted in *Sport on two* the following Saturday afternoon. The panel consisted of a columnist like Jim Manning or Peter Wilson and two top sport stars. It was a useful forum for presenting opinions, criticisms and informal discussion on any sporting topic.

I have known Peter West since he joined me on TV cricket in the late forties, and he has been the most versatile of all the TV commentators. His wide range of sports has included cricket, lawn tennis, rugby football, athletics and hockey plus of course his winter invasion of the dancing world as the genial compère of *Come dancing*. I suppose it could be said that he has tried to do too much, but I am sure that his reply to that would be that he is still on friendly terms with his bank manager!

Peter has been booked for so many different types of programmes because he is the TV producers' ideal choice – a thorough professional who will always do a good job and never let anyone down. There are quite a few behind-the-scenes crises on TV, which the viewer never knows about thanks to the aplomb, unflappability and experience of people like Peter. I enjoyed my years with him on the TV cricket commentary team immensely. With Peter and Denis Compton about there was always plenty of laughter and I honestly cannot remember a cross word ever passing between the three of us.

Much of the rest of my time was taken up with a Computer Test between England and Australia, the commentary on which was to be broadcast nightly on Radio 4 for a week after Christmas. The match was to be 'played' at Lord's and the two teams were to be chosen from postwar players who had played in Tests in England since the war.

The Australian team was selected by Sir Donald Bradman, cricket writer Ray Robinson and Alan McGilvray, and the England side by Sir Neville Cardus, John Arlott and myself. Both lots of selectors chose surprise captains, Alan Davidson for Australia, and Trevor Bailey for England, neither of whom had ever captained their country in a real Test.

Once the teams were chosen, a large computer firm was given full details about each player. If he were a batsman we gave his records, his temperament, whether good in a crisis or not, his best strokes or his favourite type of bowler. Similarly with the bowlers we gave details of their type of bowling, their stamina and the sort of pitch on which they performed best. In addition, we provided a weather forecast for the five days, and an estimate of how we thought the pitch would play. All this information was fed into a giant computer to be analysed and stored in the computer's brain. A week before Christmas the match was 'played' and a commentary recorded of the highlights of each day's play. Alan Davidson had flown over from Australia and after he had won the toss and chosen to bat he and Trevor sat in front of a big machine rather like a teleprinter. The batting captain could nominate his batting order and give instructions to his batsmen to attack or to defend. The captain of the fielding side could change his bowlers every five overs or whenever a wicket fell, and decide whether to set an attacking or defensive field.

The operator passed all this information into the machine and then pressed a button and the match was on. At the end of every five overs the machine produced an up-to-date score card to show how many runs had been scored or if any wickets had fallen. The captains could then change their tactics if they wished and another five overs would be played.

This went on till the end of the innings and the captains' decisions called for a high degree of skill. I'm sorry to say that Australia won easily by 142 runs thanks to some fine fast bowling by Lindwall and Miller which would have been extremely likely in the conditions which we had simulated.

When the details on the score sheet were complete John Arlott, Christopher Martin-Jenkins and myself recorded commentaries based on detailed notes of what had happened. We were backed by sound effects – applause, groans, appeals and the noise of ball on bat. It all sounded very realistic – too realistic according to some critics. They said that if we could make up commentary like that they would never know in future whether we were speaking the truth in our genuine ball-by-ball commentaries.

But they were taking it all far too seriously. The match was only meant to be a bit of fun to fill a few cold winter evenings with the sound of ball on bat.

We had our usual family Christmas with all of us having stockings and everyone (Barry 22, Clare 20, Andrew 17, Ian 14 and Joanna 6) opening them on Pauline's and my bed at 8 o'clock in the morning. I must admit I am a sucker for Christmas and we have been lucky to have our children to share it with us over so many years. Three days later I flew off to Australia.

Once again I had been invited to be a neutral commentator – this time by ABC television – and I covered the matches with Alan McGilvray and Lindsay Hassett. We were lucky enough to see one of the most fantastic innings ever played in international cricket – Gary Sobers's 254 at Melbourne.

I have never seen more thrilling stroke play, much of it unorthodox with feet a long way from the ball. By the end, even the fielders were applauding the scorching drives, hooks and cuts. ABC TV have fortunately made a film of it with a commentary by Don Bradman, who said it was the best innings which he had ever seen in *Australia*. I think he still considers Stan McCabe's 232 at Trent Bridge in 1938 as the best which he saw anywhere.

After the last match at Adelaide I flew to South Africa for a fortnight's holiday. Pauline and Andrew met me at Durban and after a week by the sea at the lovely Oyster Box Hotel we went up to St Lucia to see my sister Anne once again. We left Andrew with her to spend a year in South Africa to see a bit of life and get used to looking after himself.

I got back to England in the middle of February and on Thursday, 2 March heard the very sad news that Franklin Engelmann had died suddenly of a heart attack in the night, only a few hours after recording *Down your way* on the Wednesday. It was decided that this would still be used at the usual time on the Sunday but there was no immediate decision as to who would take over the programme at such short notice, although it would have to be recorded in six days' time.

Down your way had been running since 1946 with Stewart Macpherson and Richard Dimbleby as the two first interviewers. Richard had been succeeded by 'Jingle' in 1953 and since then after 733 programmes everyone associated *Down your way* with Franklin Engelmann. It would be an impossible task to follow him and needless to say after a couple of days I was asked to do it! Once again I was to be a stand-in but only for a week or two, I was told, while a permanent substitute was found.

In the end I did ten programmes before my cricket commitments forced me to give up and four different interviewers were selected, to fill in during the summer. I had evidently not done too badly as I was asked to take over the programme again in October when of course I would be a freelance after retiring from the BBC staff.

I must confess that the very first programme which I did at Hyde in

Cheshire the week after Jingle died was not easy and I felt very diffident and humble following in his footsteps. He had had such a large faithful following that I thought they would regard me as an intruder and resent me taking over. But I need not have worried. I received nothing but the most friendly and encouraging letters, and it is one of the most satisfying and rewarding programmes which I have ever done.

The procedure for the recording of *Down your way* is as follows. The producer – either Phyllis Robinson or Richard Burwood – go on Sunday night to the chosen location. On the Monday and most of Tuesday they talk to the Town Clerk, the local newspaper and possibly one of the town's taxi-drivers who usually know all about everyone. From these conversations they select six victims to tell us about the place and themselves.

The interviewer and an engineer with recording equipment arrive during Tuesday afternoon and three or possibly four interviews are done that day. We visit the people in their homes or places of work and after briefing from Phyllis or Richard, I usually chat them up for about quarter of an hour, to gain their confidence and to check up which questions are likely to get the most interesting answers.

At the end of each interview I ask them for their choice of music. This is left entirely to them so long as what they choose has not been played the previous week. Sometimes, too, if they ask for something very rare which we think the BBC Gramophone Library might not have, we ask them to give us an alternative. We usually finish by lunch time on the Wednesday, when the producer returns to London to spend the next two days putting the programme together.

This may mean cutting or editing the interviews to bring them down to the right time and also, of course, slotting in the music at the end of each interview.

The interviews are used for the Sunday programme which lasts for forty minutes from 5.15 pm to 5.55 pm on Radio 4. It is repeated on Tuesday from 11.05 am to 11.45 am still on Radio 4.

In April we enjoyed a happy family occasion when we went along to the Savoy to hear Barry's group 'Design', who were appearing as the main act in the cabaret. Barry had left Eton at the age of 17½ after getting two 'A' and five 'O'-Levels. It would be untrue to say either that he had left his mark on the school or that Eton had left its mark on him. He was always a bit of a rebel and found it difficult to conform to discipline and regulations, so unlike me had never enjoyed his school days.

But he has always acknowledged that Eton gave him the valuable gift of confidence, and also the opportunity to learn to play the guitar and compose songs. I thought at the time that it was an expensive way of attaining the latter two objectives but as things have turned out it may well have been worth it. Anyway, again unlike me, he knew exactly what he wanted to do – to sing and to compose.

I remembered my own experience when through lack of guts I failed to train as an actor but went into the family business in which I was not really interested. I was determined that so far as possible all the children could start by doing what they wanted. If they then failed they could never complain that they had not been given the chance. So Pauline and I tried to help and encourage Barry in every way we could.

Thanks to the kindness of Sir Edward Lewis he went to work at the Decca Recording Studios in West Hampstead within a few weeks of leaving Eton. He stayed there for nine months and learnt all the tricks of the recording business. He then spent the next two years behind the counter in various record shops, living with us at home and using all his spare time composing songs, often late into the night.

Barry got to know various people on the recording side of the BBC and in 1969 with three other boys and two girls formed the harmony, singing group Design. They had a tough struggle to start with but gradually got recording dates on many different programmes on Radio 2. Then came television with a number of appearances on a variety of comedy shows.

The comedians seemed to like their style and songs, and among those for whom they have appeared are Morecambe and Wise, Rolf Harris, Al Read, Mike and Bernie Winters, Tommy Cooper, Spike Milligan and Larry Grayson. They have also been in the musical programmes of Vera Lynn, Val Doonican and Nana Mouskouri. The group all live together in a flat and have produced several LPs and singles but have yet to have a hit. Their LPs especially have been highly praised by the critics but neither they nor the singles reached the charts.

One of the troubles is that their type of music is a trifle square for Radio 1 producers and disc jockeys and unless a record gets a good airing on this channel it evidently does not stand a chance. I must confess though to being puzzled how it all works. I have gone into quite a few record shops and asked for one of Design's records, only to hear 'Sorry we have not got it in stock.'

When I ask why not, I am told 'Oh we only stock records which are in the charts.' And yet we are assured that the charts are compiled from the number of records sold in the shops. But if they don't stock them how can anyone buy them? It seems to be the old story of the chicken and the egg.

Anyhow all goes well with Design and they were so successful at the Savoy that they were asked back ten months later at a bigger fee and for three weeks instead of a fortnight. They certainly make a pleasant sound and are slick and professional with their arrangements and harmonies. They go round the clubs, especially in the North, have done a summer show at Skegness with Tommy Cooper and keep popping up on the TV and radio. All they need now is that elusive hit.

The Australians were welcome visitors for my last summer on the BBC staff, and it was one of the best series since the war, very closely fought with each side winning two Tests. This meant that England kept the Ashes which Illingworth's side had won in Australia.

The Australians gave me an opportunity to play my nickname game. Laguna was obvious for Lillee but I was quite pleased with Chusetts and Melon for Massie and Colley respectively. They were a most friendly side admirably managed by Ray Steele and Fred Bennett and extremely well-captained by Ian Chappell both on and off the field.

Ian's younger brother Greg established himself as one of the leading batsmen in the world. I well remember his hundred against England in his first Test at Perth. It was on a Sunday and I felt compelled to say that the English bowlers looked as if they had had too much Chappell on Sunday.

Besides the reliable batting of Keith Stackpole the other great success of the tour was Dennis Lillee who took thirty-one wickets in the series. With his long, dark mane and even longer run he is a genuine fast bowler and a magnificent sight as he runs up – so long as you are not the batsman! It looks as if he will be plagued with a bad back unless he cuts down his run. At the moment he takes far too much out of himself.

Lillee's partner Bob Massie had his great triumph on his Test début at Lord's when he took eight wickets in each innings – sixteen for 137 in the match. It was an incredible performance which broke all Australian bowling records and was not surprisingly the best ever by any bowler on his first Test appearance.

Bob achieved it by bowling prodigious swingers from round the wicket mostly out swing but with the occasional late in-swinger in ideal heavy atmosphere. He completely flummoxed the England batsmen but one felt at the time that it was probably a once-only performance and so it proved. By adjusting their technique – in most cases using a more open stance – the England batsmen finally mastered him and in the last two Tests he only took two wickets.

The most surprising thing about the series was that no England batsman managed to score a hundred in the five Tests, but John Snow as usual produced his best against Australia and took twenty-four wickets.

For the first time there were three one-day Internationals sponsored by the Prudential. For these Brian Close was dramatically recalled to captain England in place of Ray Illingworth who had an injured ankle which he had turned over in the Oval Test. England won the mini-series 2–1 and in spite of dull weather the matches were good fun and attracted satisfactory crowds, though the Australians, at the end of a long and tiring tour were not too enthusiastic about them.

From England's point of view the main satisfaction was the impressive form of Dennis Amiss who proved that he was no longer affected by the big occasion. The Prudential made a fifty-five-minute film of the three matches for which I wrote the script and did the commentary. I was amused that the only reaction to it was because of something nothing to do with cricket. At Lord's the sun came out suddenly for a short time and its reflection shone into the batsman's eyes off a board advertising Prudential. The umpires ordered it to be turned face downwards on the grass so I said: 'That must be the only time the Sun has got the better of the Prudential,' which caused some chuckles in the insurance world.

After the three Internationals there was only a fortnight left before I retired as a member of the BBC staff. I had been due to leave on 30 September but I was owed some leave. So I had to rush around arranging things like pensions and clearing up all the clutter in my office. I also had to sign a contract for *Down your way* which I was to restart in October and for which now as a freelance I would be paid. I had agreed with Robert Hudson that all goodbyes and leaving parties should wait until October or November as most people in OBs took their leave in September when the summer activities died down.

Meanwhile I had two cricket commitments before I left. First the annual Gillette Cup Final at Lord's which has become the biggest day in the cricket season. The rival supporters really care who wins, and St John's Wood rings with their cheers and applause. This year it was between Lancashire and Warwickshire, and Lancashire completed a hat-trick of victories for the third time running under Jackie Bond's captaincy.

Clive Lloyd made a magnificent 126, one of the most exciting innings which I have ever seen, and once again my good luck held. One of the sport's programmes came over to me for a score flash at exactly the moment when Clive reached his hundred. From Lord's I went to Edgbaston to see Warwickshire clinch the County Championship by beating Derbyshire. So I finished on a high note so far as cricket was concerned, and went off to Swanage for my holiday – self-employed for the first time in my life.

It was not long before I got my first job, and strangely enough it was for Thames TV – the opposition. They were planning a series of thirteen weekly programmes called *A place in the country* in which they were to visit a National Trust property every week.

Each programme was to be introduced by a different presenter and they had asked me to do the one from the beautiful village and abbey of Lacock in Wiltshire. Although I was still with the BBC till the end of the month, with their usual kindness they allowed me to go to Lacock for a day's filming on 16 September. The main filming was to be done in November but they wanted to catch the local fair, a village cricket match and the harvest festival. It was strange to be working for the opposite side but they were most friendly and one hundred per cent efficient.

So I thoroughly enjoyed my first day's work as a freelance, especially as Larry the Ram escaped from his pen, where he was on view for people to guess his weight. We were filming the cricket at the time and Larry obligingly ran right across the pitch followed by half the village trying to catch him. Ram stopped play but it made a good shot for our film.

I returned to my interrupted holiday in Swanage where Pauline had recently bought the two top floors of a house on the cliffs, looking out on a magnificent view of the bay and Old Harry's Rocks between

Swanage and Studland. Pauline had made it very comfortable and from now on this was to be our second home. The idea was that I should write this book there in peace, away from the telephone, and looking out to sea for inspiration. I have in fact written much of it there but have always found the sun and the sea more of a temptation than an inspiration, and have often found myself sneaking off to the beach.

My immediate future was mapped out for the autumn based on *Down your way* every Tuesday and Wednesday and this book for the remainder of my spare time. I had one important thing to do and that was to register at the local Labour Exchange. The BBC had advised me to do this on the first day after I had officially left their employment. So I took their advice and I am still not sure if what happened really did!

I went along and a nice man recognised me and directed me to a counter reserved for the professions. There I asked another nice chap what I had to do, explaining that the BBC had told me to come. He asked if I was working that day. I said that I had no actual job to do, but would be doing some writing for this book and the next day would be off to record *Down your way*. He advised me to go to another counter to register as out of work as, so I understood it, I would be entitled to some pay. I couldn't believe what he had said, and asked whether the unemployment figures would go up by one if I signed and he said yes they would.

I was staggered that in my sort of profession I could draw the dole for a day on which I had no actual job. I asked if the rule would apply to a famous singing star who gave, shall we say, a concert at the Albert Hall on the Wednesday for which he might be paid a thousand pounds or more. Supposing he rested on the other four working days would he be entitled to draw the dole for those days? The answer was yes he would. I still cannot believe it – perhaps I was dreaming or he was pulling my leg.

And yet I can remember once seeing that an actor was on the dole, though I knew he had just been in quite a long run. Anyway I thanked the nice man and declined to register and at least felt that I had reduced the unemployment figures by one. It still worries me, but perhaps explains why the figures are still so high even though most people say they have a shortage of staff or labour.

When working at No. 98 I tucked myself away at the top of the house in my daughter Clare's bedroom, which I turned into an office. She had gone to Australia for a year's look-around as we wanted her to see this wonderful country which offers so many opportunities to young people. After a month or so of temporary secretarial work she landed herself a super job as the sales representative of the Island of New Caledonia in Australia and New Zealand, with her base in Sydney.

New Caledonia is a French island in the Pacific off the coast of Queensland, and Clare got the job because of her fluent French. Pauline had wisely sent her to La Rochelle as soon as she left school. There she stayed with a French family and was the only English girl to attend the local lycée.

The family consisted of the police inspector, his wife, three sons and daughter. The latter four were all more or less Clare's age or a bit older and taught her all she wanted to know. After six months she returned speaking the language like a Frenchwoman and she also taught herself Spanish, Italian and a smattering of German. This ability to speak languages coupled with all the necessary secretarial skills got her some good jobs here before she left for Australia. Already she has been to New Zealand, Fiji, New Hebrides and Singapore, and when in Sydney she has been wonderfully looked after by all our friends. So that's Number Two happily settled and I am beginning to wonder whether we shall ever get her back!

There were three parties to 'celebrate' my leaving. First Pauline and I gave a supper party at Lord's for all my old OB colleagues and their wives. It was fun collecting them all together and Barry helped to entertain them with some of his songs. Then 'owing to universal demand' John Ellison and I did our old cross-talk act with a few extra gags which had not been considered 'suitable' when we originally broadcast it in *In town tonight*.

B.J. I call my dog Carpenter.

J.E. Why?

B.J. Because he's always doing odd jobs about the house. You should see him make a bolt for the door.

J.E. I haven't seen him about lately.

B.J. No. I had to shoot him.

J.E. Was he mad?

B.J. Well, he wasn't too pleased. I must go now to see my wife.

J.E. What do you call *her*?

B.J. Radio 4.

J.E. Why on earth Radio 4?

B.J. Because she has nothing on after midnight.

Luckily, our guests had been well wined, and John and I knew enough about the business to take it all at a great pace, so it went down quite well.

Next followed a cocktail party given by the Managing Director of Radio, Ian Trethowan, in the Governors' dining-room. When I had gratefully accepted the invitation I had begged that there should be none of those farewell speeches which are usually so embarrassing to all present. But Ian did give me a beautiful brief-case and a clock from all my colleagues and I made a 'brief' speech of thanks.

Finally, OB Department gave me a dinner at Lord's with all the old heads of OBs present – Michael Standing, Lobby, Charles Max-Muller with Robert Hudson in the chair. Robert had taken over from Charlie as Head of OBs and in character was very much in the Lobby mould. He was an excellent and sympathetic boss, because he himself is a first-rate commentator – not just for ceremonials but for cricket and rugger. He therefore understands the difficulties and problems which commentators have to face, and he has always been a most helpful critic and friend. He was always of enormous help to me in arranging various cricket trips abroad.

It was an hilarious evening though I'm afraid Robert did make a very kind speech, and I could not resist making one far too long in reply.

Then came the surprise. Four of my closest friends in the department had secretly recorded a 'tribute' on tape to the tune of Noël Coward's *The stately homes of England*. The words were written by John Haslam and I am including them, not out of vanity, but because they are an accurate re-cap of the many things which I did at the BBC, and also an astute insight into one or two of my characteristics.

> *Geoff Dobson, John Fenton, John Haslam, Michael T.,*
> *We used to lunch with him every day,*
> *What shall we do without B.J.?*
>
> *Here we are the four of us*
> *And there are so many more of us,*
> *Producers at the BBC*

We know the men that we employ
All give our listeners great joy,
But only a few in our submission
Carry on the tradition
of Dimbleby, MacPherson,
Glendenning, Snagge and Alston,
Giants all you must agree.
In that list another name deserves inscription
For powers of description
And versatility.

The name of Brian Johnston
We proudly celebrate.
We think that all his broadcasts
Are utterly first rate,
In cricket of course he's number one,
But we mustn't forget other things he's done:
Like Boat Race commentary
Down at Chiswick Bridge,
Or chatting up racing fans
In the Aintree stands.
His series Let's go somewhere
Was one that brought him fame,
He's been posted as a parcel
And run over by a train,
He's even sold
Pound notes we're told,
To a very unwilling crowd.
We're proud
Of the name of Brian Johnston.

Here you see the pick of us,
You may be heartily sick of us,
Still there's more we must recall.
His introductions of Today,
His interviews in Down your way
So many programmes we can mention,
Like good old Twenty questions,
Sporting chance *and* Treble chance
Those competitions of the dance

He compèred from the Albert Hall.
At Christmas time he entertained us from the circus,
He also worked for us
From a 'seat' in the stalls.

The wit of Brian Johnston
Is famed for miles and miles,
His double-act with Ellison
Has us rolling in the aisles.
He's a terrible one for the ghastly pun,
And nicknames that make the owners run
The length of Oxford Street
To escape from them.
The luckier ones get '-ers'
Stuck onto the end of their's.
His after-dinner speeches
Are something quite unique,
His fund of risqué stories
Lasts right into next week,
And if you can thrill
To the jokes of MacGill
On postcards from the beach,
You'll screech
At the wit of Brian Johnston.

Our dear friend Brian Johnston
Has travelled near and far,
To South Africa, the West Indies
And Australasia.
In foreign climes he can be quite rude
About the muck that they serve as food,
And he must have a room with a bath,
When away from home.
While if you're ordering booze,
It must be white wine you choose.
And now he's going to leave us –
Life won't be the same at all,
When our corridor no longer resounds
To that well-known trumpet call.

But if he agrees
To work for small fees,
We'll book him for years and years.
Three cheers
For our dear friend Brian Johnston.

A couple of explanations are perhaps needed. The reference to 'ers' refers to my habit of adding 'ers' to everyone's name so that if I have not given them a nickname they become Boycers, Unders, Chappers, Stackers – yes and even Titters. As a result most of the cricket world retaliate by calling me Johnners.

This habit seems especially to amuse the West Indians and I often carry on a conversation with them adding 'ers' to every word. The mention of the trumpet-call refers to my rather poor imitation of a trumpet which became quite famous in Broadcasting House, as I trumpeted my way round the corridors 'playing' various tunes. It has also become well-known in cricket dressing-rooms all round the world, and whenever I enter one there is usually a chorus of trumpets to greet me.

34
A silver lining

My 'retirement' was proving far busier than I had expected. There was always the book and *Down your way*, and in addition to four days' filming at Lacock, I was also asked to do the commentary on the Lord Mayor's Show for BBC TV. It was nice to be back at a job of this sort and even after quite a long lay-off my past experience came in useful on this occasion.

The producer Willie Cave and myself had been assured by the City of London Police that the procession would stick meticulously to the advertised timings. But there can be no rehearsal for this long procession and with motor vehicles, horse-drawn coaches, animals, and bands marching as they play, it needs a miracle for everything to work to plan.

This time a pipe band had difficulty in keeping up and a large gap of at least a mile developed so that for ten minutes or more we had nothing passing our cameras in front of St Paul's Cathedral. It took quite a bit of filling in but with the help of some film and by switching to our roving camera on a float in the procession we managed somehow.

In fact it worked out very well for us in the end, as at the moment we were due to hand back the Lord Mayor's coach came to a halt bang in front of our cameras, and Lord Mais poked his head out and waved to the viewers.

The attraction and fascination of TV has always been that when things go wrong, as they frequently do, it really *is* a challenge, and demands the closest co-operation between producer, commentator and camera crews.

During the winter MCC were touring India and Pakistan but as I was no longer their Cricket Correspondent there was no question of my going there for the BBC. Even if I had still been a member of the staff I would have had to use all my powers of persuasion to get them to send me. They had never yet sent anyone to India and in fact did not do so on this occasion, using Crawford White of the *Daily Express* for reports.

There are several reasons for the BBC not sending a representative. Up till now this tour had never been considered a major one, and reception from some of the grounds had always been a bit dicey. The two hour difference in time also meant that any live broadcast of commentary would be during the morning or afternoon when most cricket enthusiasts are at work.

However, I had got so used to my winter sunshine that I was determined to get some somewhere. I toyed with the idea of the West Indies, either to follow Kent on their whirlwind tour of the islands as John Player champions, or to see a couple of Tests between West Indies and Australia. But I finally settled for five weeks in South Africa where Derrick Robins was taking a team to play the Provinces and two representative sides and I arranged with *Down your way* to be absent for four programmes.

Once again I was dead lucky. I happened to mention casually to Derrick that I would be following his team around and he immediately offered me the job of Press Liaison Officer – all expenses paid and to travel as one of the team. It was a marvellous offer and I naturally accepted at once, and SABC kindly asked me to broadcast all the matches for them.

Before I left, we had our first Christmas at Swanage with Barry, Ian and Joanna, but minus Clare in Australia and Andrew still in South Africa. It was a pleasant novelty for all of us to open our stockings in our bedroom on a winter morning overlooking the sea.

Just before we went down to Swanage I had been asked to do an unusual type of broadcast for me – the short religious programme *Thought for the day*. I was interviewed and asked to say exactly what Christmas means to me. Besides the mundane things which I have mentioned earlier this gave me an opportunity to put across one point which has always worried me. At Christmas time people are kind and friendly. Everyone has a cheerful greeting for each other, people are generous and take pleasure in giving. Overnight they become good neighbours. What a pity therefore that this spirit of goodwill does not exist for the rest of the year. What a better place the world would be if only it did. That was one thing I said, trite and unoriginal perhaps, but no less true for all that.

The other thing I was able to explain was my simple philosophy of life. I am afraid that I have never been a very good Christian. I believe in God and in some sort of after-life, though I don't pretend to understand how it will work.

As a child and at school, I went to church regularly, probably far too often. Instead of an occasion it just became part of a hum-drum curriculum. As a grown-up I have always gone to communion at Easter and Christmas and have attended one or two other services during the year. Pauline and I have always taken the children to Sunday School or children's services, but they like me have had a surfeit of chapel while at school.

We both feel guilty at not making them go to church on Sunday but as we don't go ourselves we have felt it wrong to expect them to do so. I really regret not showing them a better example as we have always had such a flourishing Christian community at St John's Church, and I enjoy the services when I do attend.

But somehow, Sunday morning is the time to do all the things one has not done during the week. That's no excuse. Just a very poor reason. I do in private try to say thank you to God for everything, and to pray for people less fortunate than myself in the way of health and living conditions.

In addition, I have also given myself a standard to try to follow, based on that character in Charles Kingsley's *Water babies* – Mrs Doasyouwouldbedoneby. I try to apply this philosophy in all my dealings with people, and say to myself. 'How would *I* like it if he spoke to *me* like that?' or 'if someone did that to *me* how would *I* feel?' Of course I frequently fail, or speak or act too swiftly to give myself time to ask myself the questions. But it is a useful guide-line for a workable Christian way of life and it has undoubtedly helped me. Here endeth the sermon and I do hope it doesn't sound too terribly smug.

The Robins tour was a great success and the most enjoyable of all those I have accompanied. There were none of the stresses and strains of Test matches. The team had been carefully selected for character as well as form and there were no prima-donnas.

I had no daily reports nor countless interviews to worry about as I had always had on other tours. I was accepted as a member of the team, ate, lived and travelled with them, and used their dressing-room and attended all the team meetings.

These included the famous Saturday Night Club which is a feature of all MCC tours. This is a compulsory meeting for the whole side after play every Saturday. They meet in one of the hotel rooms under a different chairman each week who ordains what dress – or lack of it – shall be worn. There are various rituals which I must not reveal, and a certain amount of drink (hard or soft) is consumed, orders for which are taken in advance by two 'barmen' appointed weekly. The whole thing only lasts about half an hour and after attending and enjoying all of them on this tour, I feel that they are a very worthwhile and informal get-together and good for a team's morale. In these days of motels, with meals and TV in the rooms, players on a tour often only meet at functions or on the field of play. This Saturday night ritual does at least bring them all together.

The weather and hospitality were superb and the cricket of high quality. The Robins team was the equivalent of an England 3rd XI with MCC in India and players like Illingworth, Snow, Boycott, Edrich and members of the Kent XI not available. Eight of the team were under twenty-six years of age and there were two definite finds, or confirmations perhaps to some of us.

Frank Hayes and John Lever both looked England class and Clive Radley, Mike Smith, Bob Willis and John Murray all had a good tour. The matches attracted enthusiastic crowds, especially the final one at the Wanderers which the South African XI not surprisingly won easily, with such names as Richards, Barlow, Procter, Bacher and Irvine in their side. South African cricket and cricket lovers owe a big debt to Derrick for giving them an opportunity to see their best players playing as a team against opposition from overseas, instead of just playing against each other. And I must add that although some of their players are not as young as they were, South Africa could still beat any other team in the world.

Derrick Robins is an amazing character, a cheerful extrovert with tremendous energy and drive. Besides founding a building firm from scratch which is now worth millions, he has made Coventry City Football Club what it is today. For the last twenty years his cricket team has also provided cheerful and aggressive cricket against overseas visitors and the Universities.

He is a splendid companion and he and I found two mutual likes – old-time music-hall comedians and the local South African white wine – a dangerous combination! We indulged in a cross-talk act on all possible occasions and he even taught me some new jokes. The one I particularly enjoyed was from one of the routines of that wonderful comic Jimmy James, of the stuttering legs.

Jimmy always had two stooges and he announced to the audience that one of them would shortly do a parachute jump from 20,000 feet. He went on to say that the stooge would not open the parachute until within 10 feet of the ground. 'What happens if the parachute doesn't open then?' asked the stooge nervously. 'You can jump 10 feet can't you?' was Jimmy's unsympathetic reply.

During the match against the South African XI I perpetuated one of my worst puns. Tony Brown of Gloucestershire, who had been flown out as a replacement for Peter Willey, had a badly poisoned toe. When he came off the field he removed his boots and socks and his toe looked an ugly sight, all red and oozing.

'What pantomime does this remind you of?' I asked the dressing-room at large. Getting no reply I said: 'Pus(s) in Boots' and received the best reward for a punster. A long sustained groan.

I shall always be grateful to Derrick for this tour as it also gave me a chance of seeing my sister Anne again, and of meeting Andrew for the first time since we had left him there a year earlier. He was very tall, fair and sun-tanned and had had a marvellous time. He has always been keen on shooting and fishing and he had enjoyed plenty of both, including a fishing trip to Mozambique.

Andrew had worked on a farm, helped to build an airstrip, and went on a wilderness trail through one of the game reserves. He also accompanied the game wardens when they darted the rhinos. They chased them through the undergrowth in a Land Rover and then fired a dart into them which did not take immediate effect. The rhino went on for a bit, and then suddenly stopped dead, completely immobilised in every limb. It could then be lifted into a truck and shipped off abroad to a zoo or to another game reserve which was short of rhino.

For the last part of his stay Andrew had hitch-hiked down to Durban and got himself a job with South African Railways driving a fork truck in Durban harbour. This was long and arduous work and meant leaving the small hotel where he lived with a number of other young people at 6.30 am, sometimes not getting back till 9 pm.

But he loved it all, especially the climate and was loath to return to England. But we thought he had had his year and that it was time he came home to decide what to do in life. As I write he is working in Foyles' bookshop in Charing Cross Road. He enjoys this but obviously still hankers after South Africa.

I returned to England at the beginning of February and immediately got down to my weekly but pleasant chore of *Down your way*, which in my absence had been introduced by that splendid character from *Tonight* – Fyfe Robertson – a real contrast in accent and pace of delivery to myself!

The most important date ahead in my diary was Sunday, 22 April, which was Pauline's and my Silver Wedding Day. This gives me an opportunity to say thank you to her for such wonderfully happy twenty-five years. She has always been of great help and given me every encouragement, though never afraid to criticise if necessary. She has also been remarkably patient and tolerant of my unusual job, with its irregular hours, few free week-ends and always working on Bank Holidays when most people are not.

I have lost count of the number of times we have had to refuse or cancel invitations to parties because of some programme which I have had to do. The twenty-second of April was a good example as I was booked to commentate on the Battersea Park Easter Parade for TV, so we could not even have a celebration lunch. Actually I nearly missed this broadcast because on the Saturday I had twenty-four hour flu but luckily was all right on the Sunday. Had I missed doing the commentary it would have broken my twenty-seven-year-old record of never missing a broadcast through ill health.

There have of course been compensations for Pauline, such as trips abroad and attending shows or ceremonies which we were broadcasting. I suppose it's also true that she has met more interesting and famous people than she would otherwise have done. But she has inevitably had to play second fiddle, except in her home town of Sheffield, where I am known as Pauline Tozer's husband!

But it must have been frustrating at times as she is artistic, musical and an expert photographer and if she had not been tied to me might have become a person in her own right. As it is of course she has had to bring up our family of five and I know they all endorse my verdict that she has been a jolly good mother.

I think our marriage proves that you don't have to be compatible in all things and that a little give and take on both sides works wonders. Our chief incompatibility has been on the question of time. She likes to go to bed late, and sleep late, and I am an early bird and can never sleep beyond 8 am. She is also very unpunctual while I, with my Grenadier training am usually five minutes early. Most of the 'little local difficulties' have been because she has kept me waiting before going out somewhere. But I gather from other husbands that this is nothing unusual! Anyhow if that's the only thing that's wrong, the next twenty-five years shouldn't be too bad either!

The summer was to be a very busy one for me as I was to combine *Down your way* with cricket commentary on all the six Tests, plus a certain number of County, Benson and Hedges, John Player and Gillette matches. This meant that when *Down your way* followed a Test match we could record on the Wednesday only, instead of the usual Tuesday/Wednesday. I also pre-recorded some to put them in the bag so that I could have my holiday in September.

As for cricket, so far as finance and weather were concerned the summer of 1973 was a bonanza. The glorious sunshine brought out the crowds and they saw Hampshire win the County Championship, Kent both the Benson and Hedges and John Player competitions and Gloucestershire the Gillette Cup for the first time. But though the cricket generally was bright and entertaining it was a sad year for England at

Test level. Although New Zealand lost the first series of the double tour 0–2 they gave England plenty of shocks in the first two Tests. At Trent Bridge they made fools of all of us so-called experts in TV, Radio and the Press. For years we had all pronounced that a score of over 400 was an impossible target for a fourth innings victory, quoting Australia's 404 for 3 at Leeds in 1948 as the one exception which would ever prove the rule. And yet at Trent Bridge New Zealand actually made 440 – only thirty-nine runs short of victory. In the series their captain Bev Congdon played two fine innings of 176 and 175, full of guts and determination while Vic Pollard also made two hundreds and Mark Burgess one. Ironically their best batsman, Glen Turner, could only average twenty-three in the Tests, obviously spent after making 1,000 runs by the end of May. For England Boycott, Fletcher and Amiss all batted well and Arnold was the star bowler. But there were ominous signs of lack of class and technique in the England batting line-up. These were even more evident in the series against West Indies who won it 2–0 because they batted superbly and England batted badly. Whereas Fredericks, Kanhai, Lloyd, Kallicharran, Boyce, Julien and the old master himself Sobers all played some brilliant innings, time and time again the England batsmen failed due to poor strokes against bowlers like Holder, Julien and Boyce whom they played regularly in county cricket.

England's crushing defeat by an innings in the 3rd Test at Lord's forced the selectors to replace Illingworth as captain after a spell of thirty-one Tests, and Mike Denness was appointed captain of the MCC Team to tour West Indies in 1974. Although slightly unfair on Illingworth who could not really be blamed for England's failure, it was probably the right time for a change. But nothing the selectors do can hide the shortage of good English-born batsmen in first-class cricket today. Both series attracted big crowds who alas were often ill-disciplined and invaded the pitch on every possible excuse. The Edgbaston authorities found the cure – no sitting on the grass and a promise to eject any invader from the ground. For some reason this Edgbaston Test – the second *versus* the West Indies – was a bad-tempered match and a poor one to watch. It also produced the unfortunate 'Fagg Incident' in which Arthur Fagg at one point had to be persuaded to continue as umpire after an ostentatious disapproval of one of his decisions by the West Indies captain Rohan Kanhai. A great pity this as in the other two Tests Kanhai proved himself to be an excellent tactician and a one hundred per cent attacking captain.

But of course the shock of the series was the bomb alert on the Saturday of the Lord's Test. A capacity crowd were basking in the sun and enjoying some splendid cricket when suddenly in the middle of an over the voice of MCC Secretary, Billy Griffith, came over the public address asking everyone to leave the ground immediately due to a bomb threat. It really was a tremendous shock and at first people just could not believe it, though everyone remained perfectly calm. After frequent requests from the police most of the crowd went out into the streets of St John's Wood while the police searched for the alleged bomb. Even so some 5,000 concentrated round the square in the middle of the ground and refused to leave.

Once again I was lucky or unlucky depending on the way you look at it. I was commentating at the time and continued to do so for the next forty-five minutes trying to keep people at home and outside the ground advised as to what was going on. It was an uncanny situation that this should be happening at Lord's of all places. But with the usual 'it can't happen to us' feeling we all stayed put in our new commentary box on the top balcony of an almost deserted pavilion. We somehow felt that if the bomb *did* go off we wouldn't have so far to go! Luckily it all proved to be a false alarm and after a loss of eighty-eight minutes play was resumed. I had been present at riots on grounds abroad but this was the first time ever that 'bomb stopped play'. A rather inauspicious start to my new career as a freelance commentator.

The Lord's Test in June prevented me going down to Bradfield to see Ian perform in their famous Greek play. There was no danger of his forgetting his lines – not that he knows any Greek – as all he had to do was to stand naked except for a loin cloth and act as a guard. So I doubt if he will follow me into the entertainment world nor alas as a cricket commentator, as he is the third of my sons to dislike the game, and in fact does not even play it at school, preferring sailing and swimming.

It was Ian who met me when I got home from a *Down your way* in Lincolnshire in July. He gave me the shock news that Joanna – now aged 7 – had diabetes. She had recently been drinking far more than usual and Pauline suspected that something was wrong and took her to our Doctor 'Cove'. He quickly discovered that she had far too much sugar in her blood, and she was immediately admitted to the Hospital for Sick Children in Great Ormond Street. There they did tests to find out how much insulin she needed and what sort of diet, because for the rest of her life she was going to have to have an injection every day – unless some cure comes up in the meantime.

It was terrible luck on poor Joanna, coming on top of everything else. She had been getting on so well. Until she was five Pauline organised a small play-school in our house with three or four other children. Joanna then went to a special school run by the Westminster Society for Mentally Handicapped Children. Here she received individual attention and unlimited kindness and thoroughly enjoyed herself.

After eighteen months she went to the Roman Catholic Convent of St Christina just off Avenue Road, where she quickly became an ordinary member of the school. The nuns and teachers were kind and understanding and all the other children seemed to love Joanna and accept her as one of them. She has made many friends there who come and play with her in our house or vice versa. We had always wanted her to mix with normal children as soon as possible and, touch wood, it has so far worked wonderfully well.

Joanna is still as happy and friendly as ever, and a perfect hostess whenever we have a party. She has grown quite tall, which is unusual, and can read and write as well as the rest of our family could at her age. This is largely due to a lovable and very efficient teacher called Vyvyen, who comes twice a week and gives special tuition. She and Joanna get on splendidly together and Joanna loves it, which is why she has made such progress. She is still behind normal children in her conversation and her reasoning and seems unable to store up memory of past events. Now that she has diabetes her life will inevitably be more restricted and disciplined with the daily injections and strict diet. But I have no doubt whatever that Pauline and Cally will cope as they always have done.

I expect by now that you have realised what a premium I put on laughter. I would like to feel that as you close this book you will be laughing or at least have a smile on your face. So here are six stories which make me laugh and I hope that at least one of them will have the same effect on you:

A man got on to a bus with a crocodile on a lead. When they had sat down the conductor came round with the tickets. 'That's a nice crocodile you have there,' he said, 'are you taking him to the zoo?' 'No', said the man, 'we went to the zoo yesterday. Today we are going to the British Museum.'

A woman took her ten-year-old son to the psychiatrist and the following conversation took place.

Psychiatrist What's the trouble?

Mother Oh, he thinks he's a hen.

Psychiatrist How long has this been going on?

Mother Ever since he was four years old.

Psychiatrist Why didn't you bring him before?

Mother Because we needed the eggs.

A man broke his finger which his doctor put into a splint. 'Will I be able to play the guitar when it's better?' asked the man. 'Yes, of course, you will,' replied the doctor. 'Funny', said the man, 'I've never been able to play one before.'

A woman was sitting nervously in a dentist's chair, waiting to have a tooth stopped. The dentist approached her with the drill and asked her to open her mouth. Suddenly he stopped and said: 'Excuse me, madam, but do you realise that your right hand is gripping me in a very painful place?' 'Yes,' said the woman sweetly, 'I do. We're not going to hurt each other *are* we?'

A man was standing in a bus queue immediately behind a very attractive blonde, who was wearing one of those dresses which fit tightly round the knees, with buttons up the back. When the bus came along she tried to get up on to the platform, but her dress was too tight. So she put her hand behind her back, undid a button and tried again with no result. So she undid another button but it was still no use.

After she had undone two more the man said: 'Excuse me, let me help,' and lifted her up on to the platform of the bus. She turned to him with an angelic smile and said: 'Thank you so much. That was very gallant of you. You've no idea how embarrassing it was undoing all those buttons in public.' 'You're telling me', said the man, 'they weren't *yours*.'

A man went into a chemist's shop and asked for a tin of talcum powder. 'Yes sir,' said the shopkeeper, coming out from behind the counter, 'please walk this way.' 'If I could walk that way,' said the man, 'I wouldn't need the talcum powder.'

★   ★   ★

Well, there it is. As I sit in my deck-chair in the garden I just can't believe it. It's Close of Play time. I have finished this book. I never really thought I would. But it has been fun to do, and if you have reached this far, I hope that you have enjoyed it too.

I would just like to say a final thank you to my wife and family and all my personal friends and relations for helping to make my life such a happy one, and for laughing occasionally at some of my jokes.

To all my friends in the BBC, and in the world of sport and entertainment I want to say how grateful I am for the way in which they have befriended and accepted a relative amateur like myself.

And finally to the general public, my warm thanks for many faithful years of viewing and listening and for the kind and generous treatment which I have always received from them.

Now I must stop. Perhaps we shall meet one day—possibly Down *Your* Way.

St John's Wood, September 1973

Index